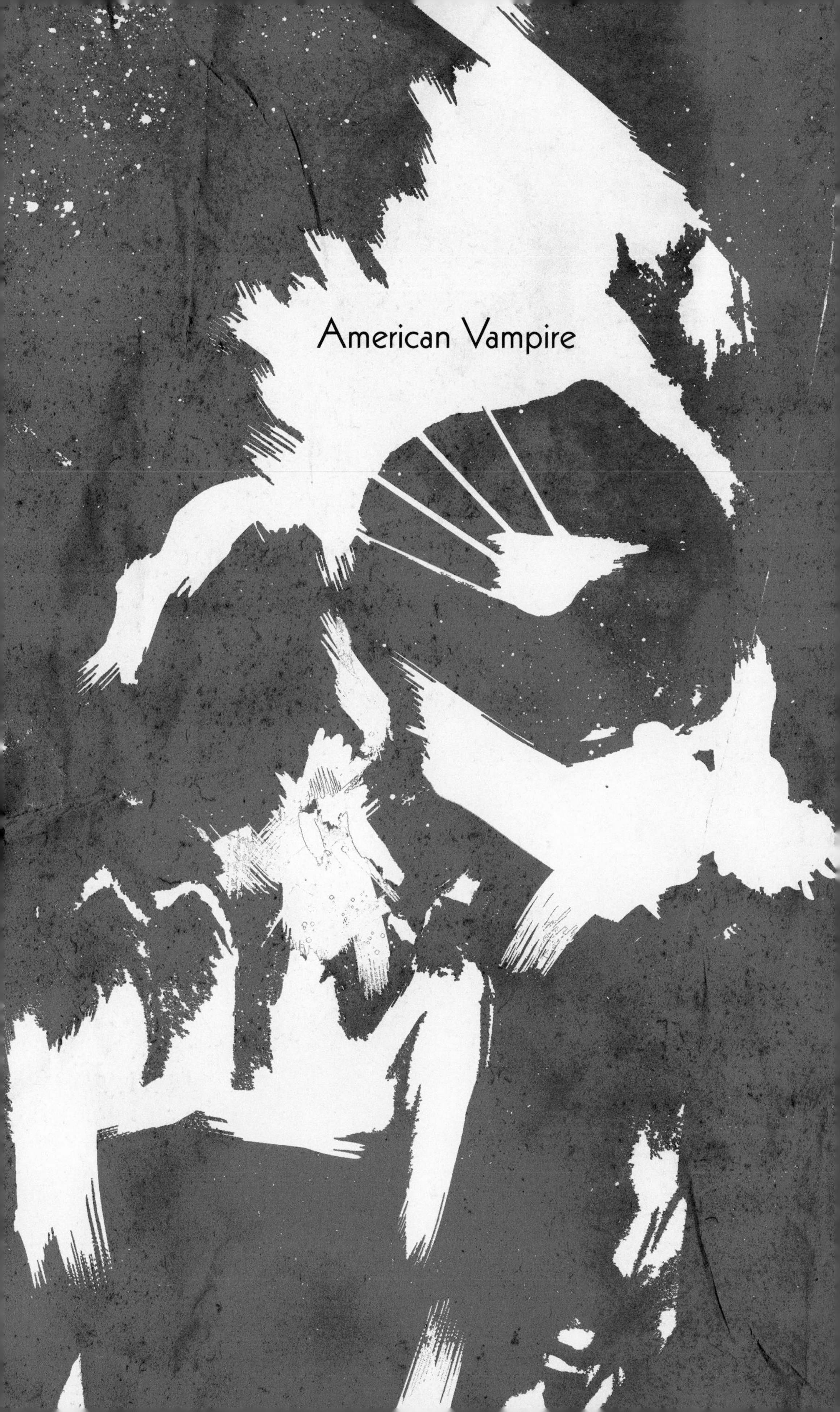
American Vampire

AMERICAN

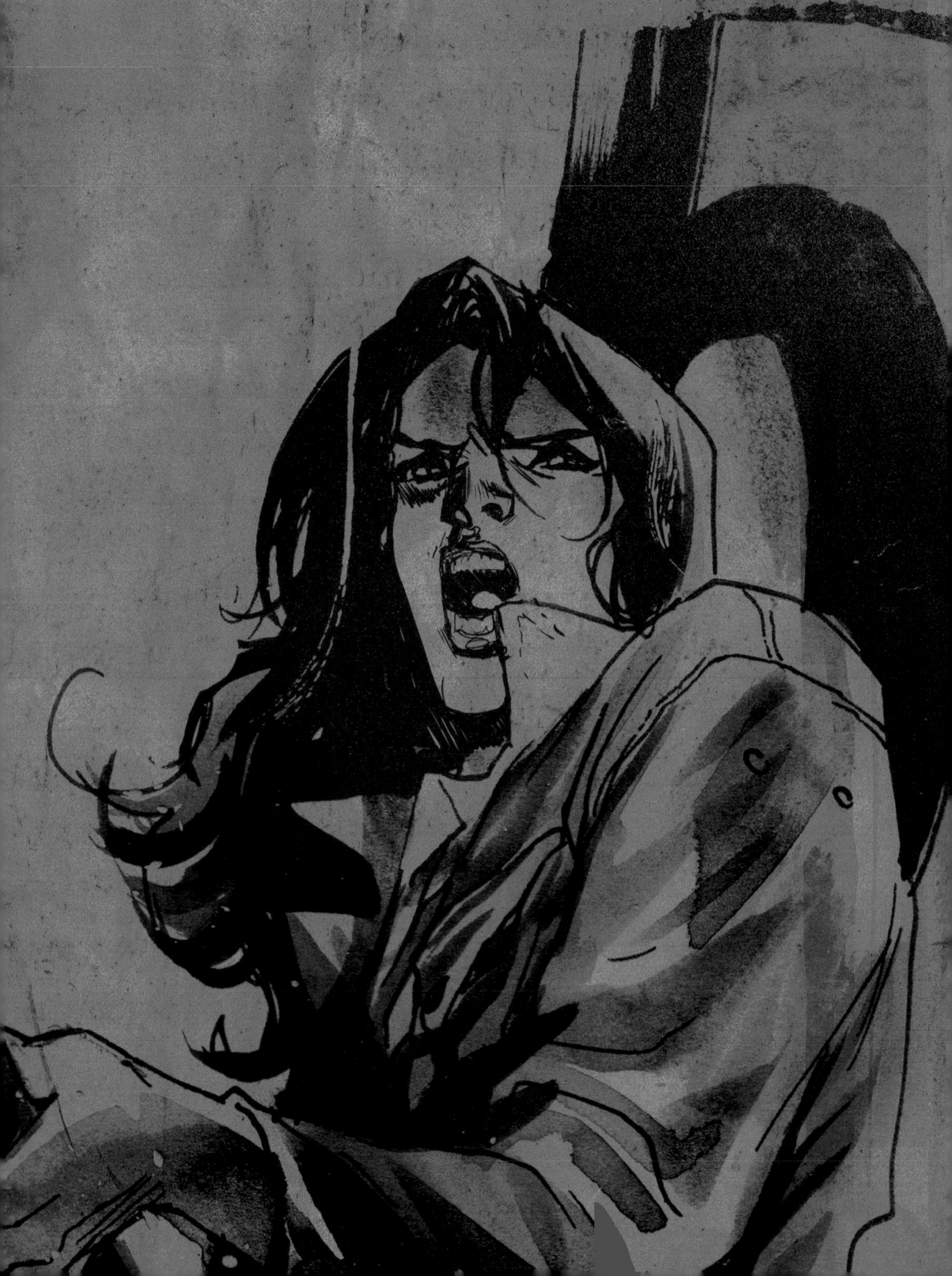

VAMPIRE

VOLUME EIGHT

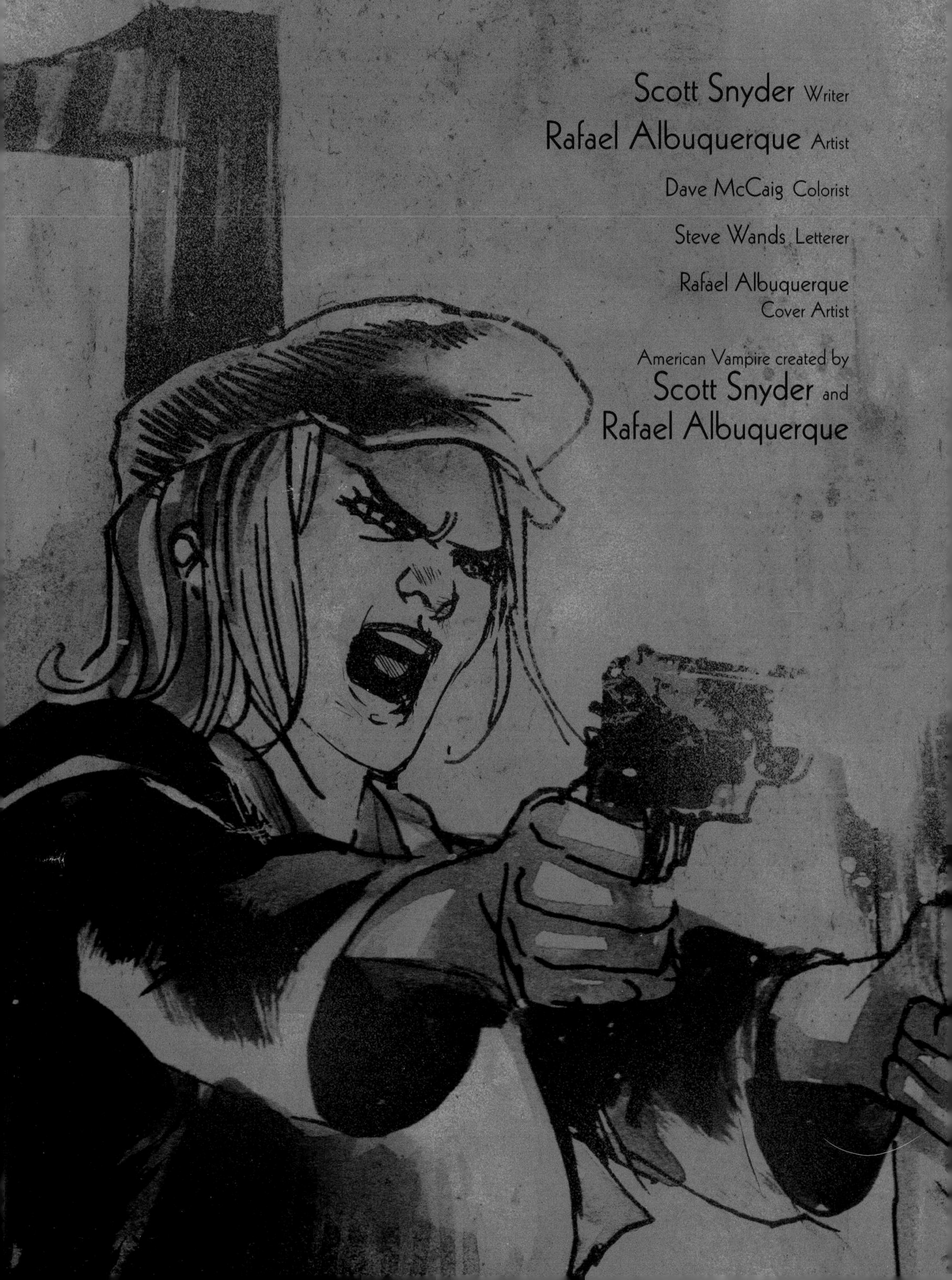

Scott Snyder Writer

Rafael Albuquerque Artist

Dave McCaig Colorist

Steve Wands Letterer

Rafael Albuquerque
Cover Artist

American Vampire created by
Scott Snyder and
Rafael Albuquerque

Ellie Pyle Mark Doyle Editors – Original Series
Sara Miller Assistant Editor – Original Series
Jeb Woodard Group Editor – Collected Editions
Robin Wildman Editor – Collected Edition
Steve Cook Design Director – Books
Louis Prandi Publication Design

Shelly Bond VP & Executive Editor – Vertigo

Diane Nelson President
Dan DiDio and Jim Lee Co-Publishers
Geoff Johns Chief Creative Officer
Amit Desai Senior VP – Marketing & Global Franchise Management
Nairi Gardiner Senior VP – Finance
Sam Ades VP – Digital Marketing
Bobbie Chase VP – Talent Development
Mark Chiarello Senior VP – Art, Design & Collected Editions
John Cunningham VP – Content Strategy
Anne DePies VP – Strategy Planning & Reporting
Don Falletti VP – Manufacturing Operations
Lawrence Ganem VP – Editorial Administration & Talent Relations
Alison Gill Senior VP – Manufacturing & Operations
Hank Kanalz Senior VP – Editorial Strategy & Administration
Jay Kogan VP – Legal Affairs
Derek Maddalena Senior VP – Sales & Business Development
Jack Mahan VP – Business Affairs
Dan Miron VP – Sales Planning & Trade Development
Nick Napolitano VP – Manufacturing Administration
Carol Roeder VP – Marketing
Eddie Scannell VP – Mass Account & Digital Sales
Courtney Simmons Senior VP – Publicity & Communications
Jim (Ski) Sokolowski VP – Comic Book Specialty & Newsstand Sales
Sandy Yi Senior VP – Global Franchise Management

AMERICAN VAMPIRE VOLUME EIGHT

Originally published in single magazine form in AMERICAN VAMPIRE:
SECOND CYCLE 6-11 Copyright © 2015 Scott Snyder and DC Comics.
All Rights Reserved. All characters, their distinctive likenesses and related ele-
ments featured in this publication are trademarks of DC Comics. VERTIGO
is a trademark of DC Comics. The stories, characters and incidents featured
in this publication are entirely fictional. DC Comics does not read or
accept unsolicited submissions of ideas, stories or artwork.

DC Comics, 2900 West Alameda Avenue, Burbank, CA 91505
Printed in the USA. First Printing.
ISBN: 978-1-4012-5433-9

LIBRARY OF CONGRESS CATALOGING-IN-
PUBLICATION DATA

Snyder, Scott, author.
  American Vampire volume eight / Scott Snyder, writer ;
Rafael Albuquerque, artist.
    pages cm
  ISBN 978-1-4012-5433-9 (hardback)
1. Vampires—Comic books, strips, etc. 2. Graphic
novels. 3. Horror comic books, strips, etc. .
Albuquerque, Rafael, 1981- illustrator. II. Title.
PN6727.S555A5 2016
741.5'973—dc23

2015031547

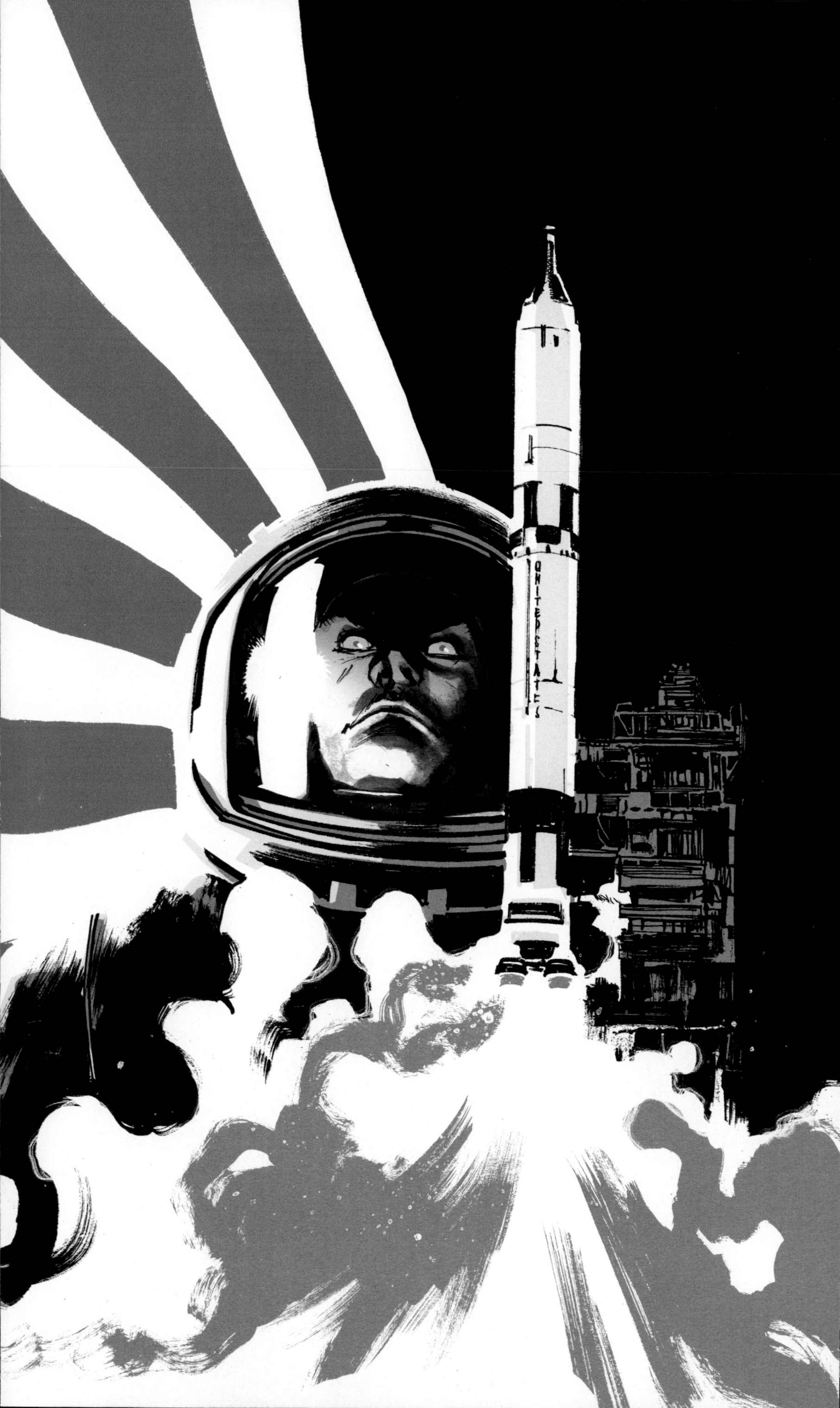
UNITED STATES

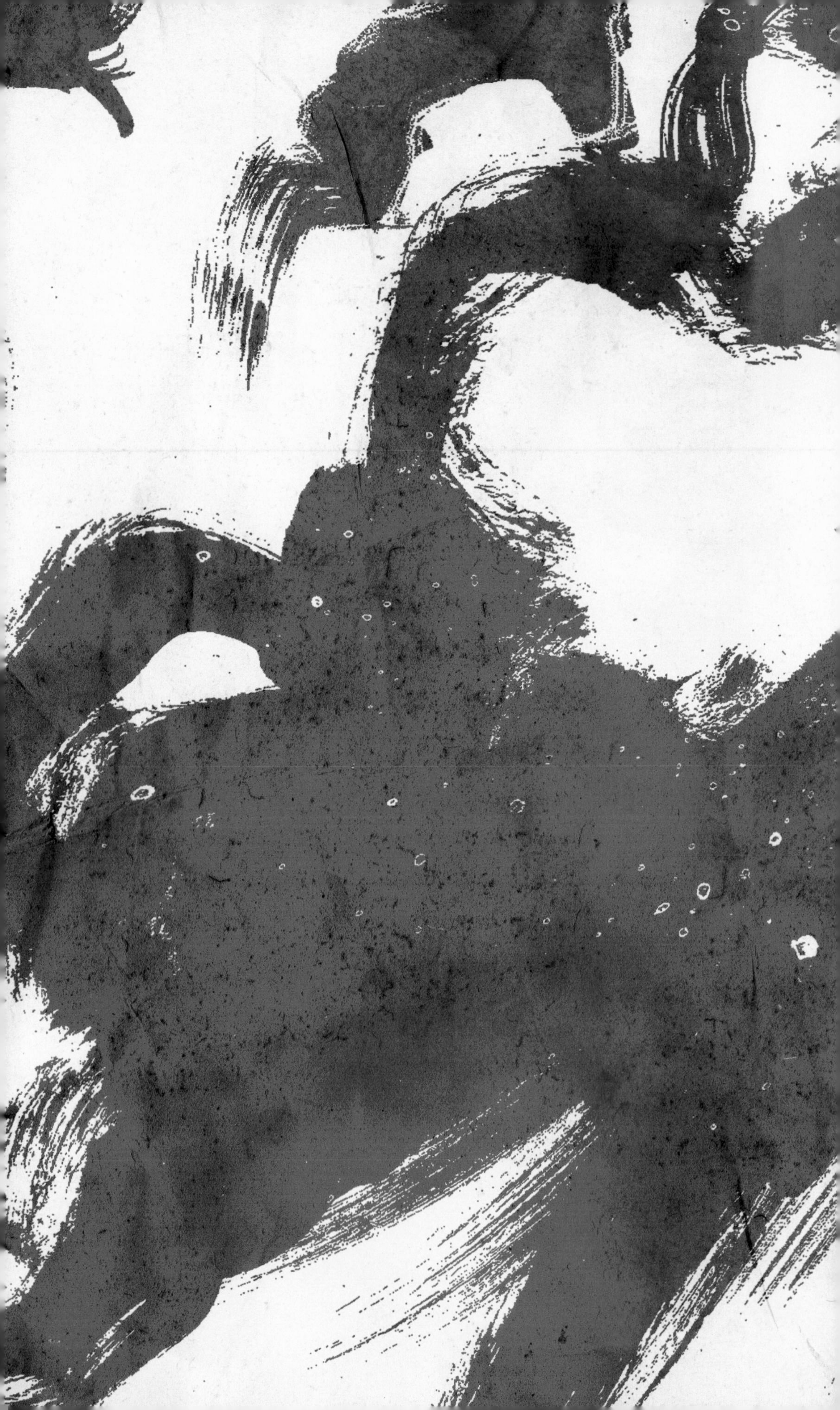

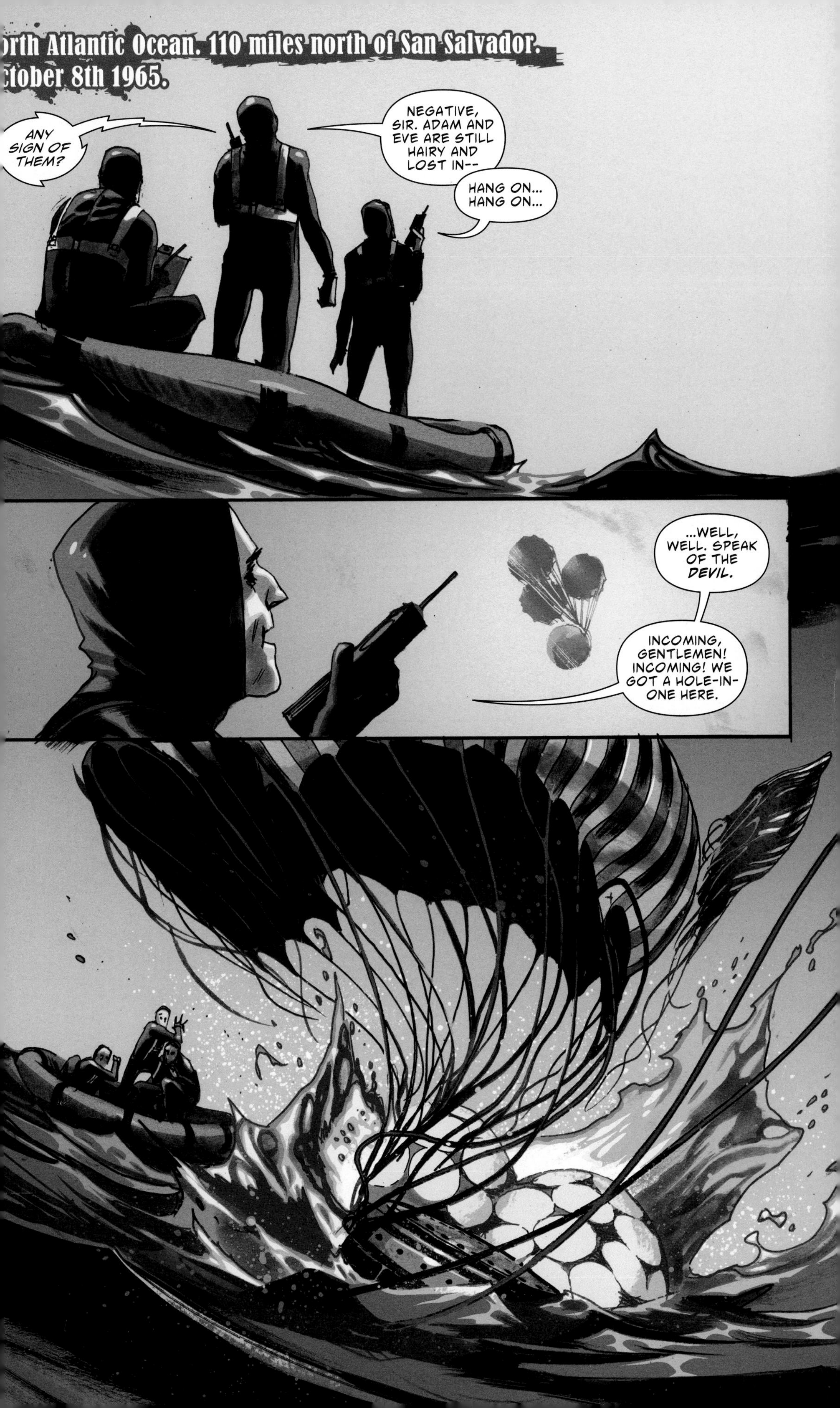
orth Atlantic Ocean. 110 miles north of San Salvador.
ctober 8th 1965.
ANY SIGN OF THEM?
NEGATIVE, SIR. ADAM AND EVE ARE STILL HAIRY AND LOST IN--
HANG ON... HANG ON...
...WELL, WELL. SPEAK OF THE *DEVIL.*
INCOMING, GENTLEMEN! INCOMING! WE GOT A HOLE-IN-ONE HERE.

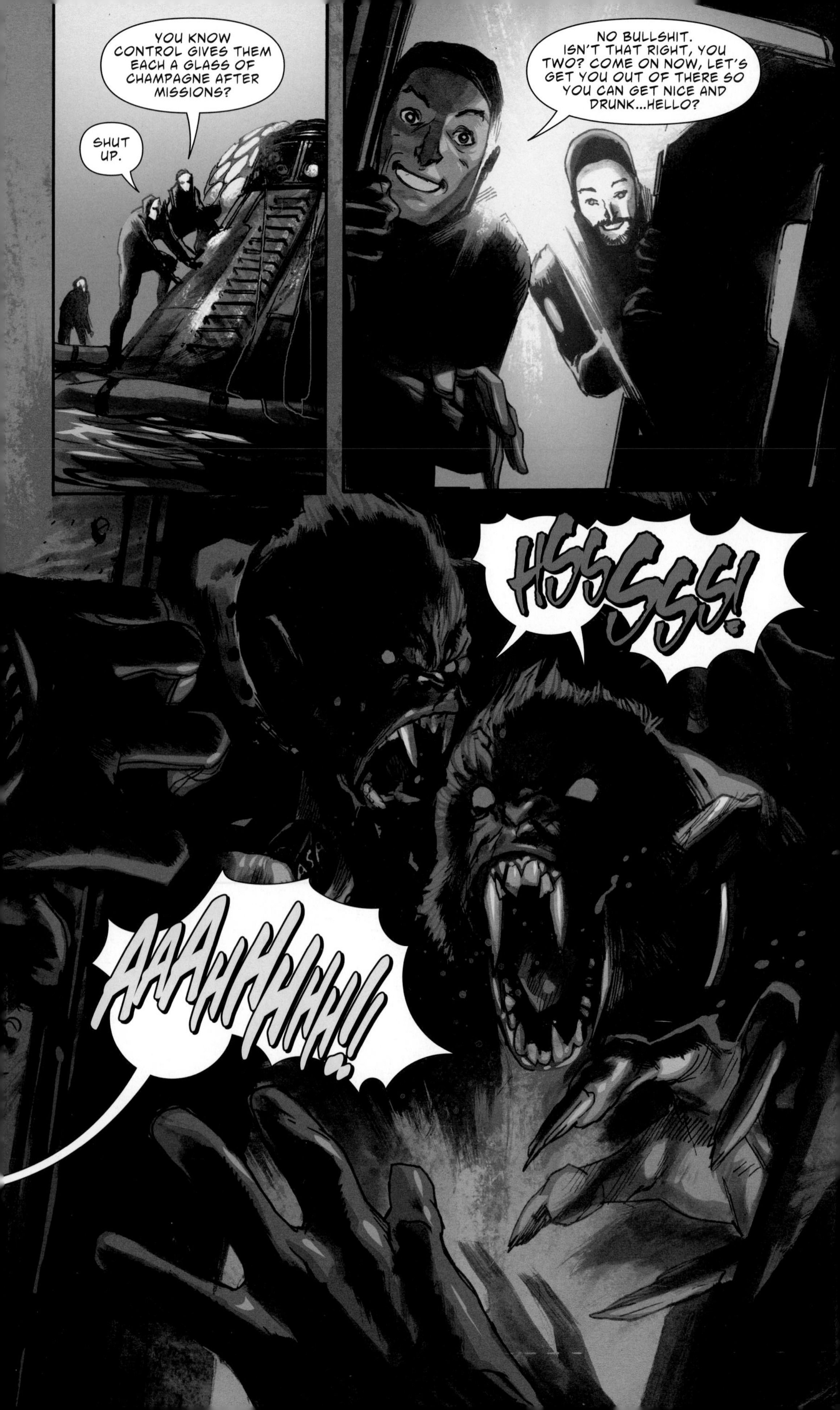

YOU KNOW CONTROL GIVES THEM EACH A GLASS OF CHAMPAGNE AFTER MISSIONS?
SHUT UP.
NO BULLSHIT. ISN'T THAT RIGHT, YOU TWO? COME ON NOW, LET'S GET YOU OUT OF THERE SO YOU CAN GET NICE AND DRUNK...HELLO?
HSSSSS!
AAAHHHHH!!

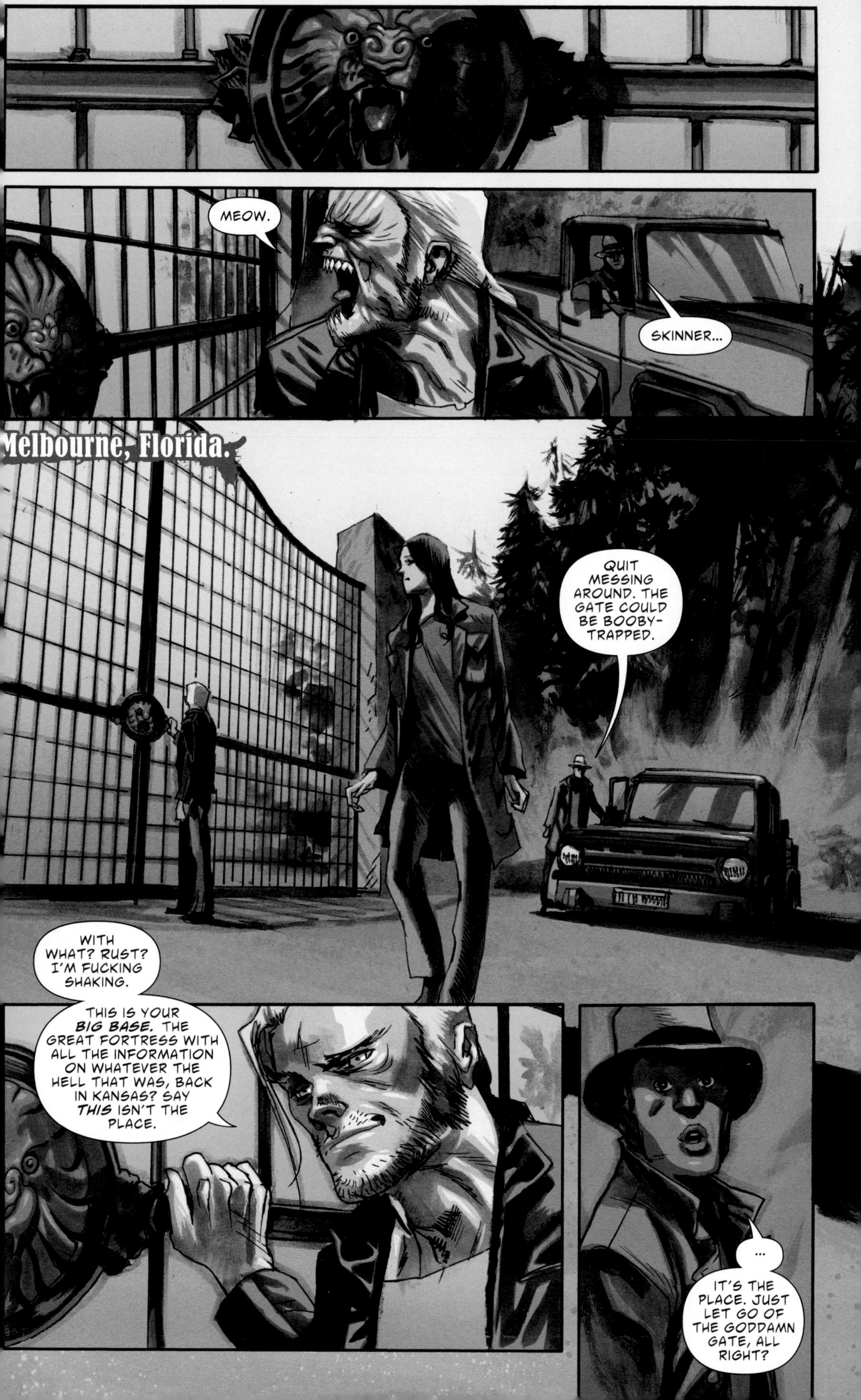

MEOW.
SKINNER...
Melbourne, Florida.
QUIT MESSING AROUND. THE GATE COULD BE BOOBY-TRAPPED.
WITH WHAT? RUST? I'M FUCKING SHAKING.
THIS IS YOUR *BIG BASE.* THE GREAT FORTRESS WITH ALL THE INFORMATION ON WHATEVER THE HELL THAT WAS, BACK IN KANSAS? SAY *THIS* ISN'T THE PLACE.
...
IT'S THE PLACE. JUST LET GO OF THE GODDAMN GATE, ALL RIGHT?

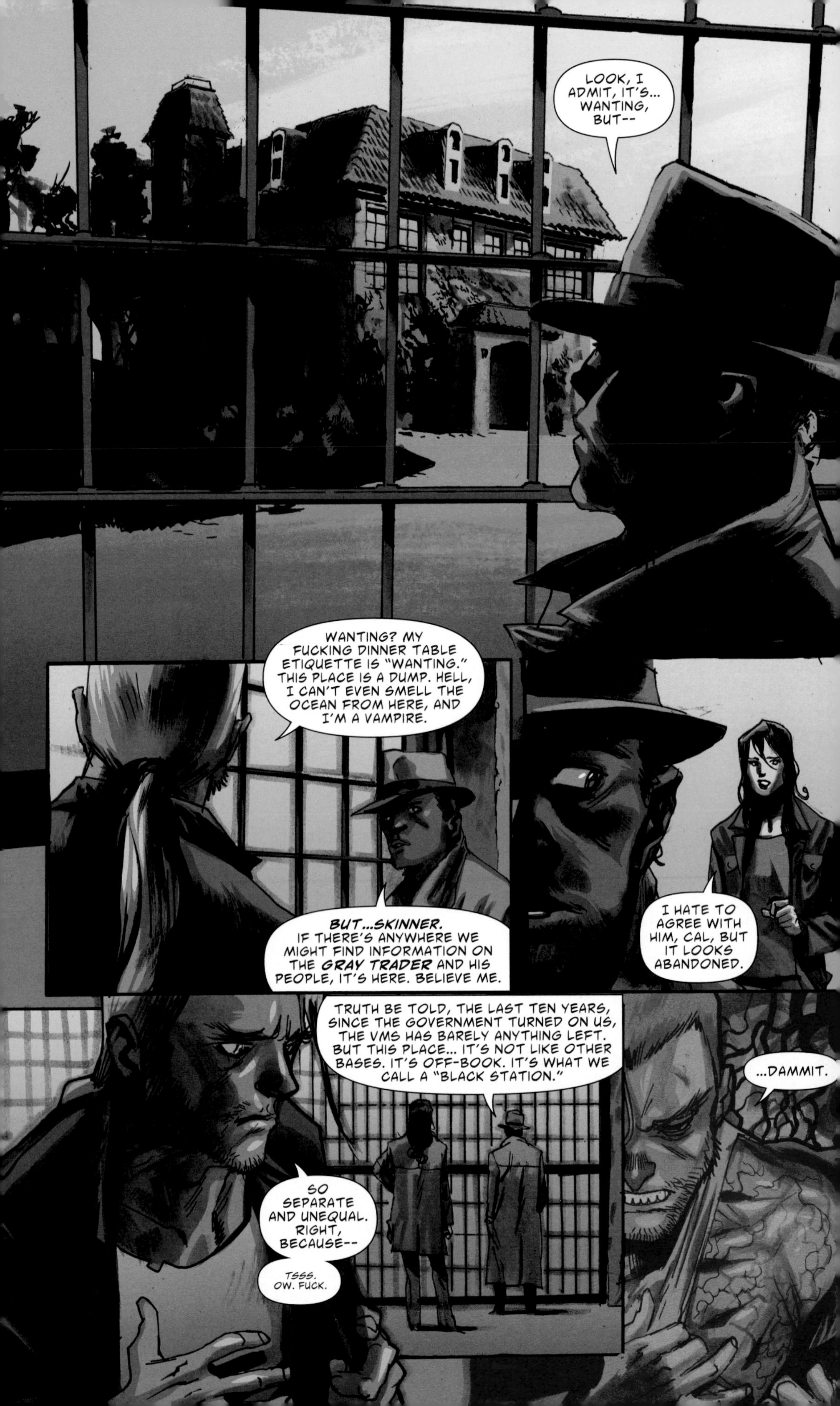
LOOK, I ADMIT, IT'S... WANTING, BUT--
WANTING? MY FUCKING DINNER TABLE ETIQUETTE IS "WANTING." THIS PLACE IS A DUMP. HELL, I CAN'T EVEN SMELL THE OCEAN FROM HERE, AND I'M A VAMPIRE.
BUT...SKINNER. IF THERE'S ANYWHERE WE MIGHT FIND INFORMATION ON THE GRAY TRADER AND HIS PEOPLE, IT'S HERE. BELIEVE ME.
I HATE TO AGREE WITH HIM, CAL, BUT IT LOOKS ABANDONED.
TRUTH BE TOLD, THE LAST TEN YEARS, SINCE THE GOVERNMENT TURNED ON US, THE VMS HAS BARELY ANYTHING LEFT. BUT THIS PLACE... IT'S NOT LIKE OTHER BASES. IT'S OFF-BOOK. IT'S WHAT WE CALL A "BLACK STATION."
SO SEPARATE AND UNEQUAL. RIGHT, BECAUSE--
TSSS. OW. FUCK.
...DAMMIT.

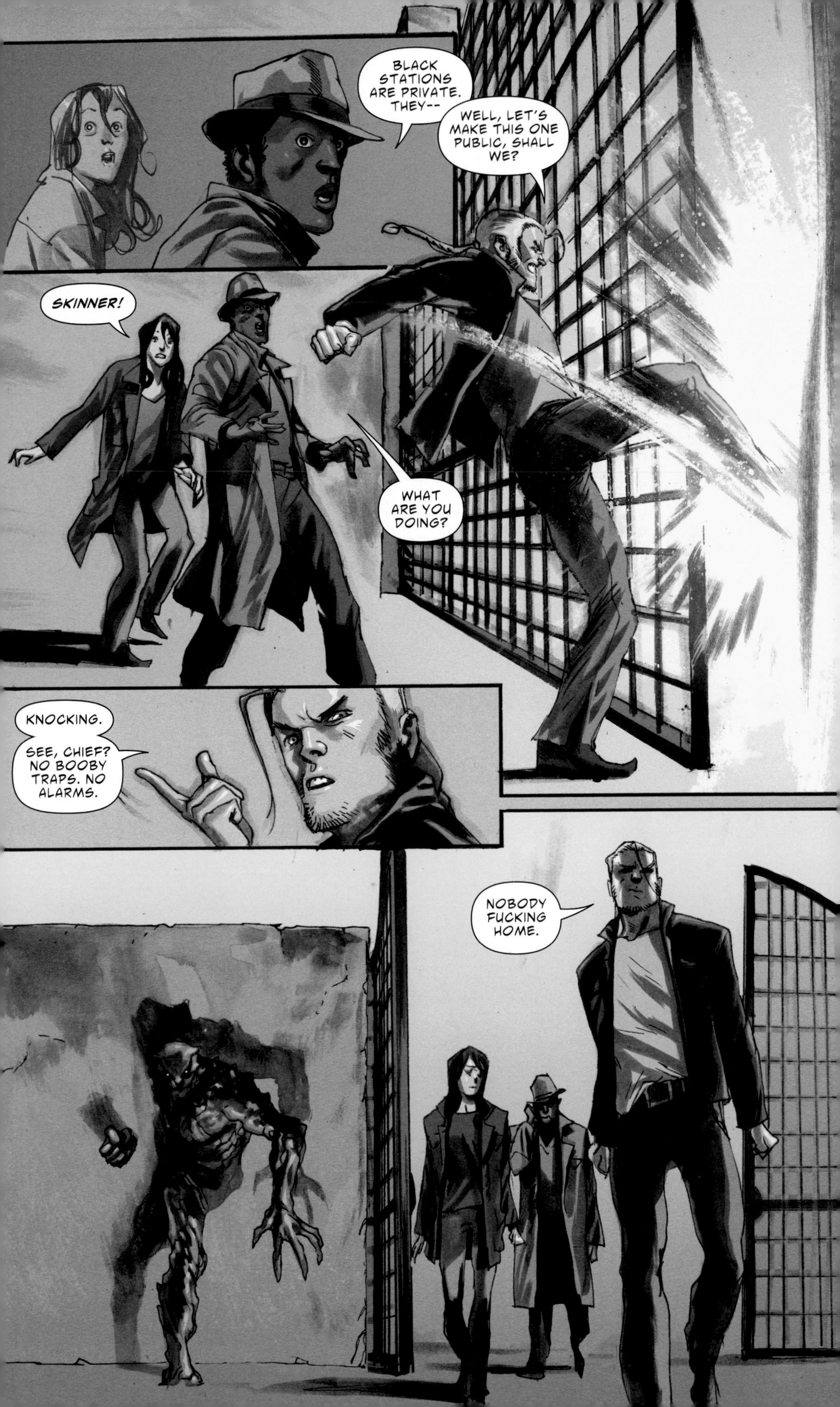
BLACK STATIONS ARE PRIVATE. THEY--
WELL, LET'S MAKE THIS ONE PUBLIC, SHALL WE?
SKINNER!
WHAT ARE YOU DOING?
KNOCKING.
SEE, CHIEF? NO BOOBY TRAPS. NO ALARMS.
NOBODY FUCKING HOME.

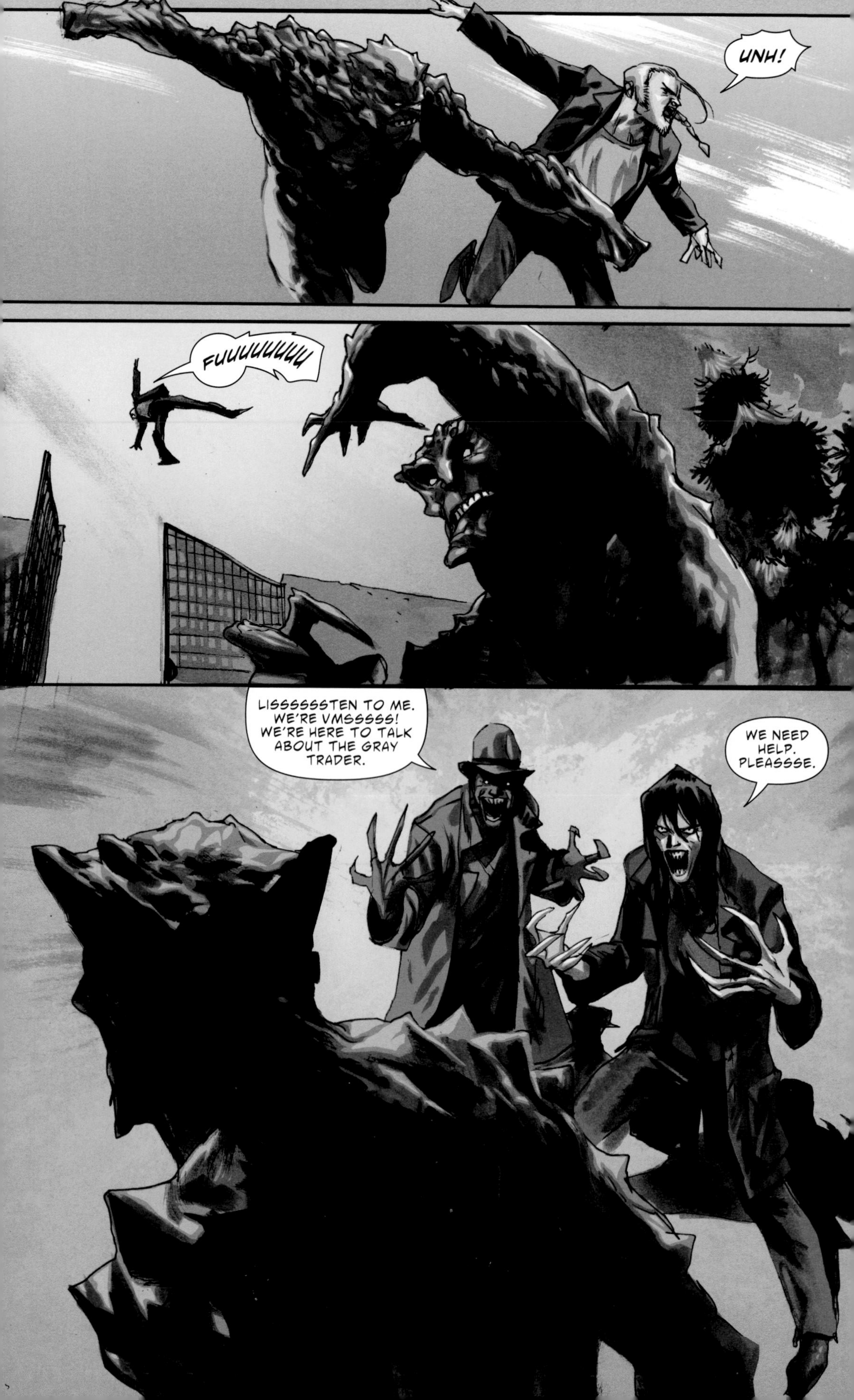
UNH!
FUUUUUUUU
LISSSSSSTEN TO ME. WE'RE VMSSSSS! WE'RE HERE TO TALK ABOUT THE GRAY TRADER.
WE NEED HELP. PLEASSSE.

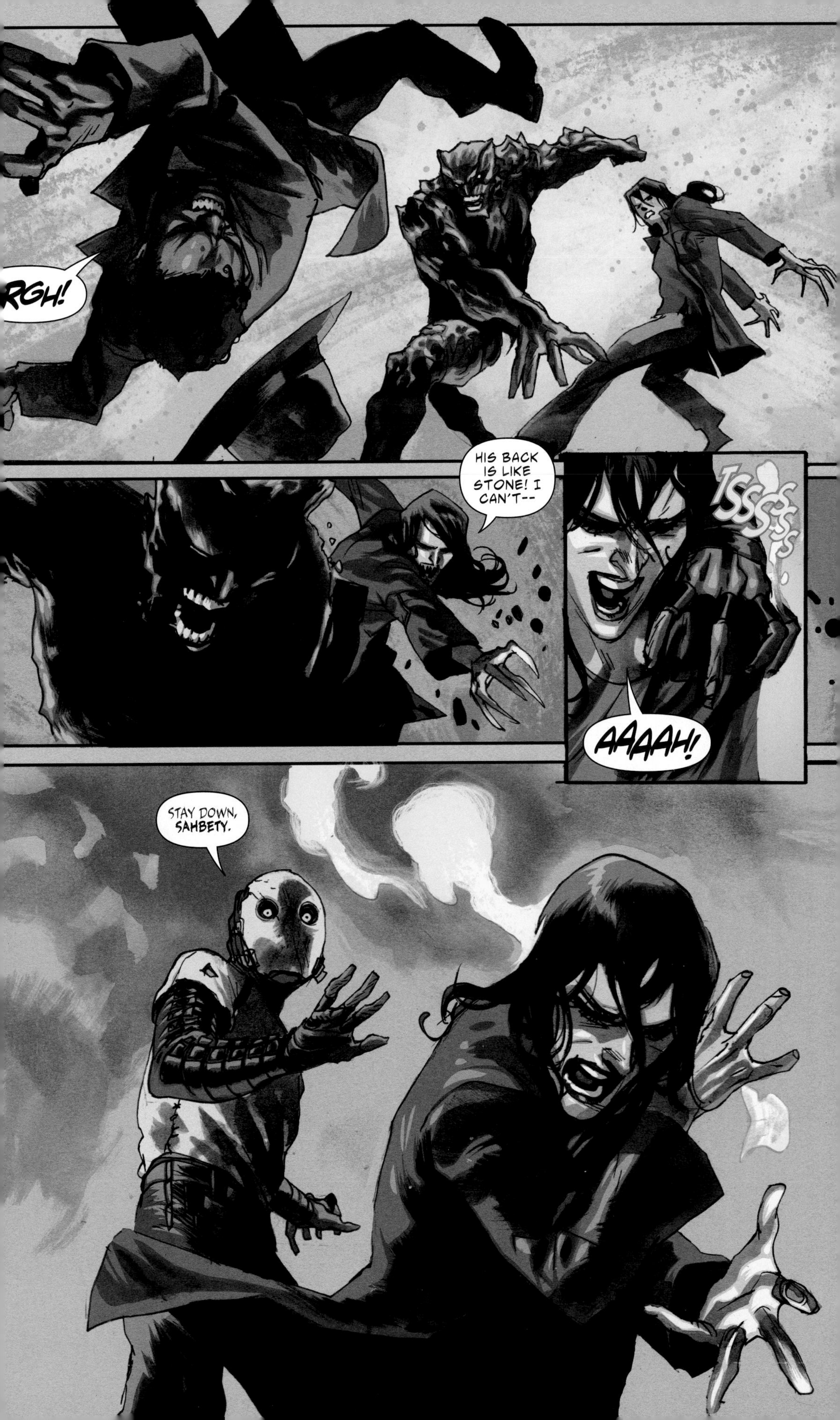
RGH!
HIS BACK IS LIKE STONE! I CAN'T--
ISSSSSSS
AAAAH!
STAY DOWN, SAHBETY.

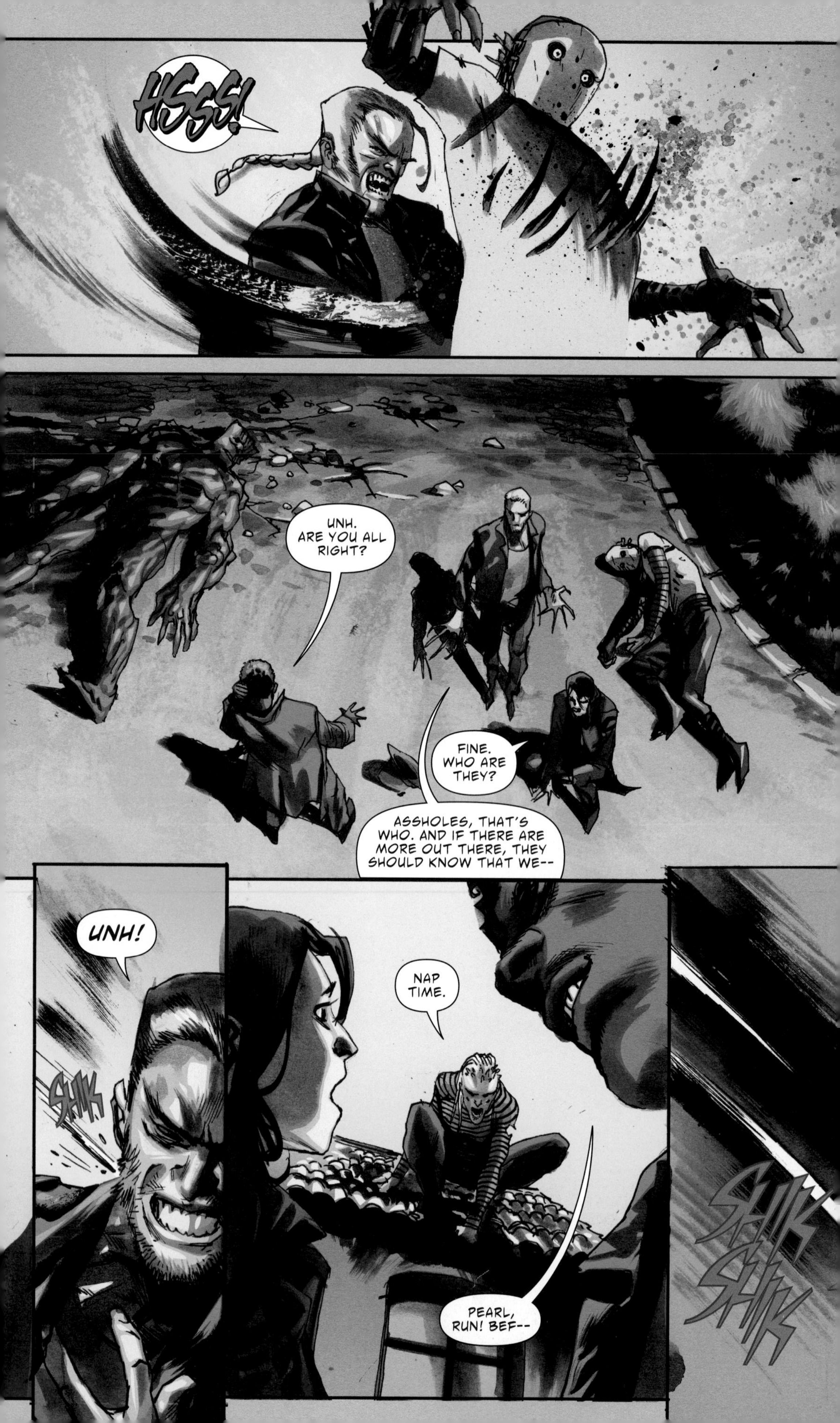
HSSS!
UNH. ARE YOU ALL RIGHT?
FINE. WHO ARE THEY?
ASSHOLES, THAT'S WHO. AND IF THERE ARE MORE OUT THERE, THEY SHOULD KNOW THAT WE--
UNH!
SHIK
NAP TIME.
PEARL, RUN! BEF--
SHIK SHIK

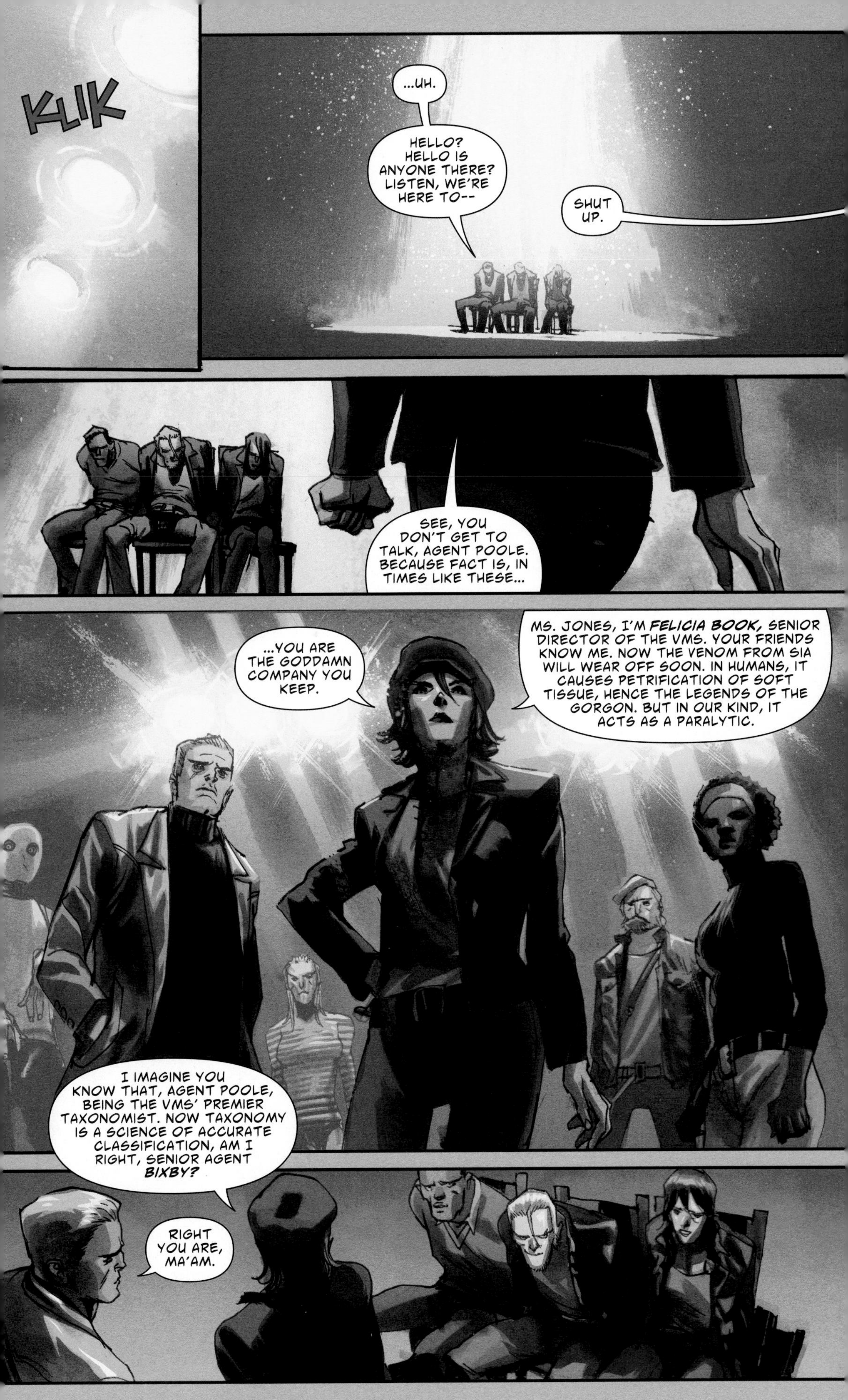
KLIK
...UH.
HELLO? HELLO IS ANYONE THERE? LISTEN, WE'RE HERE TO--
SHUT UP.
SEE, YOU DON'T GET TO TALK, AGENT POOLE. BECAUSE FACT IS, IN TIMES LIKE THESE...
...YOU ARE THE GODDAMN COMPANY YOU KEEP.
MS. JONES, I'M ***FELICIA BOOK,*** SENIOR DIRECTOR OF THE VMS. YOUR FRIENDS KNOW ME. NOW THE VENOM FROM SIA WILL WEAR OFF SOON. IN HUMANS, IT CAUSES PETRIFICATION OF SOFT TISSUE, HENCE THE LEGENDS OF THE GORGON. BUT IN OUR KIND, IT ACTS AS A PARALYTIC.
I IMAGINE YOU KNOW THAT, AGENT POOLE, BEING THE VMS' PREMIER TAXONOMIST. NOW TAXONOMY IS A SCIENCE OF ACCURATE CLASSIFICATION, AM I RIGHT, SENIOR AGENT ***BIXBY?***
RIGHT YOU ARE, MA'AM.

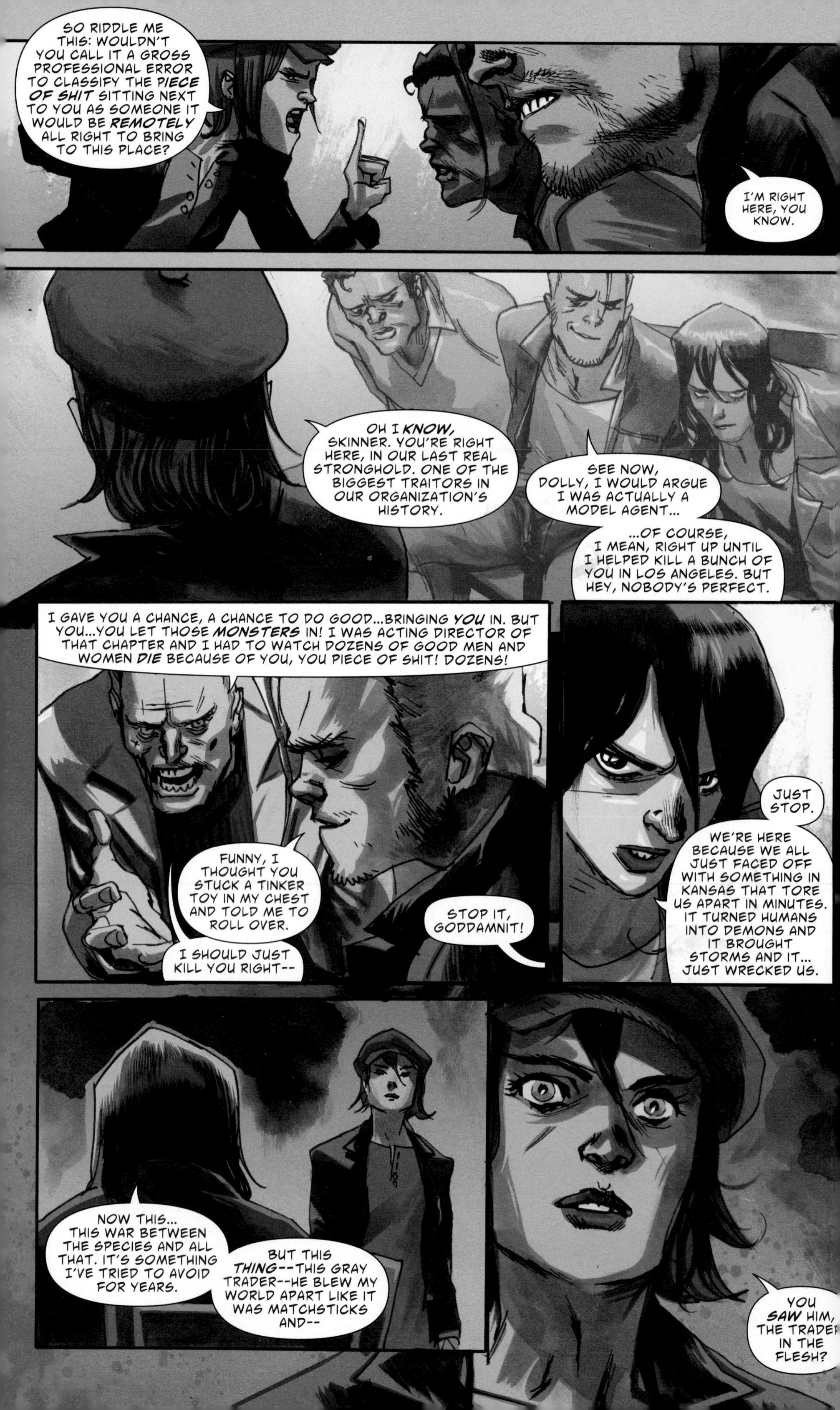
SO RIDDLE ME THIS: WOULDN'T YOU CALL IT A GROSS PROFESSIONAL ERROR TO CLASSIFY THE PIECE OF SHIT SITTING NEXT TO YOU AS SOMEONE IT WOULD BE REMOTELY ALL RIGHT TO BRING TO THIS PLACE?
I'M RIGHT HERE, YOU KNOW.
OH I KNOW, SKINNER. YOU'RE RIGHT HERE, IN OUR LAST REAL STRONGHOLD. ONE OF THE BIGGEST TRAITORS IN OUR ORGANIZATION'S HISTORY.
SEE NOW, DOLLY, I WOULD ARGUE I WAS ACTUALLY A MODEL AGENT...
...OF COURSE, I MEAN, RIGHT UP UNTIL I HELPED KILL A BUNCH OF YOU IN LOS ANGELES. BUT HEY, NOBODY'S PERFECT.
I GAVE YOU A CHANCE, A CHANCE TO DO GOOD...BRINGING YOU IN. BUT YOU...YOU LET THOSE MONSTERS IN! I WAS ACTING DIRECTOR OF THAT CHAPTER AND I HAD TO WATCH DOZENS OF GOOD MEN AND WOMEN DIE BECAUSE OF YOU, YOU PIECE OF SHIT! DOZENS!
FUNNY, I THOUGHT YOU STUCK A TINKER TOY IN MY CHEST AND TOLD ME TO ROLL OVER.
I SHOULD JUST KILL YOU RIGHT--
STOP IT, GODDAMNIT!
JUST STOP.
WE'RE HERE BECAUSE WE ALL JUST FACED OFF WITH SOMETHING IN KANSAS THAT TORE US APART IN MINUTES. IT TURNED HUMANS INTO DEMONS AND IT BROUGHT STORMS AND IT... JUST WRECKED US.
NOW THIS... THIS WAR BETWEEN THE SPECIES AND ALL THAT. IT'S SOMETHING I'VE TRIED TO AVOID FOR YEARS.
BUT THIS THING--THIS GRAY TRADER--HE BLEW MY WORLD APART LIKE IT WAS MATCHSTICKS AND--
YOU SAW HIM, THE TRADER IN THE FLESH?

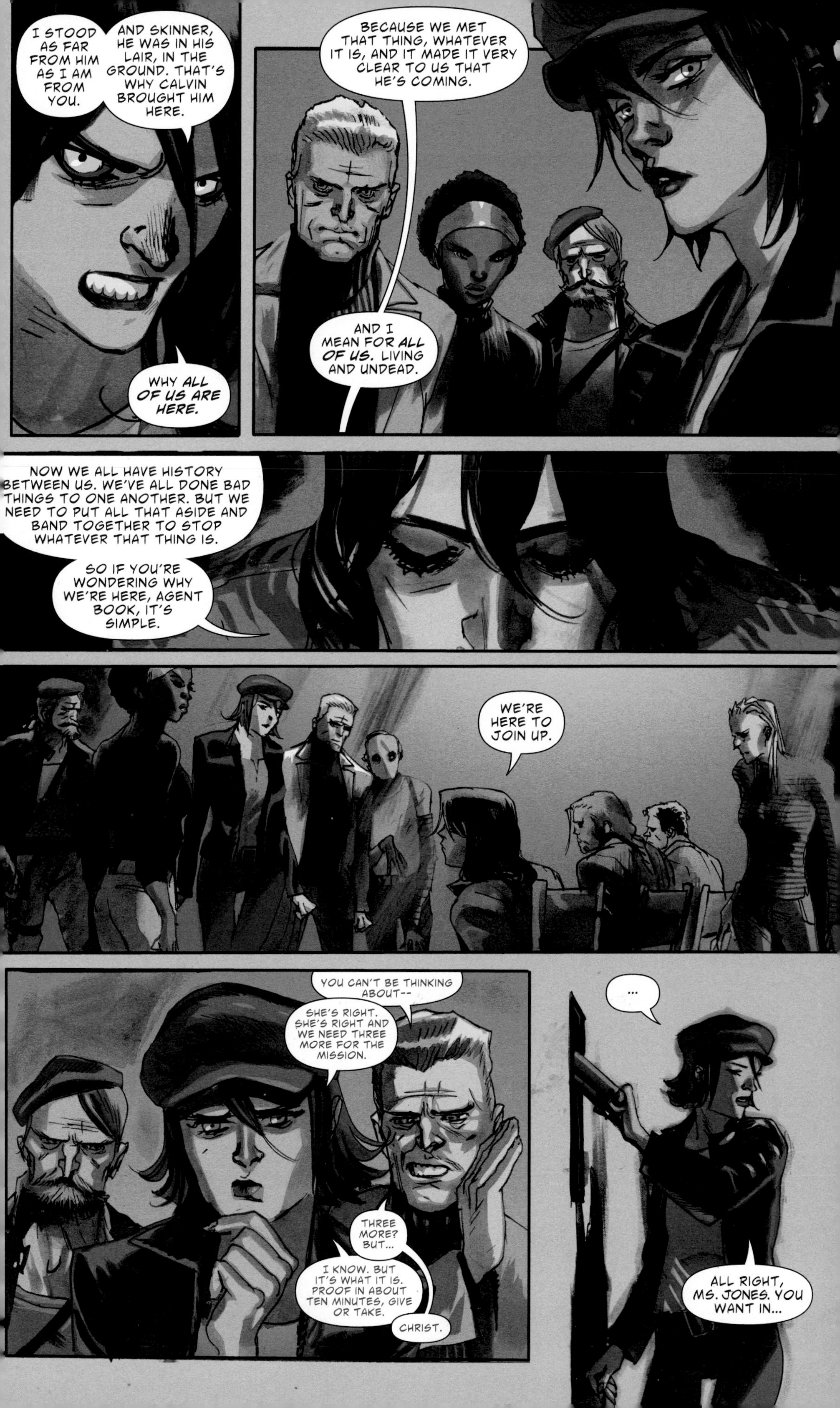
I STOOD AS FAR FROM HIM AS I AM FROM YOU.
AND SKINNER, HE WAS IN HIS LAIR, IN THE GROUND. THAT'S WHY CALVIN BROUGHT HIM HERE.
WHY *ALL OF US ARE HERE.*
BECAUSE WE MET THAT THING, WHATEVER IT IS, AND IT MADE IT VERY CLEAR TO US THAT HE'S COMING.
AND I MEAN FOR *ALL OF US.* LIVING AND UNDEAD.
NOW WE ALL HAVE HISTORY BETWEEN US. WE'VE ALL DONE BAD THINGS TO ONE ANOTHER. BUT WE NEED TO PUT ALL THAT ASIDE AND BAND TOGETHER TO STOP WHATEVER THAT THING IS.
SO IF YOU'RE WONDERING WHY WE'RE HERE, AGENT BOOK, IT'S SIMPLE.
WE'RE HERE TO JOIN UP.
YOU CAN'T BE THINKING ABOUT--
SHE'S RIGHT. SHE'S RIGHT AND WE NEED THREE MORE FOR THE MISSION.
THREE MORE? BUT...
I KNOW. BUT IT'S WHAT IT IS. PROOF IN ABOUT TEN MINUTES, GIVE OR TAKE.
CHRIST.
...
ALL RIGHT, MS. JONES. YOU WANT IN...

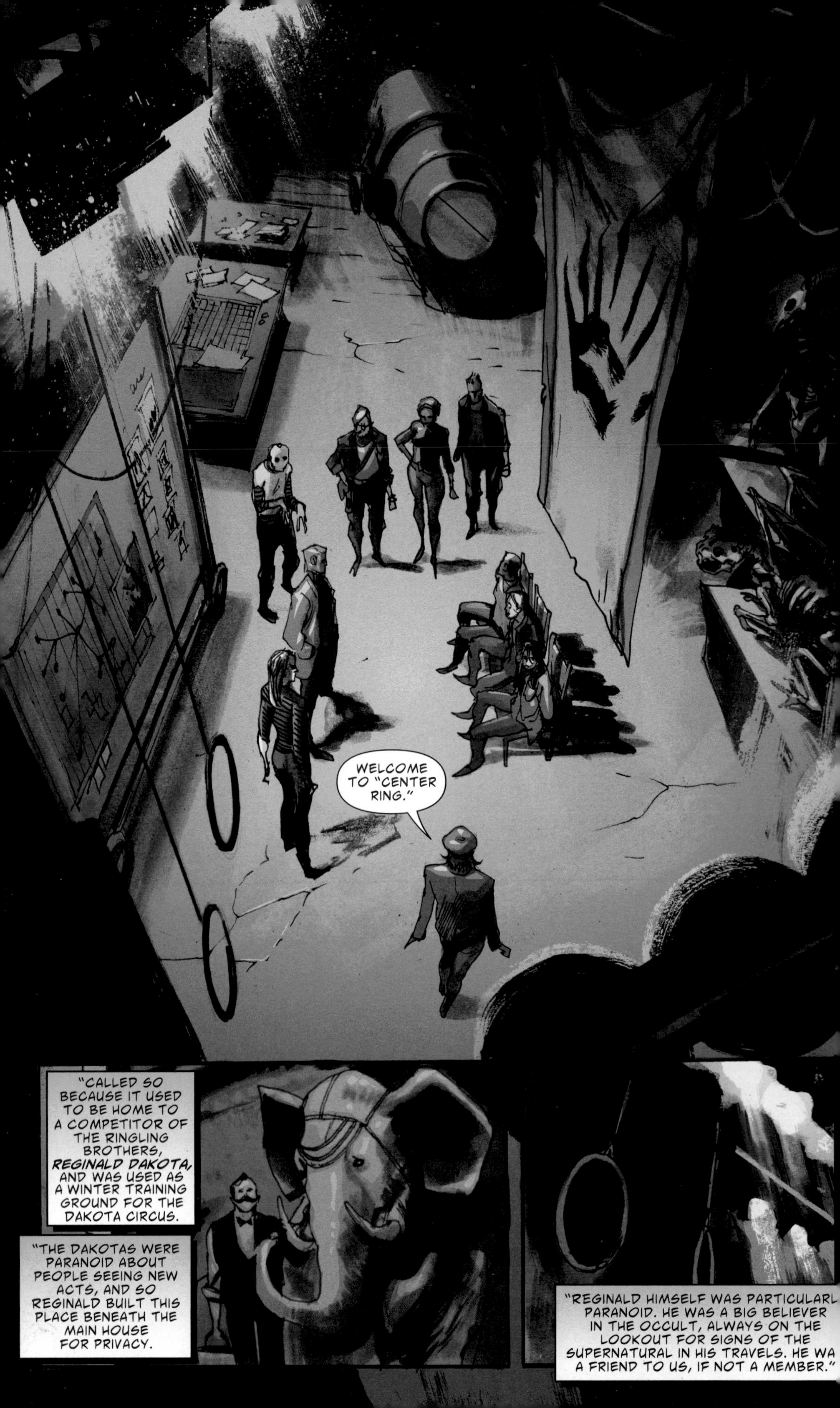

WELCOME TO "CENTER RING."
"CALLED SO BECAUSE IT USED TO BE HOME TO A COMPETITOR OF THE RINGLING BROTHERS, REGINALD DAKOTA, AND WAS USED AS A WINTER TRAINING GROUND FOR THE DAKOTA CIRCUS.
"THE DAKOTAS WERE PARANOID ABOUT PEOPLE SEEING NEW ACTS, AND SO REGINALD BUILT THIS PLACE BENEATH THE MAIN HOUSE FOR PRIVACY.
"REGINALD HIMSELF WAS PARTICULARL PARANOID. HE WAS A BIG BELIEVER IN THE OCCULT, ALWAYS ON THE LOOKOUT FOR SIGNS OF THE SUPERNATURAL IN HIS TRAVELS. HE WA A FRIEND TO US, IF NOT A MEMBER."

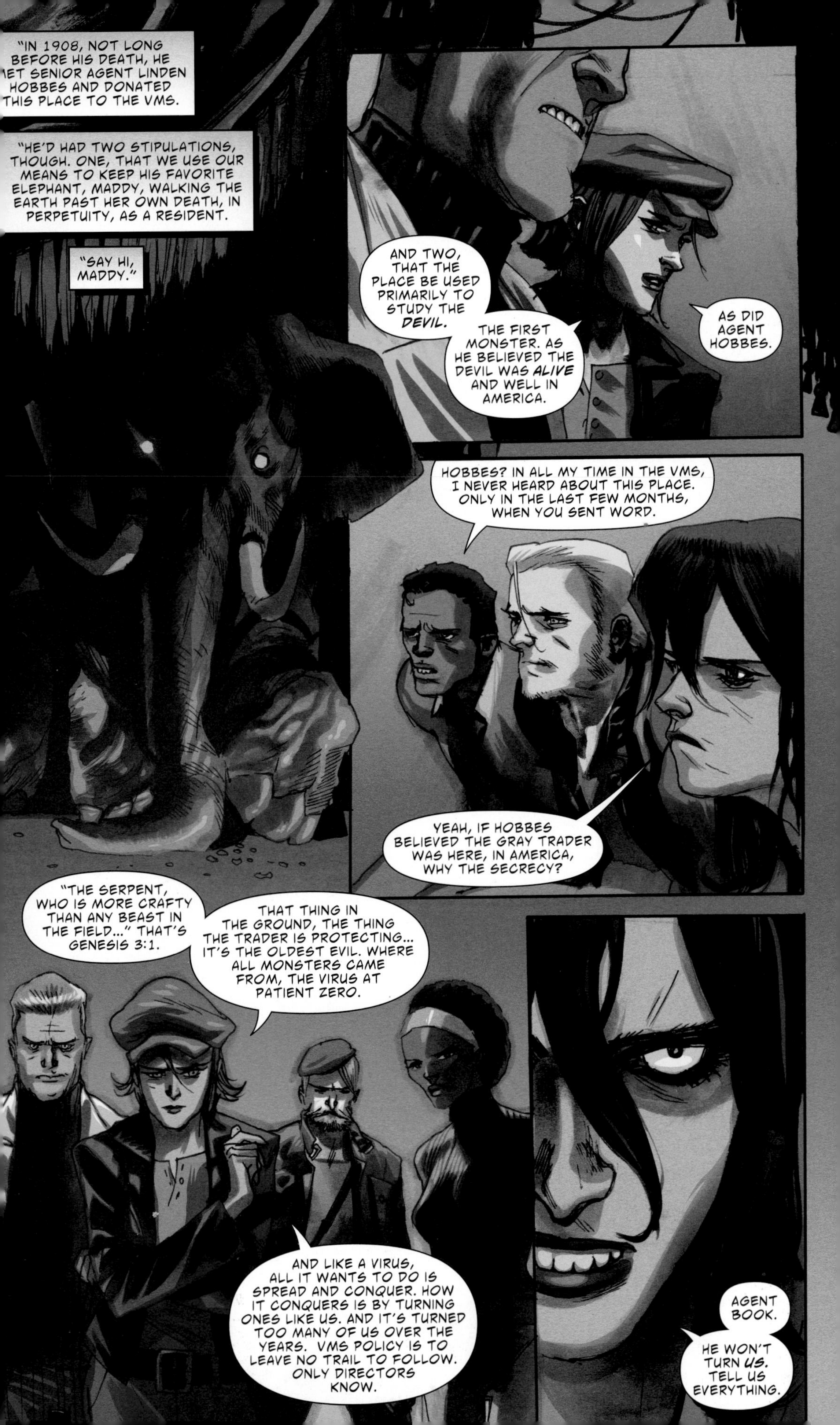
"IN 1908, NOT LONG BEFORE HIS DEATH, HE MET SENIOR AGENT LINDEN HOBBES AND DONATED THIS PLACE TO THE VMS.
"HE'D HAD TWO STIPULATIONS, THOUGH. ONE, THAT WE USE OUR MEANS TO KEEP HIS FAVORITE ELEPHANT, MADDY, WALKING THE EARTH PAST HER OWN DEATH, IN PERPETUITY, AS A RESIDENT.
"SAY HI, MADDY."
AND TWO, THAT THE PLACE BE USED PRIMARILY TO STUDY THE *DEVIL.*
THE FIRST MONSTER. AS HE BELIEVED THE DEVIL WAS *ALIVE* AND WELL IN AMERICA.
AS DID AGENT HOBBES.
HOBBES? IN ALL MY TIME IN THE VMS, I NEVER HEARD ABOUT THIS PLACE. ONLY IN THE LAST FEW MONTHS, WHEN YOU SENT WORD.
YEAH, IF HOBBES BELIEVED THE GRAY TRADER WAS HERE, IN AMERICA, WHY THE SECRECY?
"THE SERPENT, WHO IS MORE CRAFTY THAN ANY BEAST IN THE FIELD..." THAT'S GENESIS 3:1.
THAT THING IN THE GROUND, THE THING THE TRADER IS PROTECTING... IT'S THE OLDEST EVIL. WHERE ALL MONSTERS CAME FROM, THE VIRUS AT PATIENT ZERO.
AND LIKE A VIRUS, ALL IT WANTS TO DO IS SPREAD AND CONQUER. HOW IT CONQUERS IS BY TURNING ONES LIKE US. AND IT'S TURNED TOO MANY OF US OVER THE YEARS. VMS POLICY IS TO LEAVE NO TRAIL TO FOLLOW. ONLY DIRECTORS KNOW.
AGENT BOOK.
HE WON'T TURN *US.* TELL US EVERYTHING.

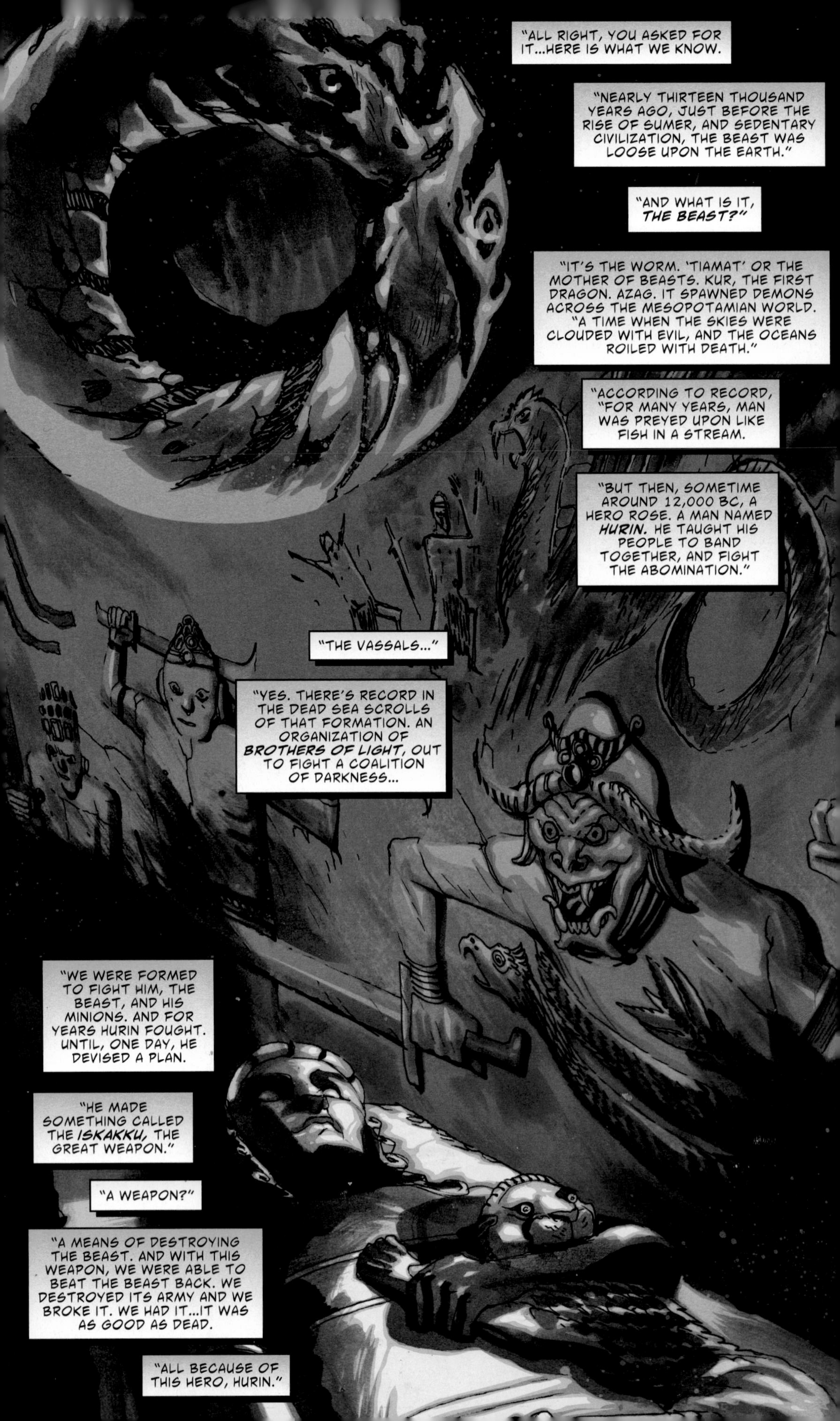
"ALL RIGHT, YOU ASKED FOR IT...HERE IS WHAT WE KNOW.
"NEARLY THIRTEEN THOUSAND YEARS AGO, JUST BEFORE THE RISE OF SUMER, AND SEDENTARY CIVILIZATION, THE BEAST WAS LOOSE UPON THE EARTH."
"AND WHAT IS IT, *THE BEAST?*"
"IT'S THE WORM. 'TIAMAT' OR THE MOTHER OF BEASTS. KUR, THE FIRST DRAGON. AZAG. IT SPAWNED DEMONS ACROSS THE MESOPOTAMIAN WORLD. "A TIME WHEN THE SKIES WERE CLOUDED WITH EVIL, AND THE OCEANS ROILED WITH DEATH."
"ACCORDING TO RECORD, "FOR MANY YEARS, MAN WAS PREYED UPON LIKE FISH IN A STREAM.
"BUT THEN, SOMETIME AROUND 12,000 BC, A HERO ROSE. A MAN NAMED *HURIN.* HE TAUGHT HIS PEOPLE TO BAND TOGETHER, AND FIGHT THE ABOMINATION."
"THE VASSALS..."
"YES. THERE'S RECORD IN THE DEAD SEA SCROLLS OF THAT FORMATION. AN ORGANIZATION OF *BROTHERS OF LIGHT,* OUT TO FIGHT A COALITION OF DARKNESS...
"WE WERE FORMED TO FIGHT HIM, THE BEAST, AND HIS MINIONS. AND FOR YEARS HURIN FOUGHT. UNTIL, ONE DAY, HE DEVISED A PLAN.
"HE MADE SOMETHING CALLED THE *ISKAKKU,* THE GREAT WEAPON."
"A WEAPON?"
"A MEANS OF DESTROYING THE BEAST. AND WITH THIS WEAPON, WE WERE ABLE TO BEAT THE BEAST BACK. WE DESTROYED ITS ARMY AND WE BROKE IT. WE HAD IT...IT WAS AS GOOD AS DEAD.
"ALL BECAUSE OF THIS HERO, HURIN."

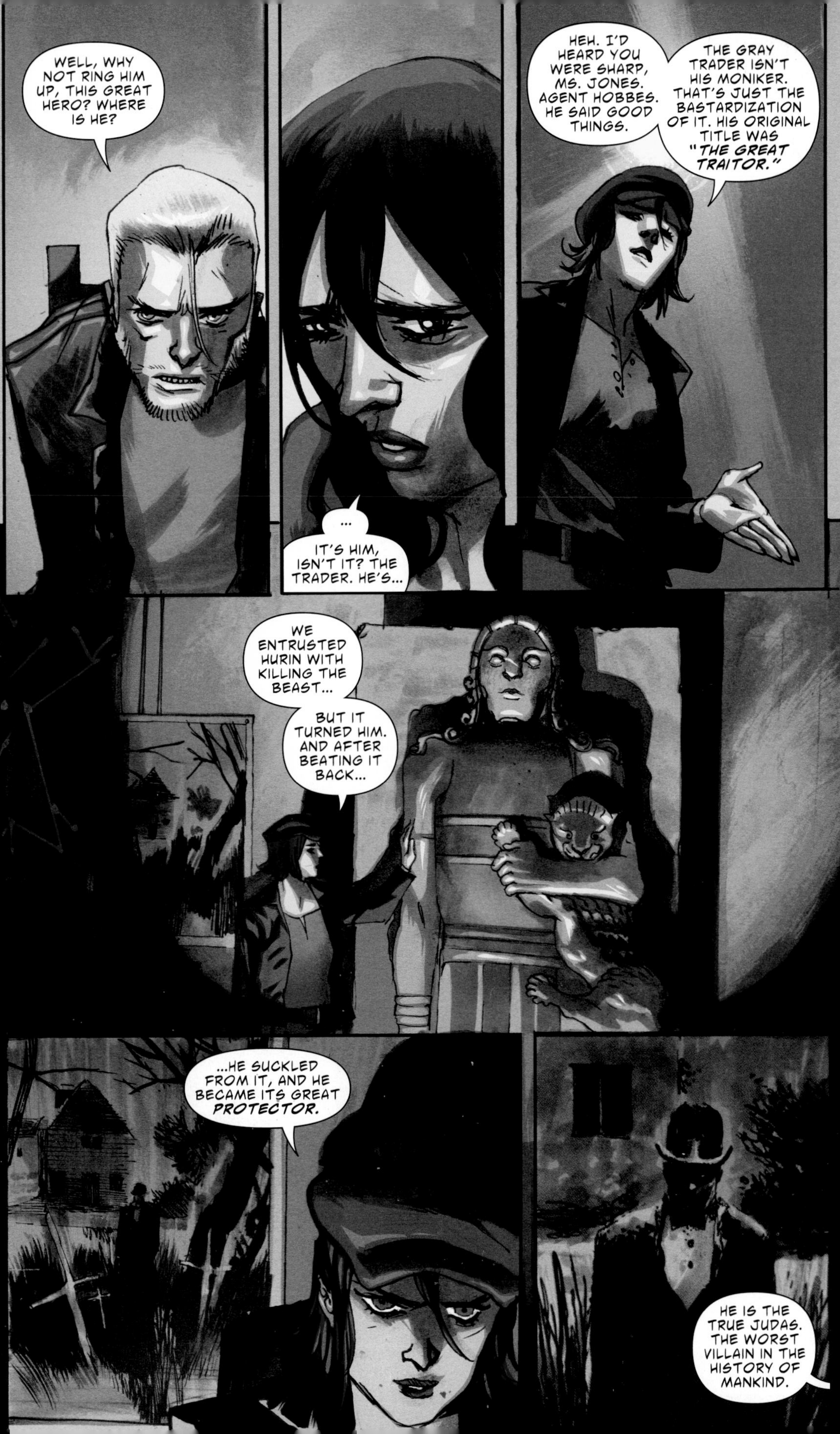
WELL, WHY NOT RING HIM UP, THIS GREAT HERO? WHERE IS HE?
...
IT'S HIM, ISN'T IT? THE TRADER. HE'S...
HEH. I'D HEARD YOU WERE SHARP, MS. JONES. AGENT HOBBES. HE SAID GOOD THINGS.
THE GRAY TRADER ISN'T HIS MONIKER. THAT'S JUST THE BASTARDIZATION OF IT. HIS ORIGINAL TITLE WAS "THE GREAT TRAITOR."
WE ENTRUSTED HURIN WITH KILLING THE BEAST...
BUT IT TURNED HIM. AND AFTER BEATING IT BACK...
...HE SUCKLED FROM IT, AND HE BECAME ITS GREAT PROTECTOR.
HE IS THE TRUE JUDAS. THE WORST VILLAIN IN THE HISTORY OF MANKIND.

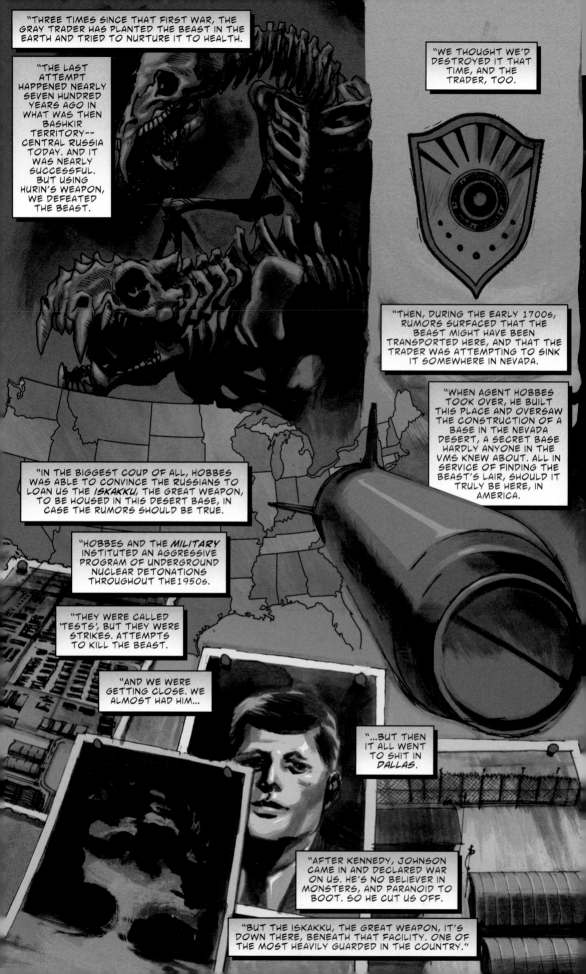

"THREE TIMES SINCE THAT FIRST WAR, THE GRAY TRADER HAS PLANTED THE BEAST IN THE EARTH AND TRIED TO NURTURE IT TO HEALTH.

"THE LAST ATTEMPT HAPPENED NEARLY SEVEN HUNDRED YEARS AGO IN WHAT WAS THEN BASHKIR TERRITORY-- CENTRAL RUSSIA TODAY. AND IT WAS NEARLY SUCCESSFUL. BUT USING HURIN'S WEAPON, WE DEFEATED THE BEAST.

"WE THOUGHT WE'D DESTROYED IT THAT TIME, AND THE TRADER, TOO.

"THEN, DURING THE EARLY 1700s, RUMORS SURFACED THAT THE BEAST MIGHT HAVE BEEN TRANSPORTED HERE, AND THAT THE TRADER WAS ATTEMPTING TO SINK IT SOMEWHERE IN NEVADA.

"WHEN AGENT HOBBES TOOK OVER, HE BUILT THIS PLACE AND OVERSAW THE CONSTRUCTION OF A BASE IN THE NEVADA DESERT, A SECRET BASE HARDLY ANYONE IN THE VMS KNEW ABOUT. ALL IN SERVICE OF FINDING THE BEAST'S LAIR, SHOULD IT TRULY BE HERE, IN AMERICA.

"IN THE BIGGEST COUP OF ALL, HOBBES WAS ABLE TO CONVINCE THE RUSSIANS TO LOAN US THE *ISKAKKU*, THE GREAT WEAPON, TO BE HOUSED IN THIS DESERT BASE, IN CASE THE RUMORS SHOULD BE TRUE.

"HOBBES AND THE *MILITARY* INSTITUTED AN AGGRESSIVE PROGRAM OF UNDERGROUND NUCLEAR DETONATIONS THROUGHOUT THE 1950s.

"THEY WERE CALLED 'TESTS', BUT THEY WERE STRIKES. ATTEMPTS TO KILL THE BEAST.

"AND WE WERE GETTING CLOSE. WE ALMOST HAD HIM...

"...BUT THEN IT ALL WENT TO SHIT IN *DALLAS*.

"AFTER KENNEDY, JOHNSON CAME IN AND DECLARED WAR ON US. HE'S NO BELIEVER IN MONSTERS, AND PARANOID TO BOOT. SO HE CUT US OFF.

"BUT THE ISKAKKU, THE GREAT WEAPON, IT'S DOWN THERE, BENEATH THAT FACILITY. ONE OF THE MOST HEAVILY GUARDED IN THE COUNTRY."

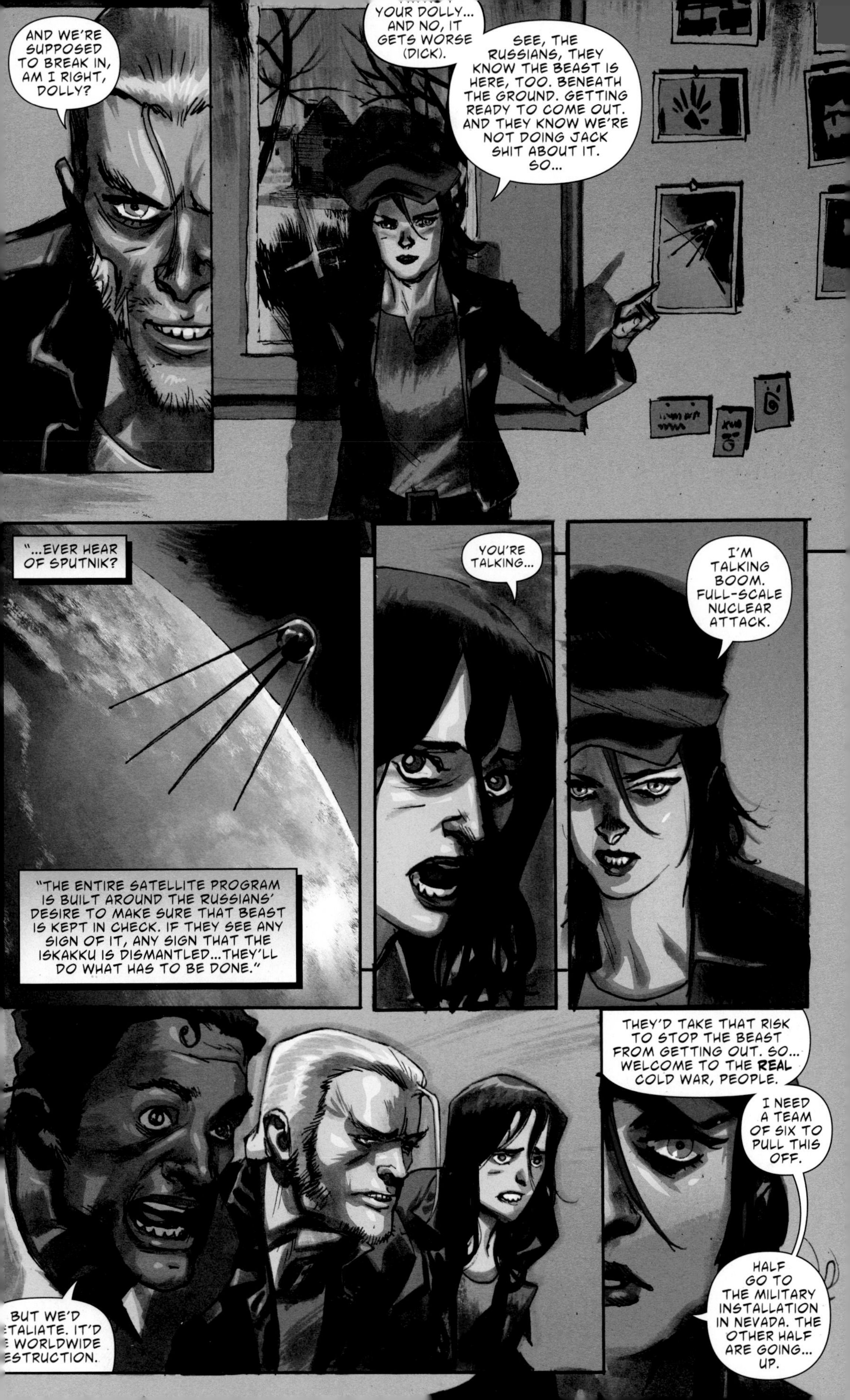

AND WE'RE SUPPOSED TO BREAK IN, AM I RIGHT, DOLLY?
YOUR DOLLY... AND NO, IT GETS WORSE (DICK).
SEE, THE RUSSIANS, THEY KNOW THE BEAST IS HERE, TOO. BENEATH THE GROUND. GETTING READY TO COME OUT. AND THEY KNOW WE'RE NOT DOING JACK SHIT ABOUT IT. SO...
"...EVER HEAR OF SPUTNIK?
"THE ENTIRE SATELLITE PROGRAM IS BUILT AROUND THE RUSSIANS' DESIRE TO MAKE SURE THAT BEAST IS KEPT IN CHECK. IF THEY SEE ANY SIGN OF IT, ANY SIGN THAT THE ISKAKKU IS DISMANTLED...THEY'LL DO WHAT HAS TO BE DONE."
YOU'RE TALKING...
I'M TALKING BOOM. FULL-SCALE NUCLEAR ATTACK.
BUT WE'D ETALIATE. IT'D E WORLDWIDE ESTRUCTION.
THEY'D TAKE THAT RISK TO STOP THE BEAST FROM GETTING OUT. SO... WELCOME TO THE **REAL** COLD WAR, PEOPLE.
I NEED A TEAM OF SIX TO PULL THIS OFF.
HALF GO TO THE MILITARY INSTALLATION IN NEVADA. THE OTHER HALF ARE GOING... UP.

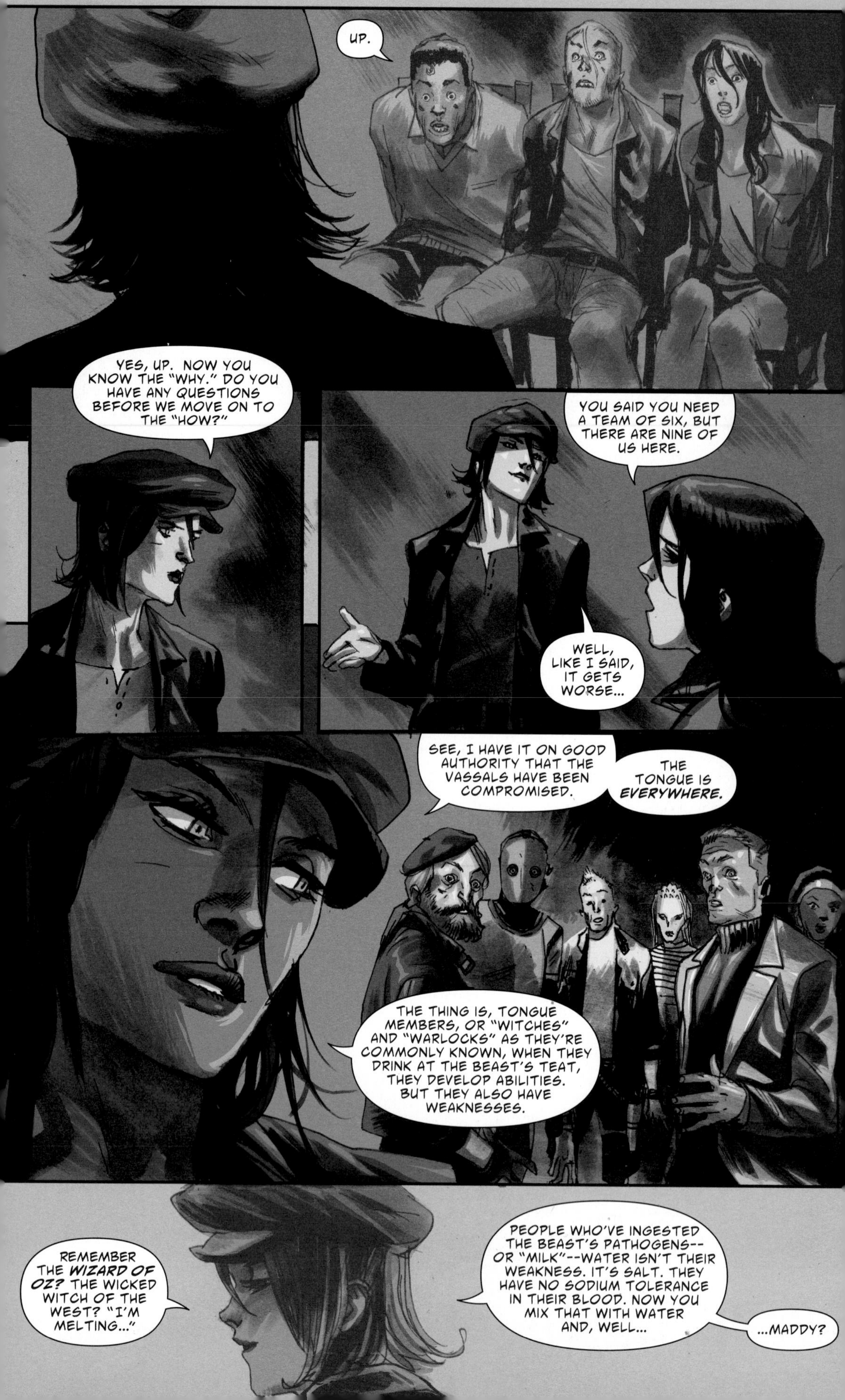
UP.
YES, UP. NOW YOU KNOW THE "WHY." DO YOU HAVE ANY QUESTIONS BEFORE WE MOVE ON TO THE "HOW?"
YOU SAID YOU NEED A TEAM OF SIX, BUT THERE ARE NINE OF US HERE.
WELL, LIKE I SAID, IT GETS WORSE...
SEE, I HAVE IT ON GOOD AUTHORITY THAT THE VASSALS HAVE BEEN COMPROMISED.
THE TONGUE IS *EVERYWHERE.*
THE THING IS, TONGUE MEMBERS, OR "WITCHES" AND "WARLOCKS" AS THEY'RE COMMONLY KNOWN, WHEN THEY DRINK AT THE BEAST'S TEAT, THEY DEVELOP ABILITIES. BUT THEY ALSO HAVE WEAKNESSES.
REMEMBER THE ***WIZARD OF OZ?*** THE WICKED WITCH OF THE WEST? "I'M MELTING..."
PEOPLE WHO'VE INGESTED THE BEAST'S PATHOGENS--OR "MILK"--WATER ISN'T THEIR WEAKNESS. IT'S SALT. THEY HAVE NO SODIUM TOLERANCE IN THEIR BLOOD. NOW YOU MIX THAT WITH WATER AND, WELL...
...MADDY?

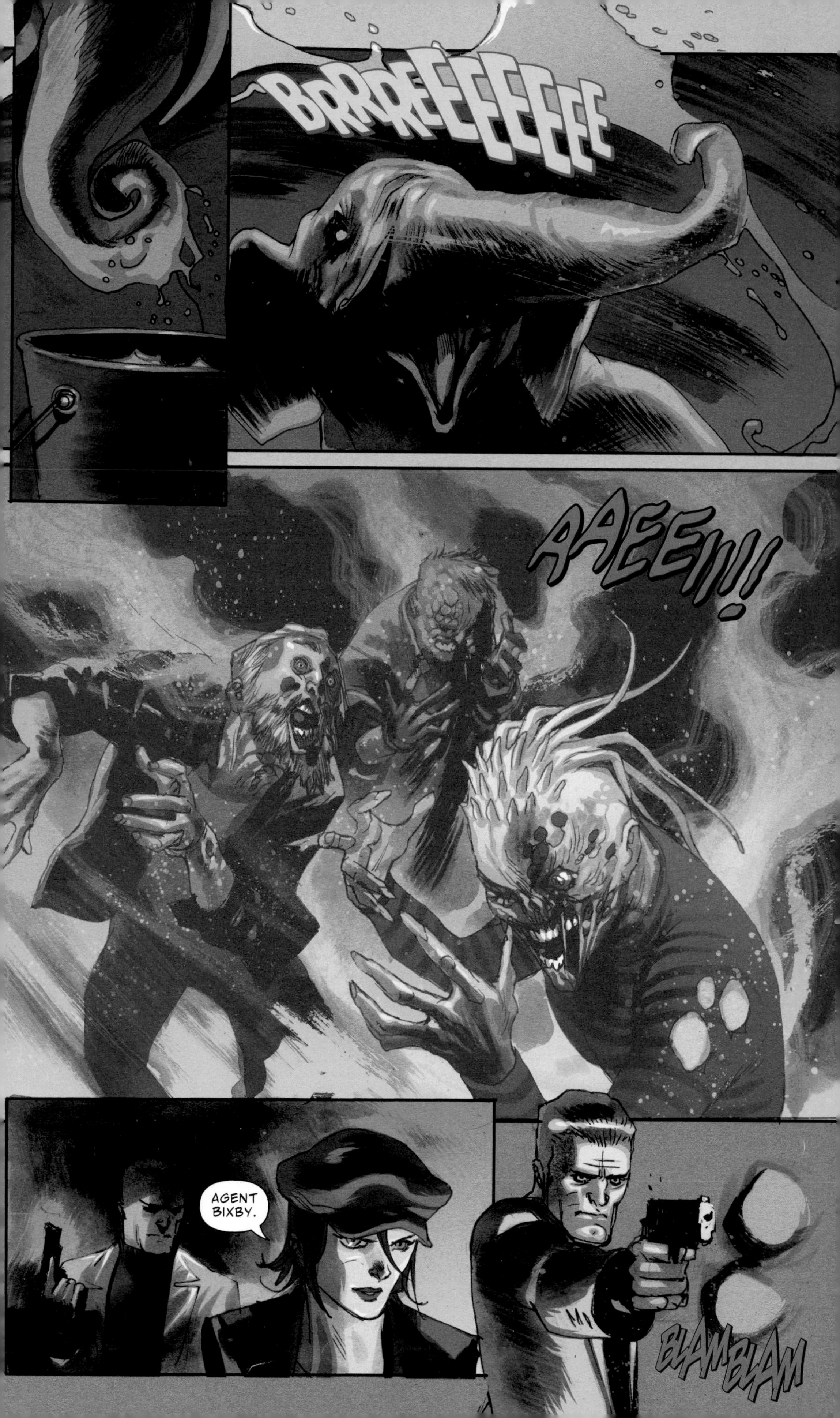
BRRREEEEEEEE
AAEEII!!
AGENT BIXBY.
BLAM BLAM

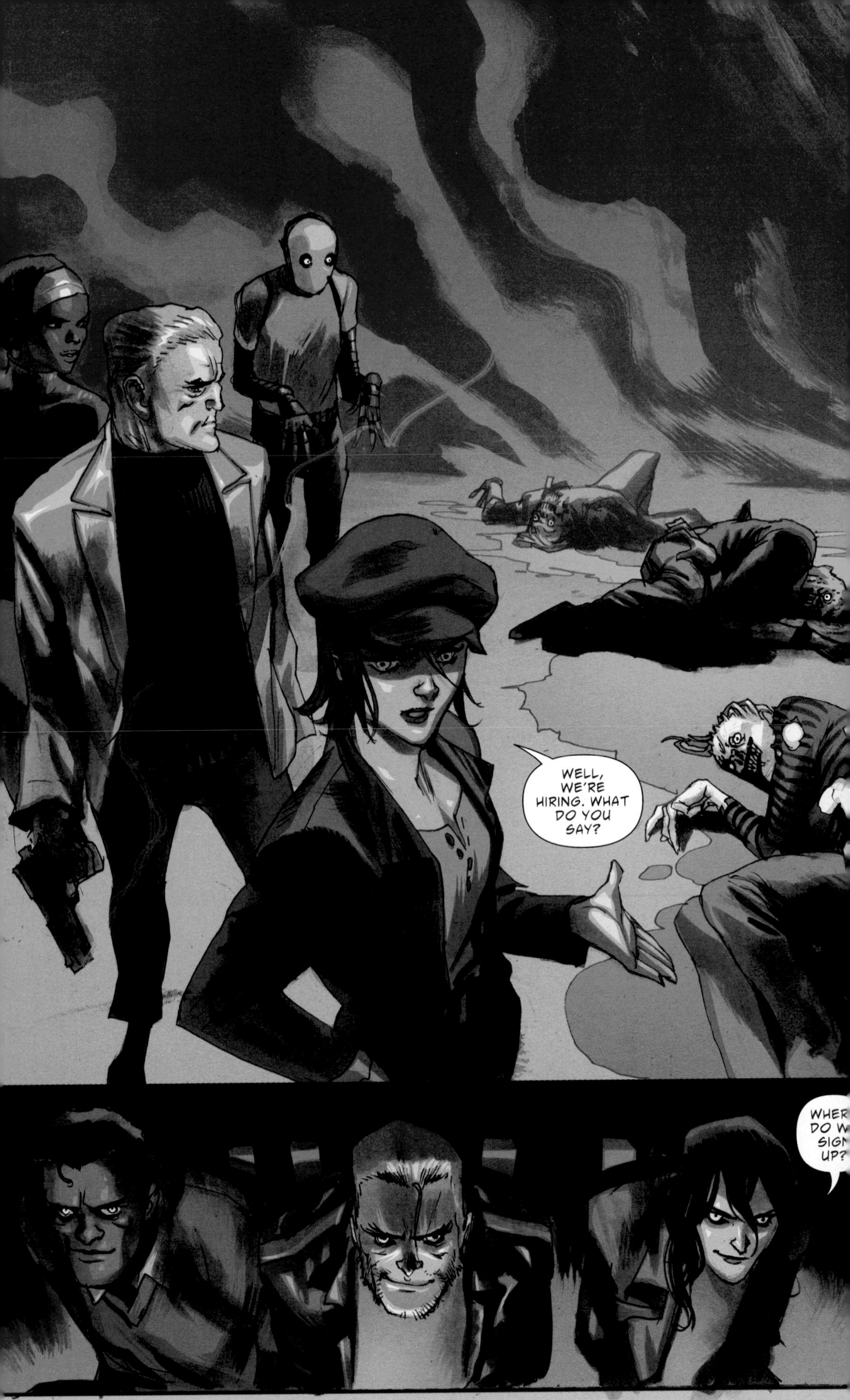
WELL, WE'RE HIRING. WHAT DO YOU SAY?
WHER DO W SIGN UP?

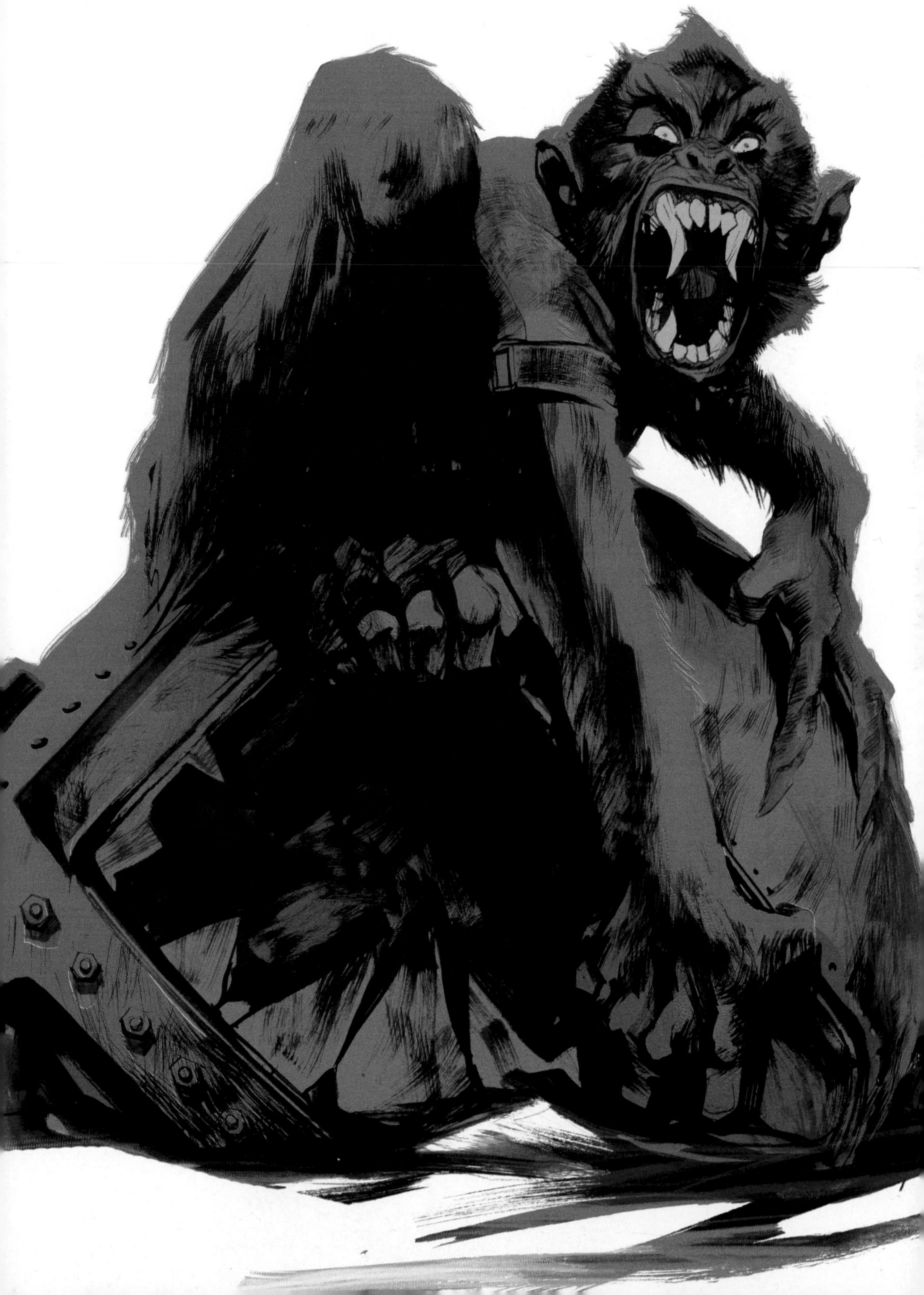

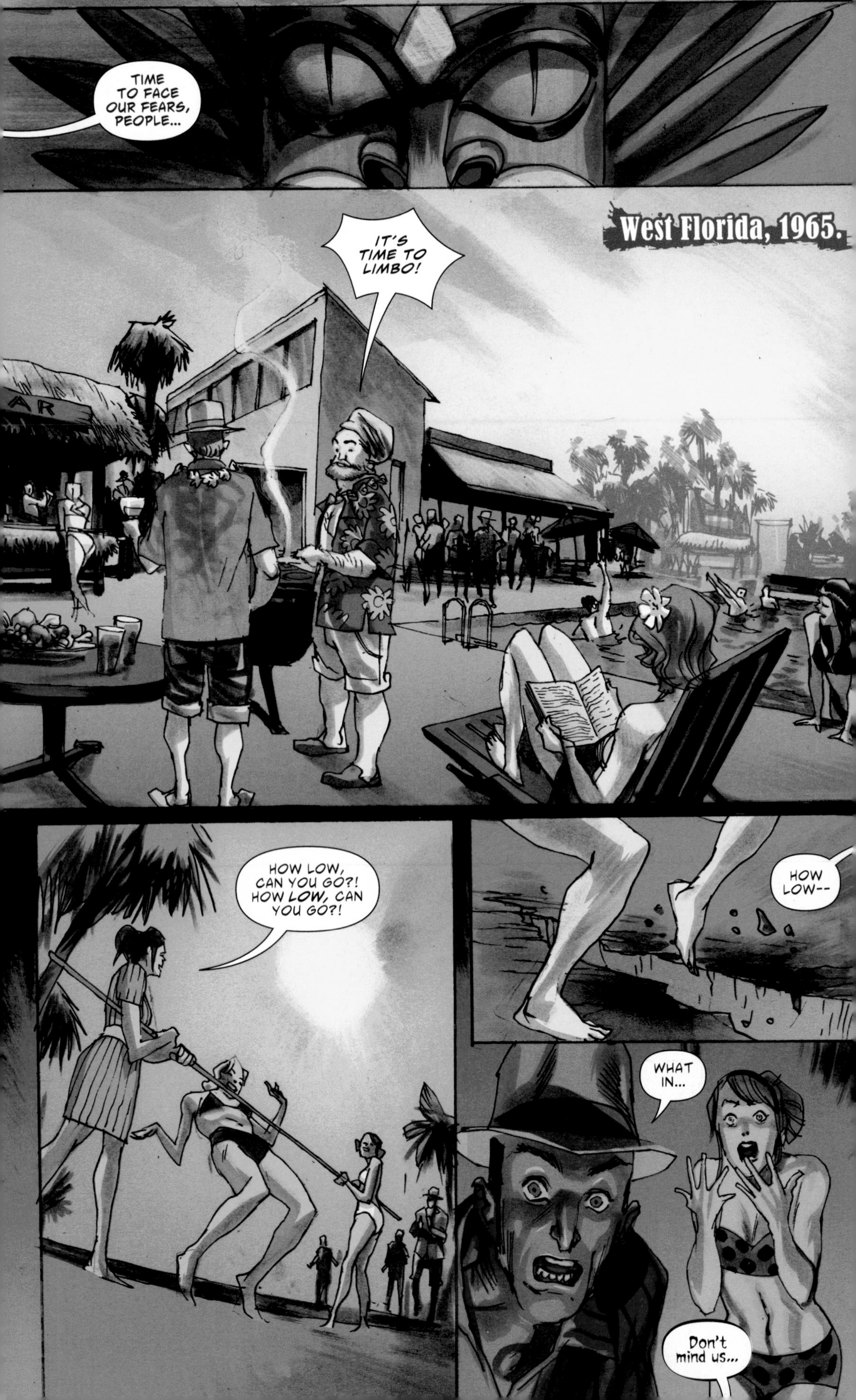
TIME TO FACE OUR FEARS, PEOPLE...
West Florida, 1965.
IT'S TIME TO LIMBO!
AR
HOW LOW, CAN YOU GO?! HOW LOW, CAN YOU GO?!
HOW LOW--
WHAT IN...
Don't mind us...

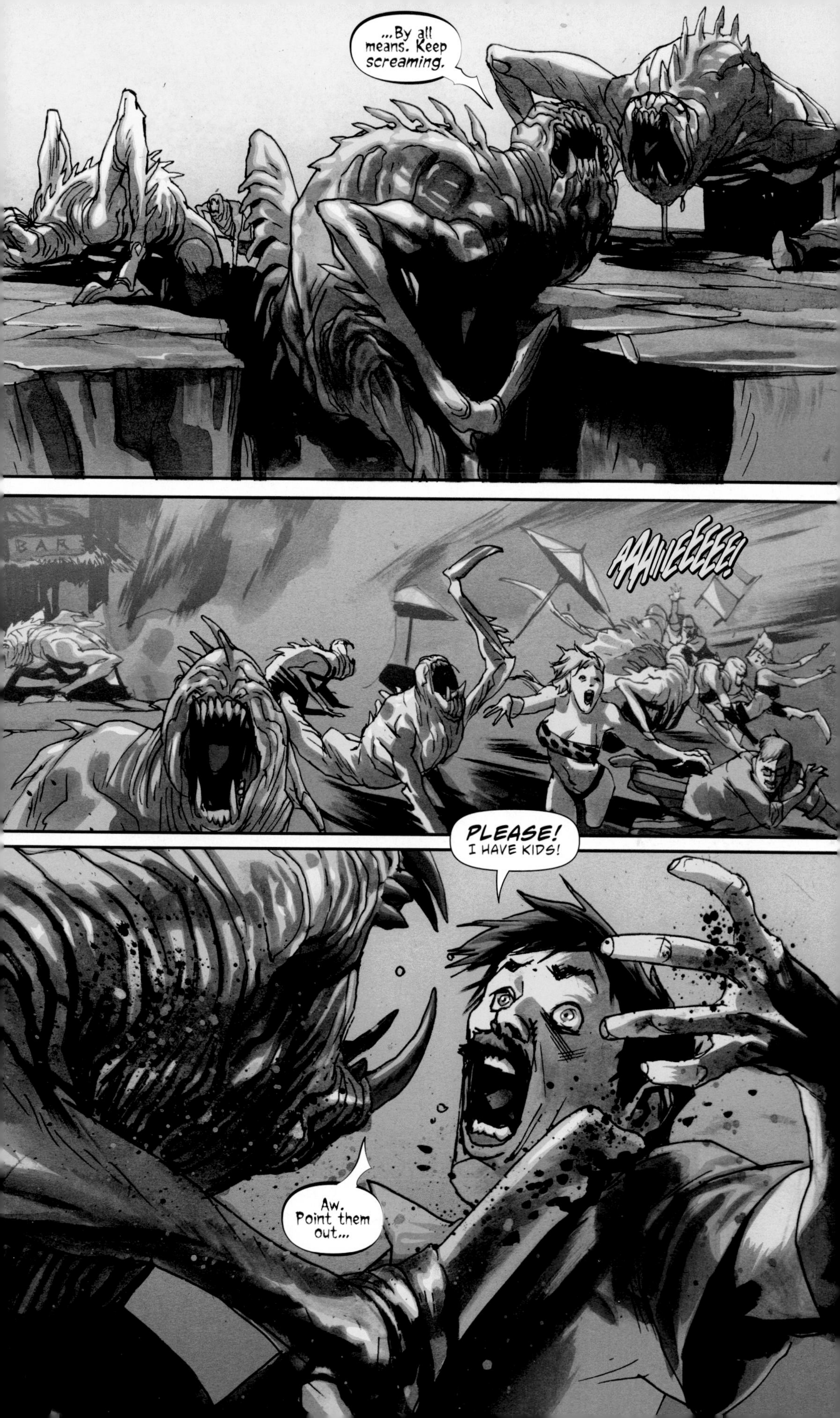
...By all means. Keep screaming.
AAAIIEEEEE!
BAR
PLEASE! I HAVE KIDS!
Aw. Point them out...

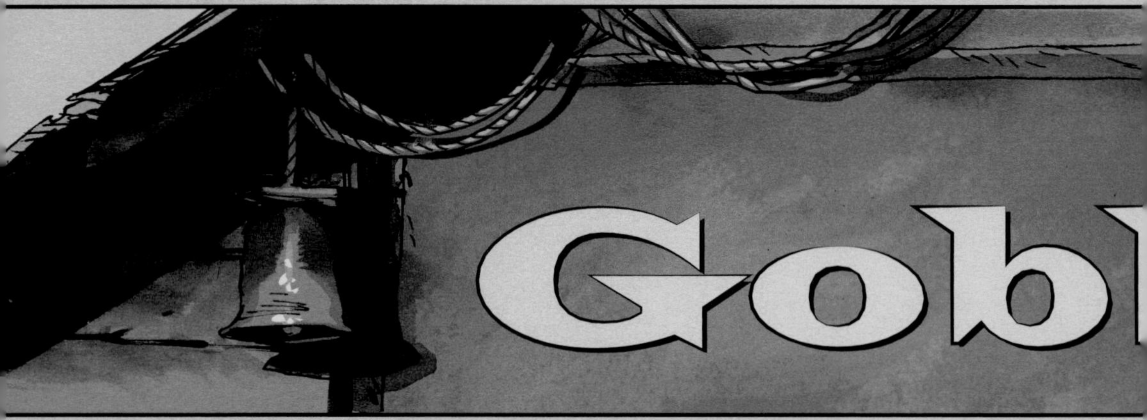
Gobb

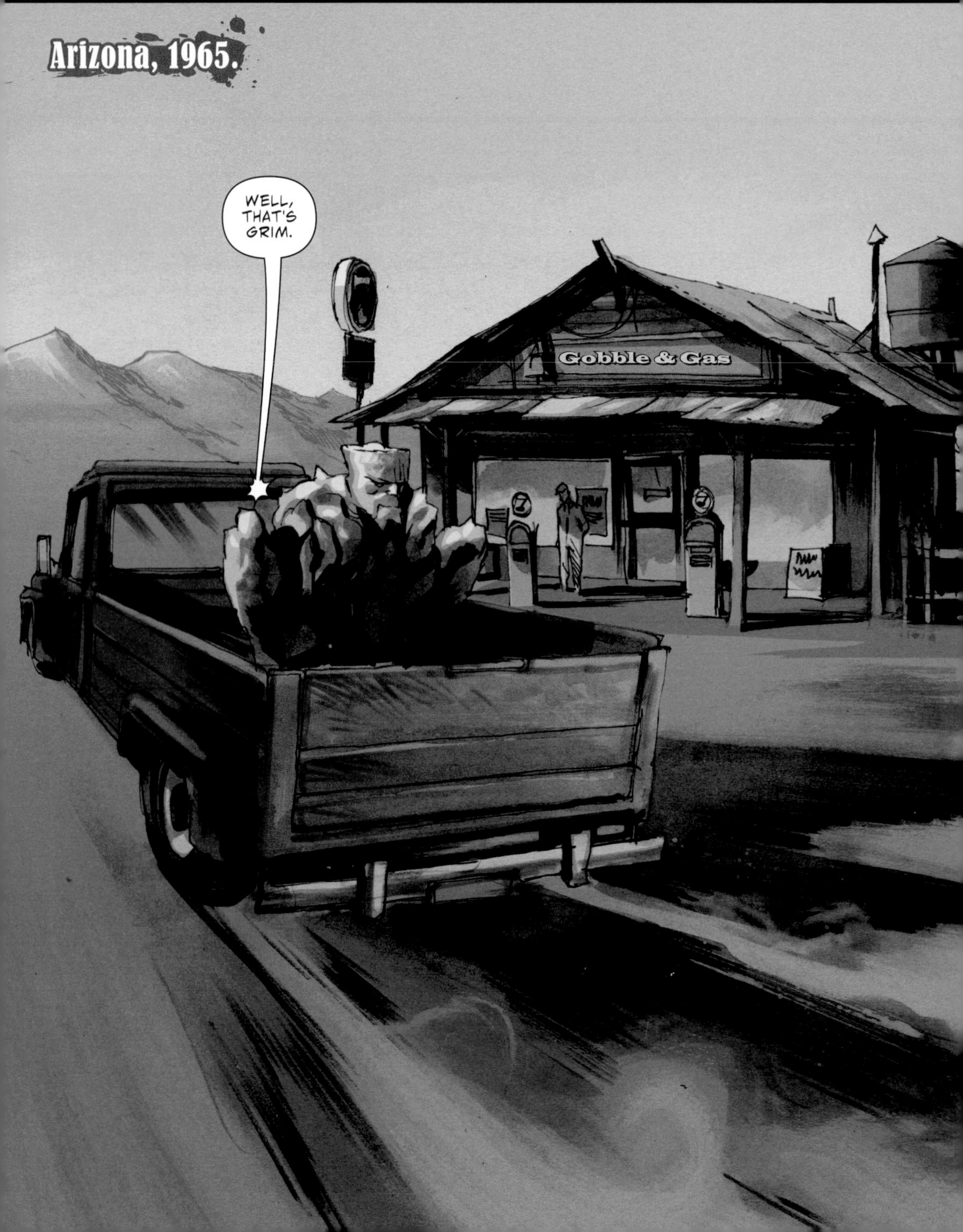
Arizona, 1965.
WELL, THAT'S GRIM.
Gobble & Gas

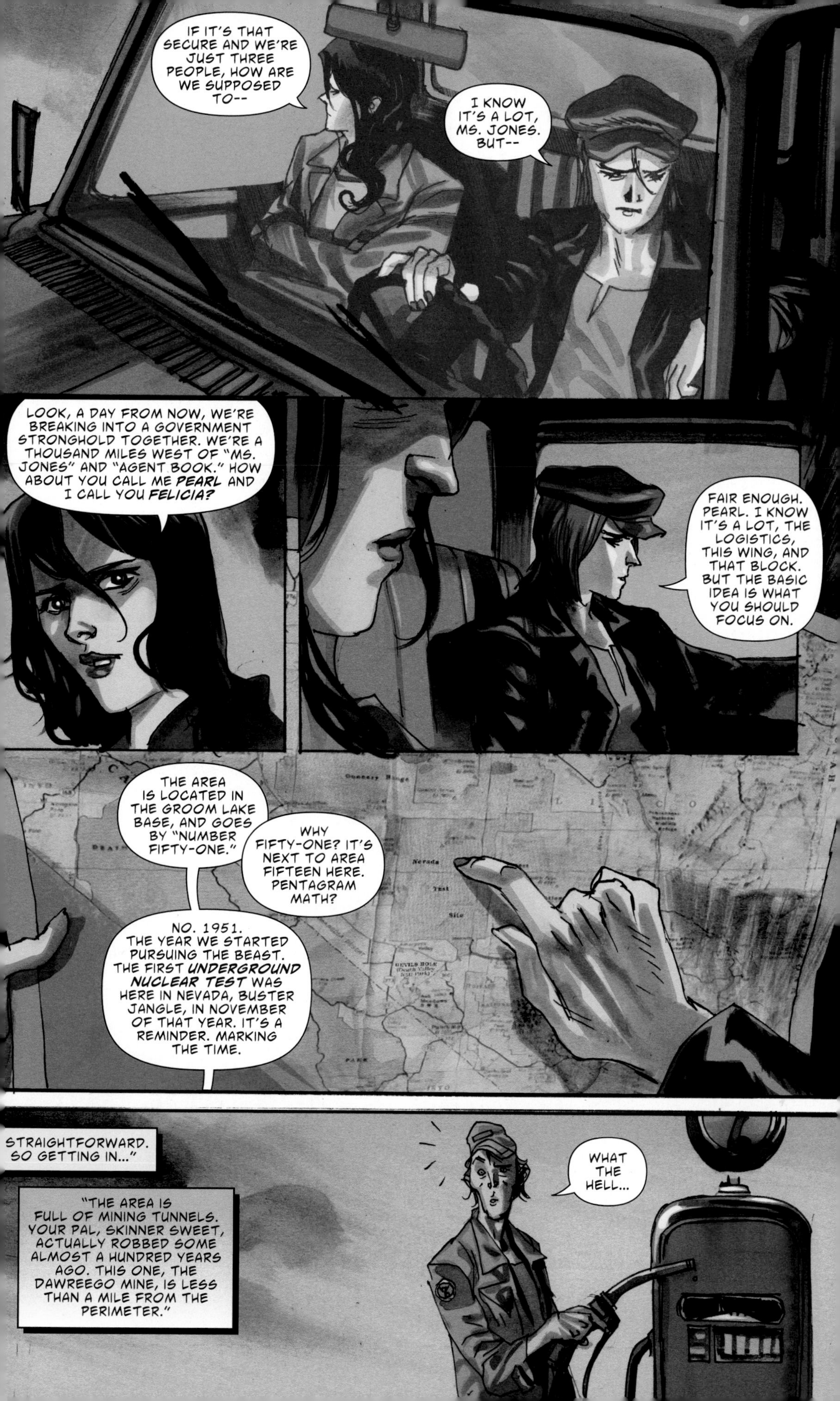
IF IT'S THAT SECURE AND WE'RE JUST THREE PEOPLE, HOW ARE WE SUPPOSED TO--
I KNOW IT'S A LOT, MS. JONES. BUT--
LOOK, A DAY FROM NOW, WE'RE BREAKING INTO A GOVERNMENT STRONGHOLD TOGETHER. WE'RE A THOUSAND MILES WEST OF "MS. JONES" AND "AGENT BOOK." HOW ABOUT YOU CALL ME PEARL AND I CALL YOU FELICIA?
FAIR ENOUGH. PEARL. I KNOW IT'S A LOT, THE LOGISTICS, THIS WING, AND THAT BLOCK. BUT THE BASIC IDEA IS WHAT YOU SHOULD FOCUS ON.
THE AREA IS LOCATED IN THE GROOM LAKE BASE, AND GOES BY "NUMBER FIFTY-ONE."
WHY FIFTY-ONE? IT'S NEXT TO AREA FIFTEEN HERE. PENTAGRAM MATH?
NO. 1951. THE YEAR WE STARTED PURSUING THE BEAST. THE FIRST UNDERGROUND NUCLEAR TEST WAS HERE IN NEVADA, BUSTER JANGLE, IN NOVEMBER OF THAT YEAR. IT'S A REMINDER. MARKING THE TIME.
STRAIGHTFORWARD. SO GETTING IN..."
"THE AREA IS FULL OF MINING TUNNELS. YOUR PAL, SKINNER SWEET, ACTUALLY ROBBED SOME ALMOST A HUNDRED YEARS AGO. THIS ONE, THE DAWREEGO MINE, IS LESS THAN A MILE FROM THE PERIMETER."
WHAT THE HELL...

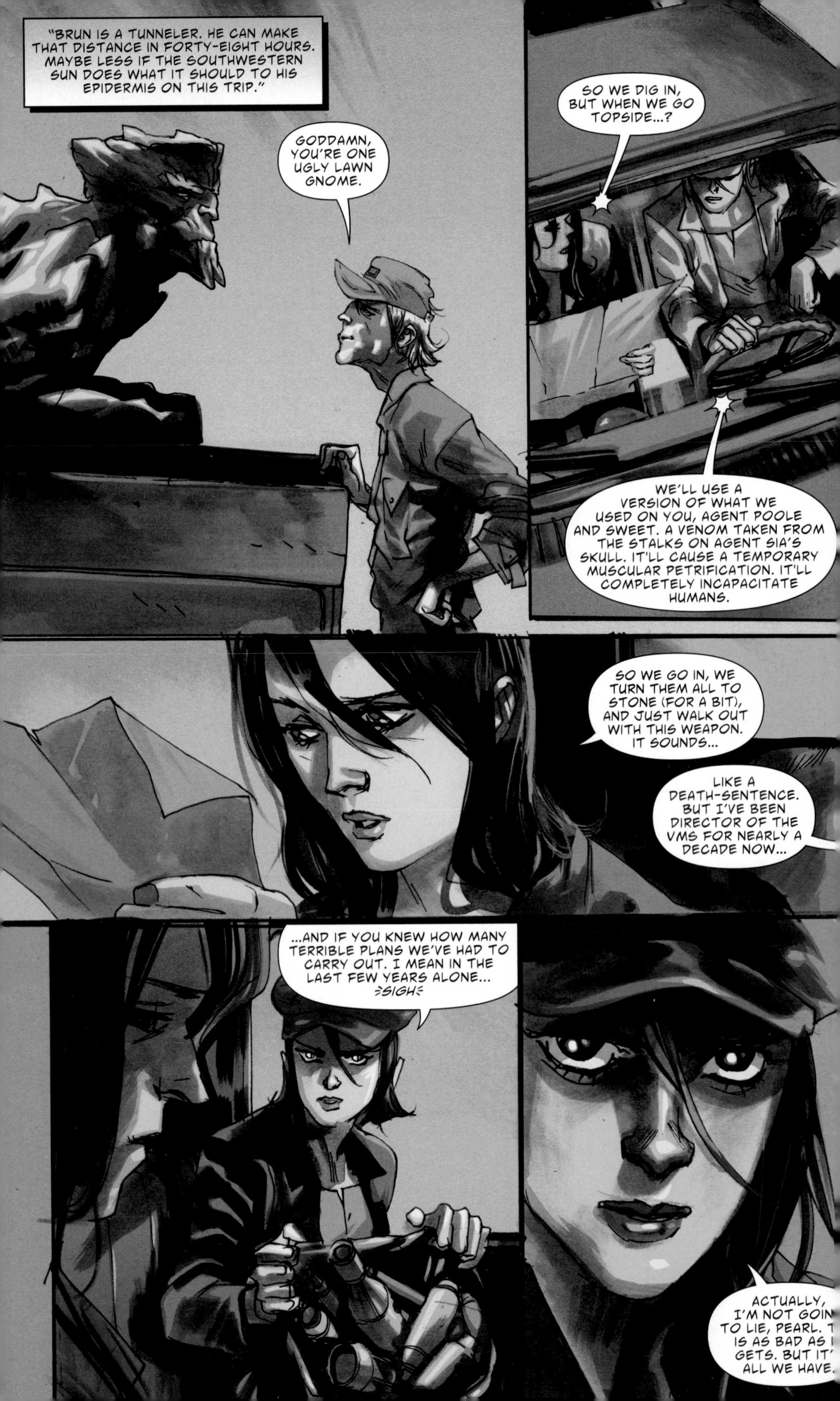
"BRUN IS A TUNNELER. HE CAN MAKE THAT DISTANCE IN FORTY-EIGHT HOURS. MAYBE LESS IF THE SOUTHWESTERN SUN DOES WHAT IT SHOULD TO HIS EPIDERMIS ON THIS TRIP."
GODDAMN, YOU'RE ONE UGLY LAWN GNOME.
SO WE DIG IN, BUT WHEN WE GO TOPSIDE...?
WE'LL USE A VERSION OF WHAT WE USED ON YOU, AGENT POOLE AND SWEET. A VENOM TAKEN FROM THE STALKS ON AGENT SIA'S SKULL. IT'LL CAUSE A TEMPORARY MUSCULAR PETRIFICATION. IT'LL COMPLETELY INCAPACITATE HUMANS.
SO WE GO IN, WE TURN THEM ALL TO STONE (FOR A BIT), AND JUST WALK OUT WITH THIS WEAPON. IT SOUNDS...
LIKE A DEATH-SENTENCE. BUT I'VE BEEN DIRECTOR OF THE VMS FOR NEARLY A DECADE NOW...
...AND IF YOU KNEW HOW MANY TERRIBLE PLANS WE'VE HAD TO CARRY OUT. I MEAN IN THE LAST FEW YEARS ALONE... SIGH
ACTUALLY, I'M NOT GOIN TO LIE, PEARL. T IS AS BAD AS GETS. BUT IT' ALL WE HAVE.

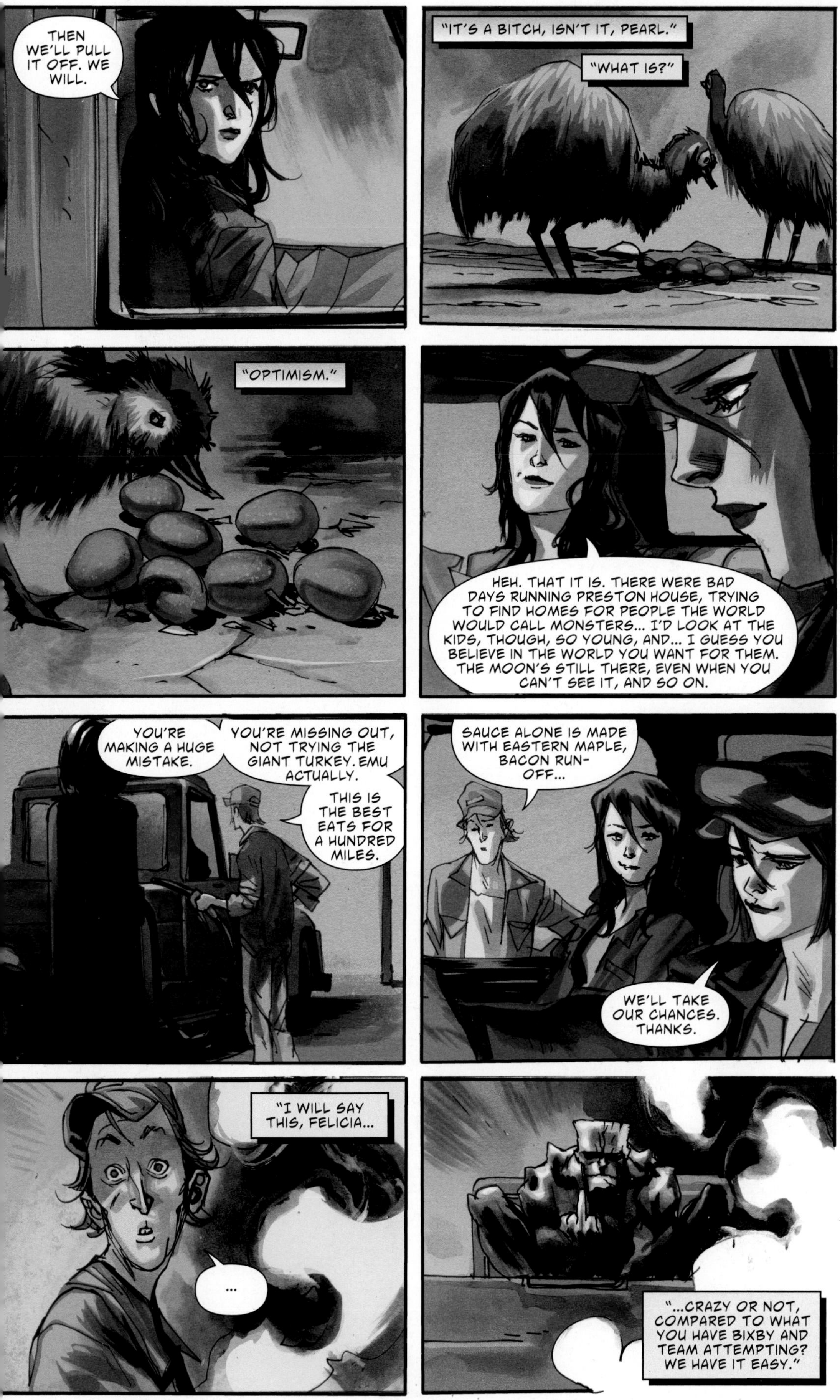
THEN WE'LL PULL IT OFF. WE WILL.
"IT'S A BITCH, ISN'T IT, PEARL."
"WHAT IS?"
"OPTIMISM."
HEH. THAT IT IS. THERE WERE BAD DAYS RUNNING PRESTON HOUSE, TRYING TO FIND HOMES FOR PEOPLE THE WORLD WOULD CALL MONSTERS... I'D LOOK AT THE KIDS, THOUGH, SO YOUNG, AND... I GUESS YOU BELIEVE IN THE WORLD YOU WANT FOR THEM. THE MOON'S STILL THERE, EVEN WHEN YOU CAN'T SEE IT, AND SO ON.
YOU'RE MAKING A HUGE MISTAKE.
YOU'RE MISSING OUT, NOT TRYING THE GIANT TURKEY. EMU ACTUALLY.
THIS IS THE BEST EATS FOR A HUNDRED MILES.
SAUCE ALONE IS MADE WITH EASTERN MAPLE, BACON RUN-OFF...
WE'LL TAKE OUR CHANCES. THANKS.
"I WILL SAY THIS, FELICIA...
...
"...CRAZY OR NOT, COMPARED TO WHAT YOU HAVE BIXBY AND TEAM ATTEMPTING? WE HAVE IT EASY."

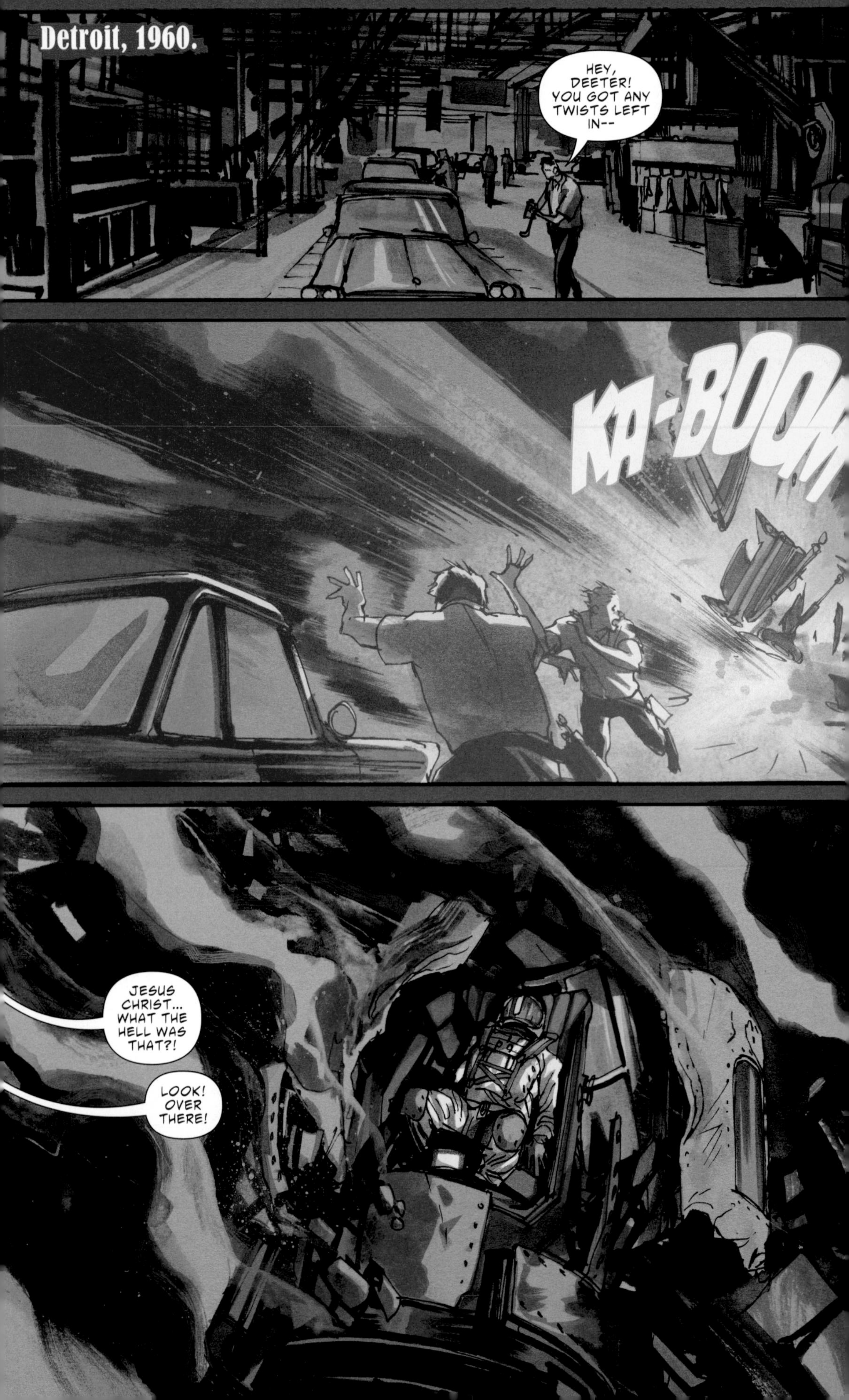
Detroit, 1960.
HEY, DEETER! YOU GOT ANY TWISTS LEFT IN--
KA-BOOM
JESUS CHRIST... WHAT THE HELL WAS THAT?!
LOOK! OVER THERE!

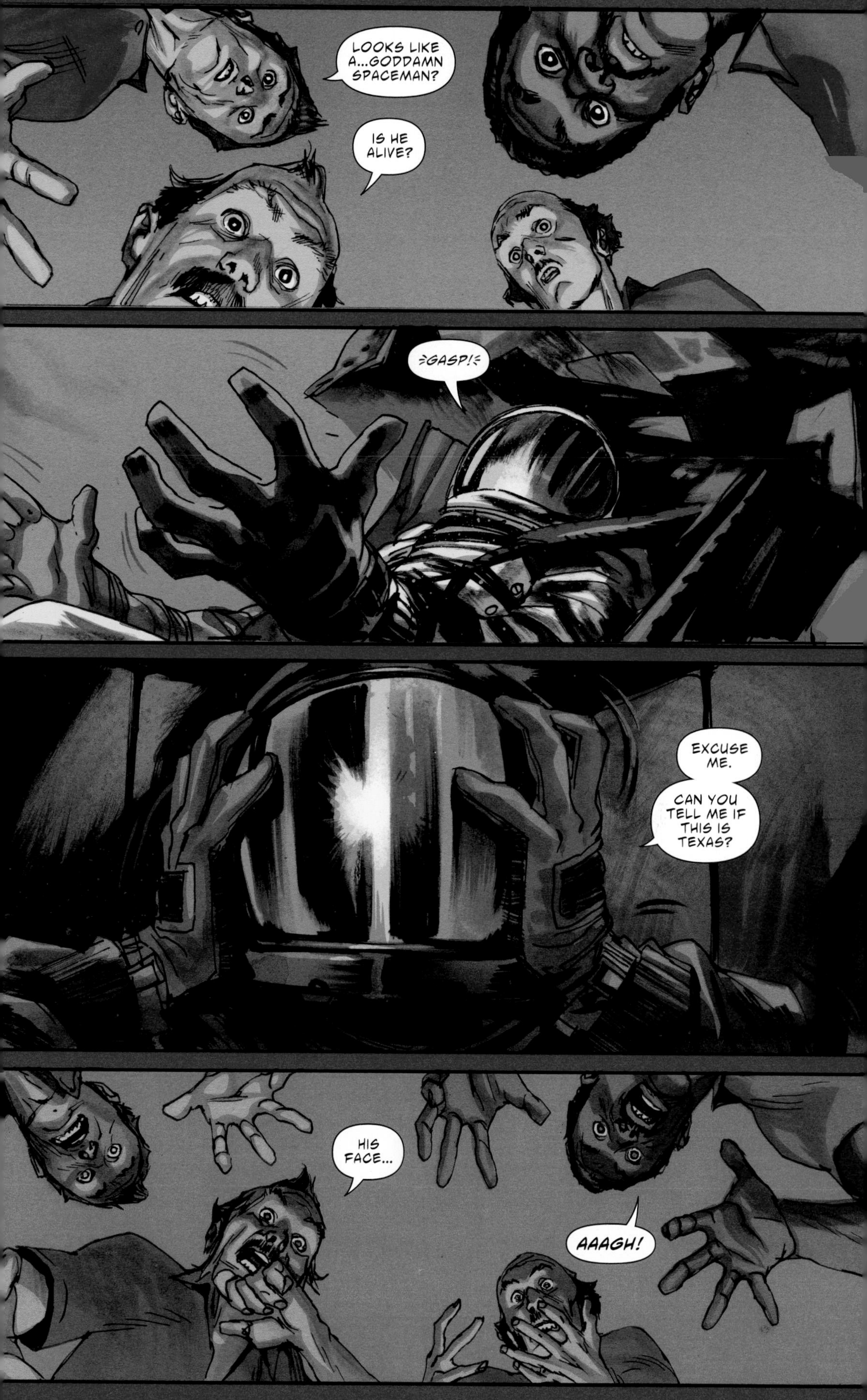
LOOKS LIKE A...GODDAMN SPACEMAN?
IS HE ALIVE?
GASP!
EXCUSE ME.
CAN YOU TELL ME IF THIS IS TEXAS?
HIS FACE...
AAAGH!

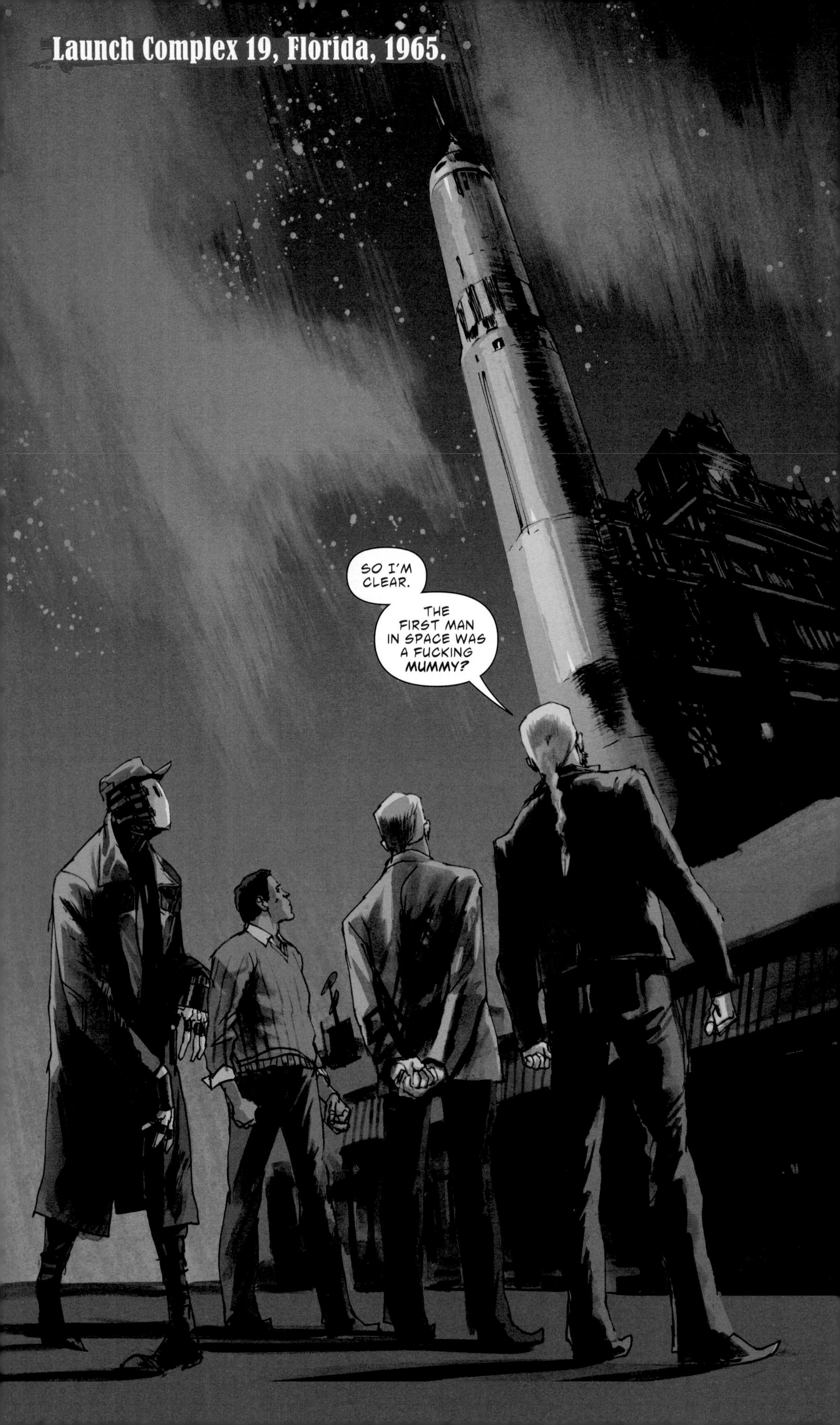
Launch Complex 19, Florida, 1965.
SO I'M CLEAR.
THE FIRST MAN IN SPACE WAS A FUCKING MUMMY?

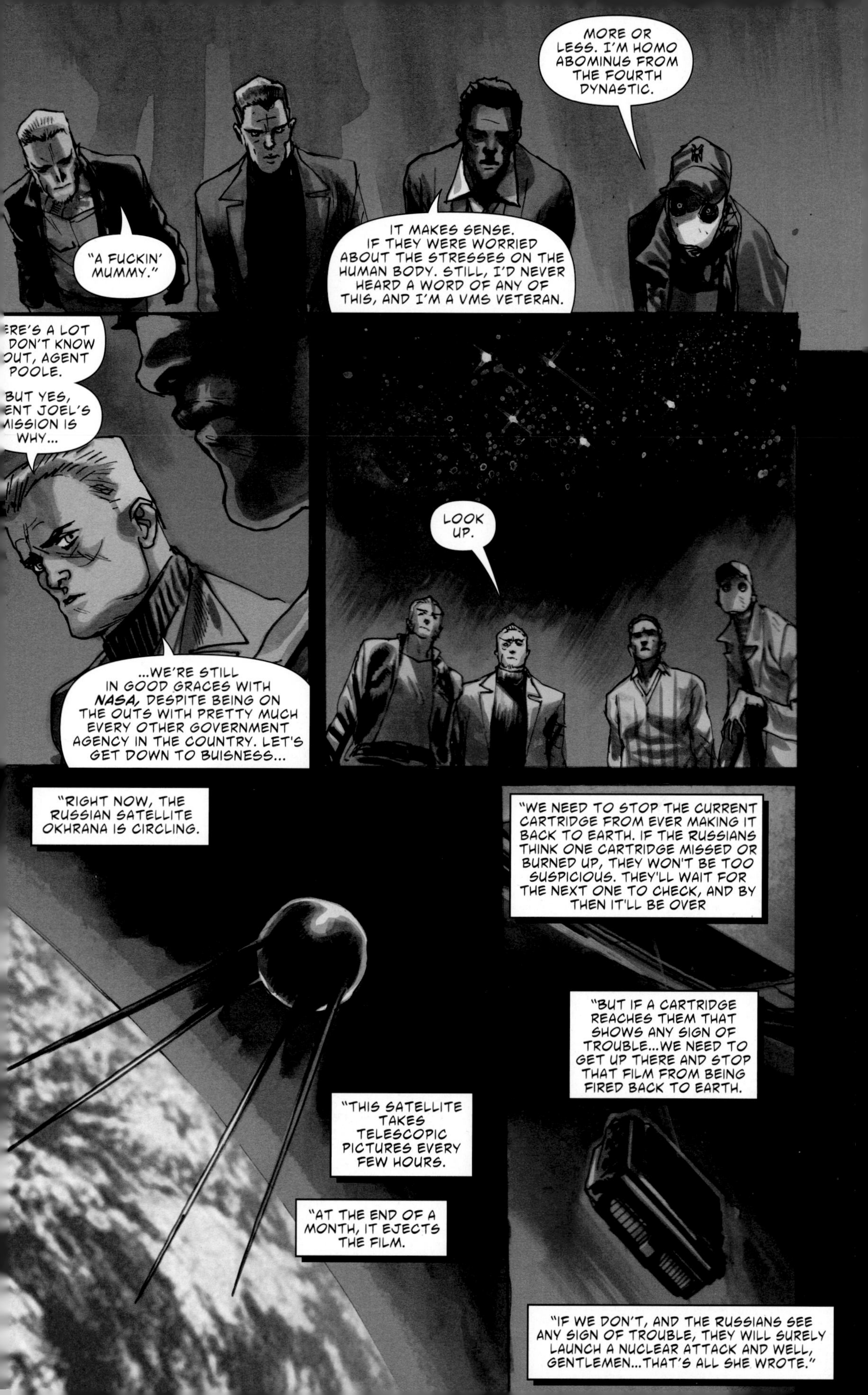
MORE OR LESS. I'M HOMO ABOMINUS FROM THE FOURTH DYNASTIC.
"A FUCKIN' MUMMY."
IT MAKES SENSE. IF THEY WERE WORRIED ABOUT THE STRESSES ON THE HUMAN BODY. STILL, I'D NEVER HEARD A WORD OF ANY OF THIS, AND I'M A VMS VETERAN.
ERE'S A LOT DON'T KNOW OUT, AGENT POOLE.
BUT YES, ENT JOEL'S MISSION IS WHY...
...WE'RE STILL IN GOOD GRACES WITH NASA, DESPITE BEING ON THE OUTS WITH PRETTY MUCH EVERY OTHER GOVERNMENT AGENCY IN THE COUNTRY. LET'S GET DOWN TO BUISNESS...
LOOK UP.
"RIGHT NOW, THE RUSSIAN SATELLITE OKHRANA IS CIRCLING.
"THIS SATELLITE TAKES TELESCOPIC PICTURES EVERY FEW HOURS.
"AT THE END OF A MONTH, IT EJECTS THE FILM.
"WE NEED TO STOP THE CURRENT CARTRIDGE FROM EVER MAKING IT BACK TO EARTH. IF THE RUSSIANS THINK ONE CARTRIDGE MISSED OR BURNED UP, THEY WON'T BE TOO SUSPICIOUS. THEY'LL WAIT FOR THE NEXT ONE TO CHECK, AND BY THEN IT'LL BE OVER
"BUT IF A CARTRIDGE REACHES THEM THAT SHOWS ANY SIGN OF TROUBLE...WE NEED TO GET UP THERE AND STOP THAT FILM FROM BEING FIRED BACK TO EARTH.
"IF WE DON'T, AND THE RUSSIANS SEE ANY SIGN OF TROUBLE, THEY WILL SURELY LAUNCH A NUCLEAR ATTACK AND WELL, GENTLEMEN...THAT'S ALL SHE WROTE."

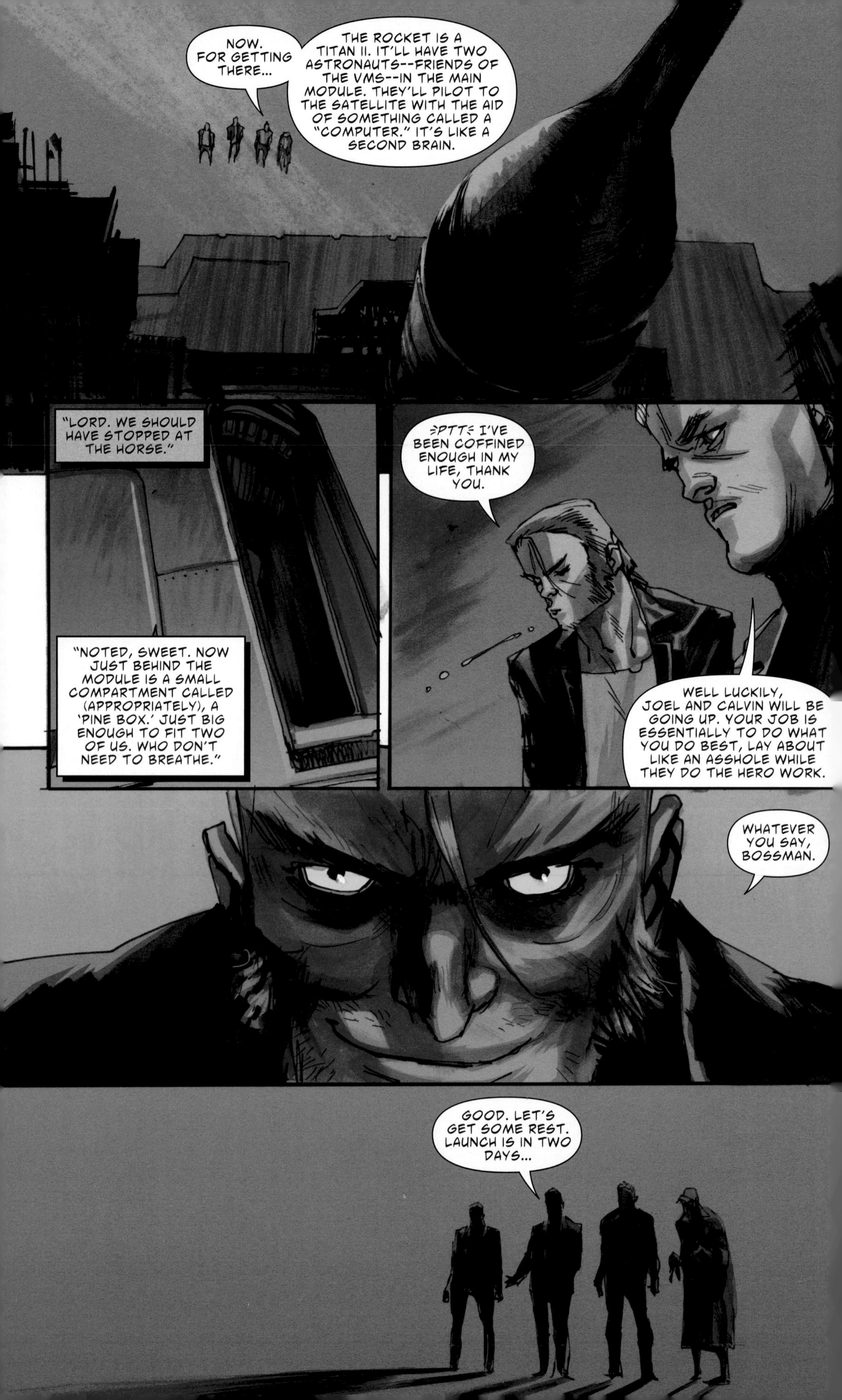
NOW. FOR GETTING THERE...
THE ROCKET IS A TITAN II. IT'LL HAVE TWO ASTRONAUTS--FRIENDS OF THE VMS--IN THE MAIN MODULE. THEY'LL PILOT TO THE SATELLITE WITH THE AID OF SOMETHING CALLED A "COMPUTER." IT'S LIKE A SECOND BRAIN.
"LORD. WE SHOULD HAVE STOPPED AT THE HORSE."
"NOTED, SWEET. NOW JUST BEHIND THE MODULE IS A SMALL COMPARTMENT CALLED (APPROPRIATELY), A 'PINE BOX.' JUST BIG ENOUGH TO FIT TWO OF US. WHO DON'T NEED TO BREATHE."
=PTT= I'VE BEEN COFFINED ENOUGH IN MY LIFE, THANK YOU.
WELL LUCKILY, JOEL AND CALVIN WILL BE GOING UP. YOUR JOB IS ESSENTIALLY TO DO WHAT YOU DO BEST, LAY ABOUT LIKE AN ASSHOLE WHILE THEY DO THE HERO WORK.
WHATEVER YOU SAY, BOSSMAN.
GOOD. LET'S GET SOME REST. LAUNCH IS IN TWO DAYS...

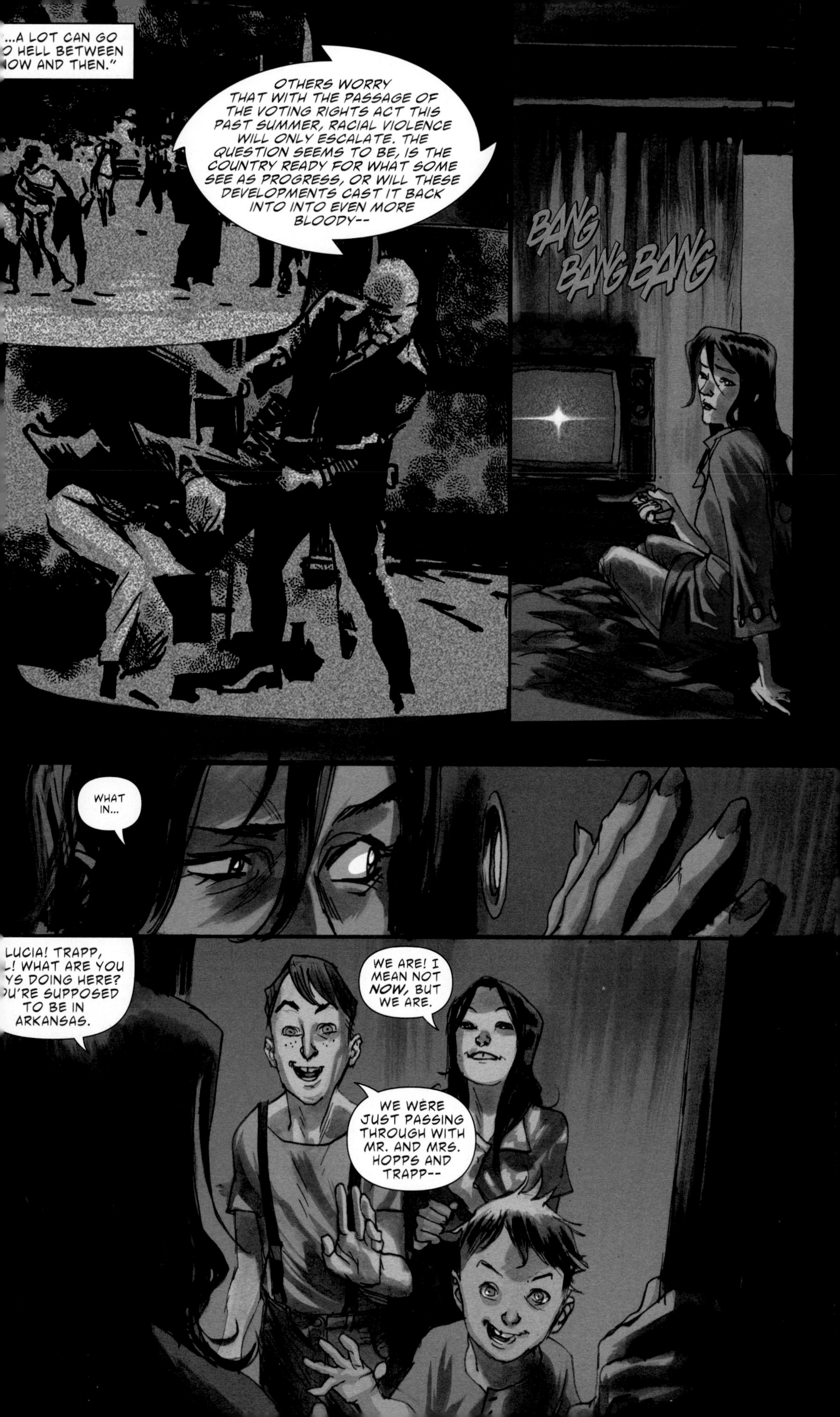

...A LOT CAN GO
O HELL BETWEEN
NOW AND THEN."
OTHERS WORRY THAT WITH THE PASSAGE OF THE VOTING RIGHTS ACT THIS PAST SUMMER, RACIAL VIOLENCE WILL ONLY ESCALATE. THE QUESTION SEEMS TO BE, IS THE COUNTRY READY FOR WHAT SOME SEE AS PROGRESS, OR WILL THESE DEVELOPMENTS CAST IT BACK INTO INTO EVEN MORE BLOODY--
BANG BANG BANG
WHAT IN...
LUCIA! TRAPP, L! WHAT ARE YOU YS DOING HERE? U'RE SUPPOSED TO BE IN ARKANSAS.
WE ARE! I MEAN NOT NOW, BUT WE ARE.
WE WERE JUST PASSING THROUGH WITH MR. AND MRS. HOPPS AND TRAPP--

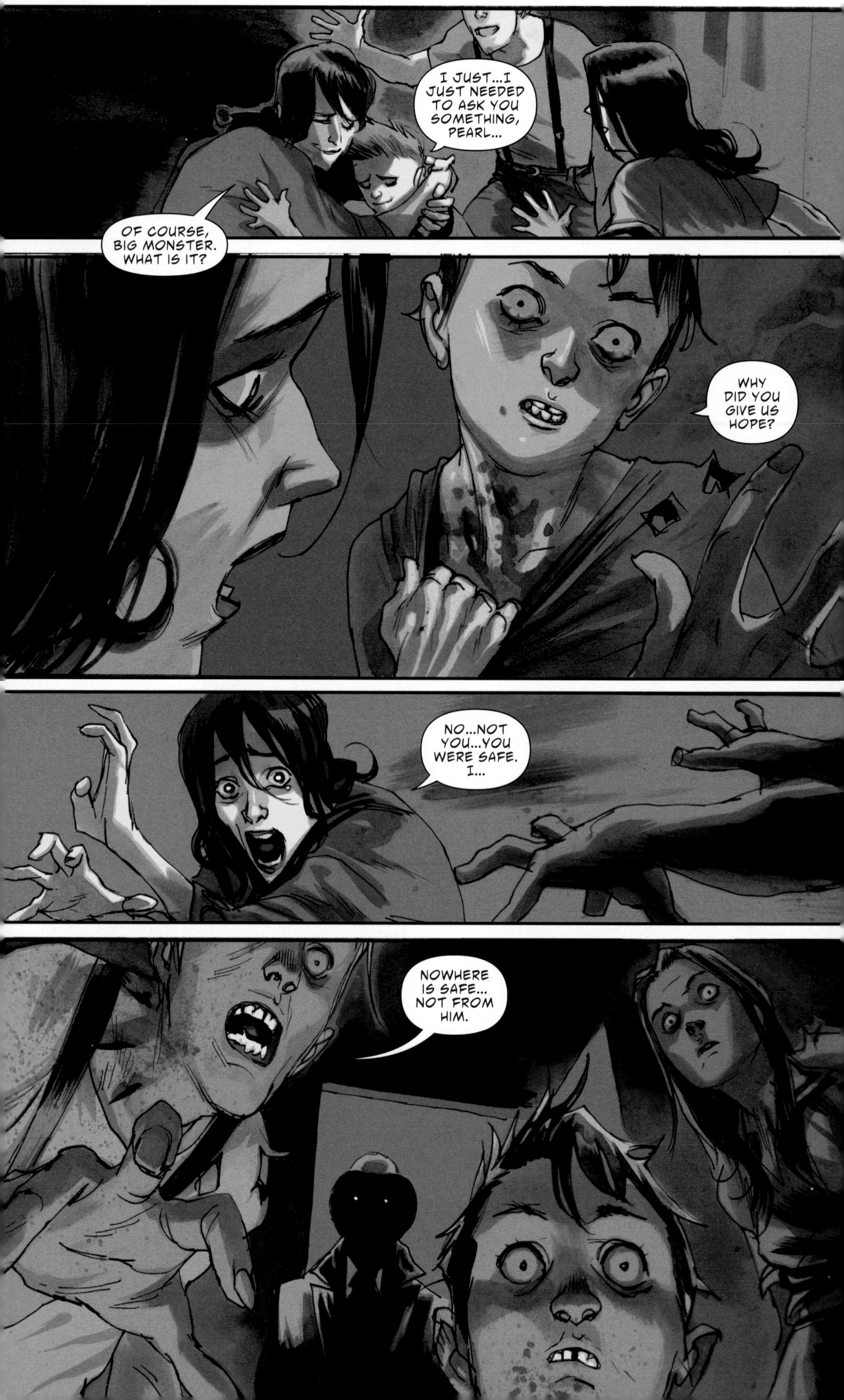
I JUST...I JUST NEEDED TO ASK YOU SOMETHING, PEARL...
OF COURSE, BIG MONSTER. WHAT IS IT?
WHY DID YOU GIVE US HOPE?
NO...NOT YOU...YOU WERE SAFE. I...
NOWHERE IS SAFE... NOT FROM HIM.

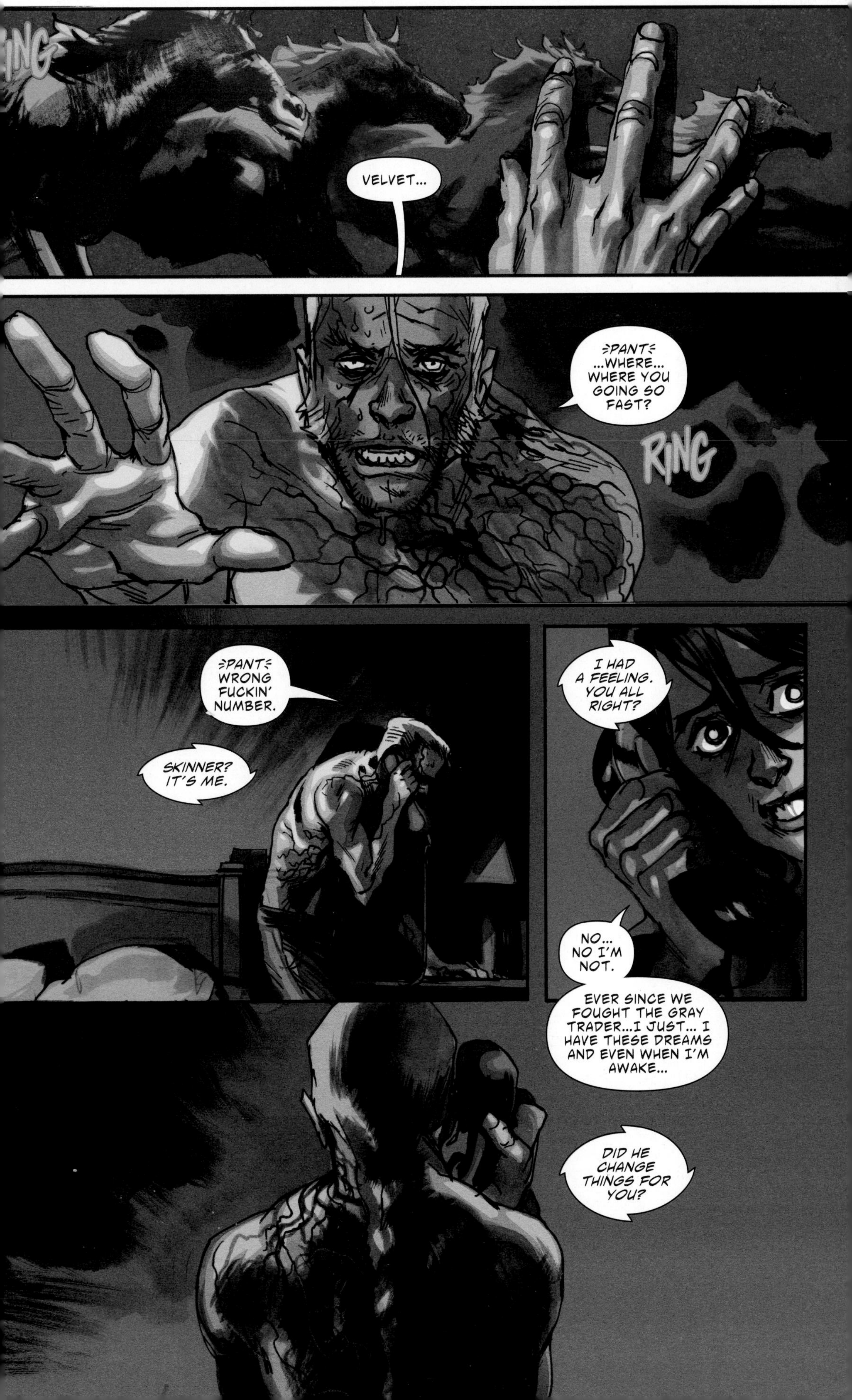
ING
VELVET...
=PANT=
...WHERE...
WHERE YOU
GOING SO
FAST?
RING
=PANT=
WRONG
FUCKIN'
NUMBER.
SKINNER?
IT'S ME.
I HAD
A FEELING.
YOU ALL
RIGHT?
NO...
NO I'M
NOT.
EVER SINCE WE
FOUGHT THE GRAY
TRADER...I JUST... I
HAVE THESE DREAMS
AND EVEN WHEN I'M
AWAKE...
DID HE
CHANGE
THINGS FOR
YOU?

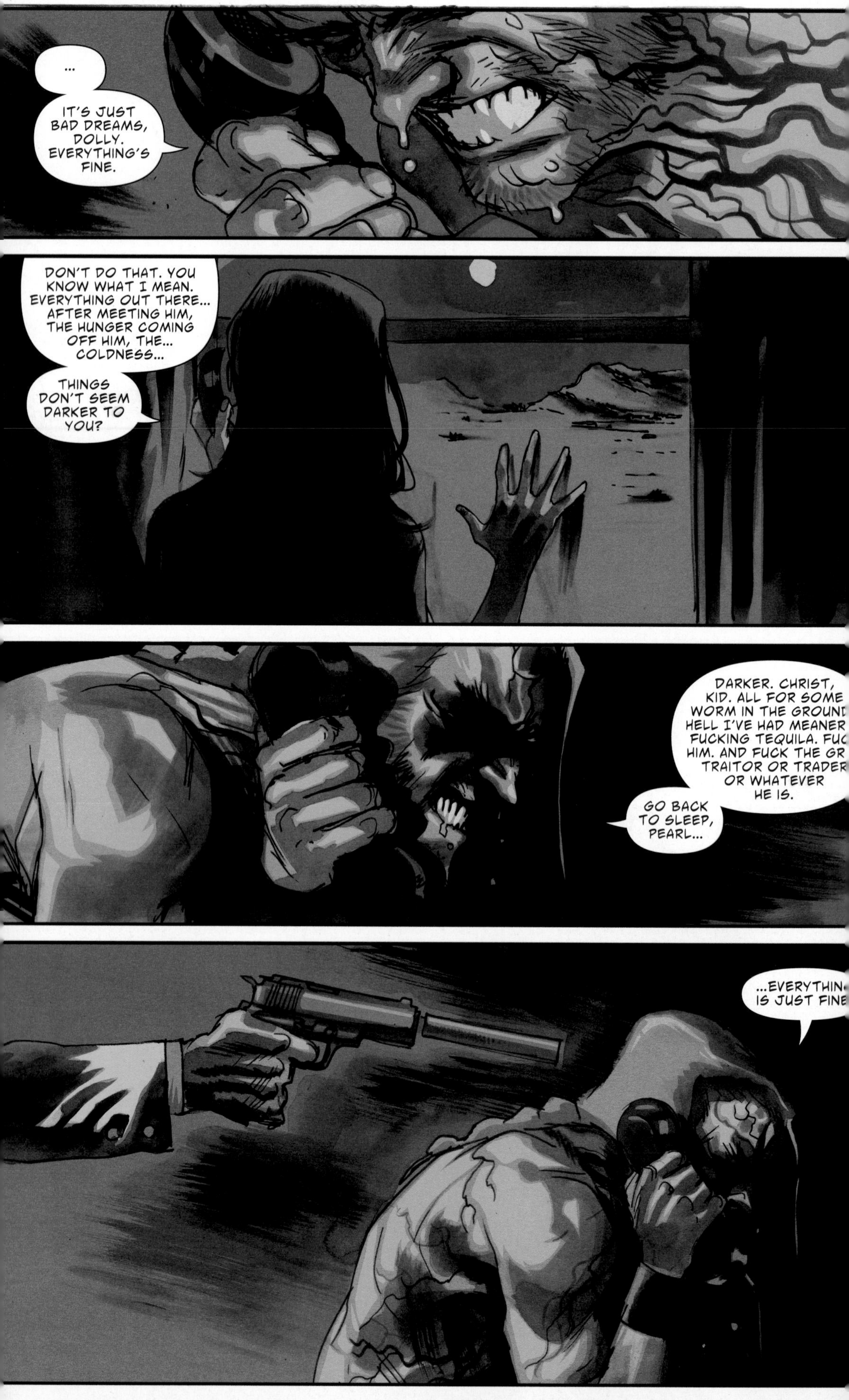
...
IT'S JUST BAD DREAMS, DOLLY. EVERYTHING'S FINE.
DON'T DO THAT. YOU KNOW WHAT I MEAN. EVERYTHING OUT THERE... AFTER MEETING HIM, THE HUNGER COMING OFF HIM, THE... COLDNESS...
THINGS DON'T SEEM DARKER TO YOU?
DARKER. CHRIST, KID. ALL FOR SOME WORM IN THE GROUN HELL I'VE HAD MEANER FUCKING TEQUILA. FU HIM. AND FUCK THE GR TRAITOR OR TRADER OR WHATEVER HE IS.
GO BACK TO SLEEP, PEARL...
...EVERYTHIN IS JUST FINE

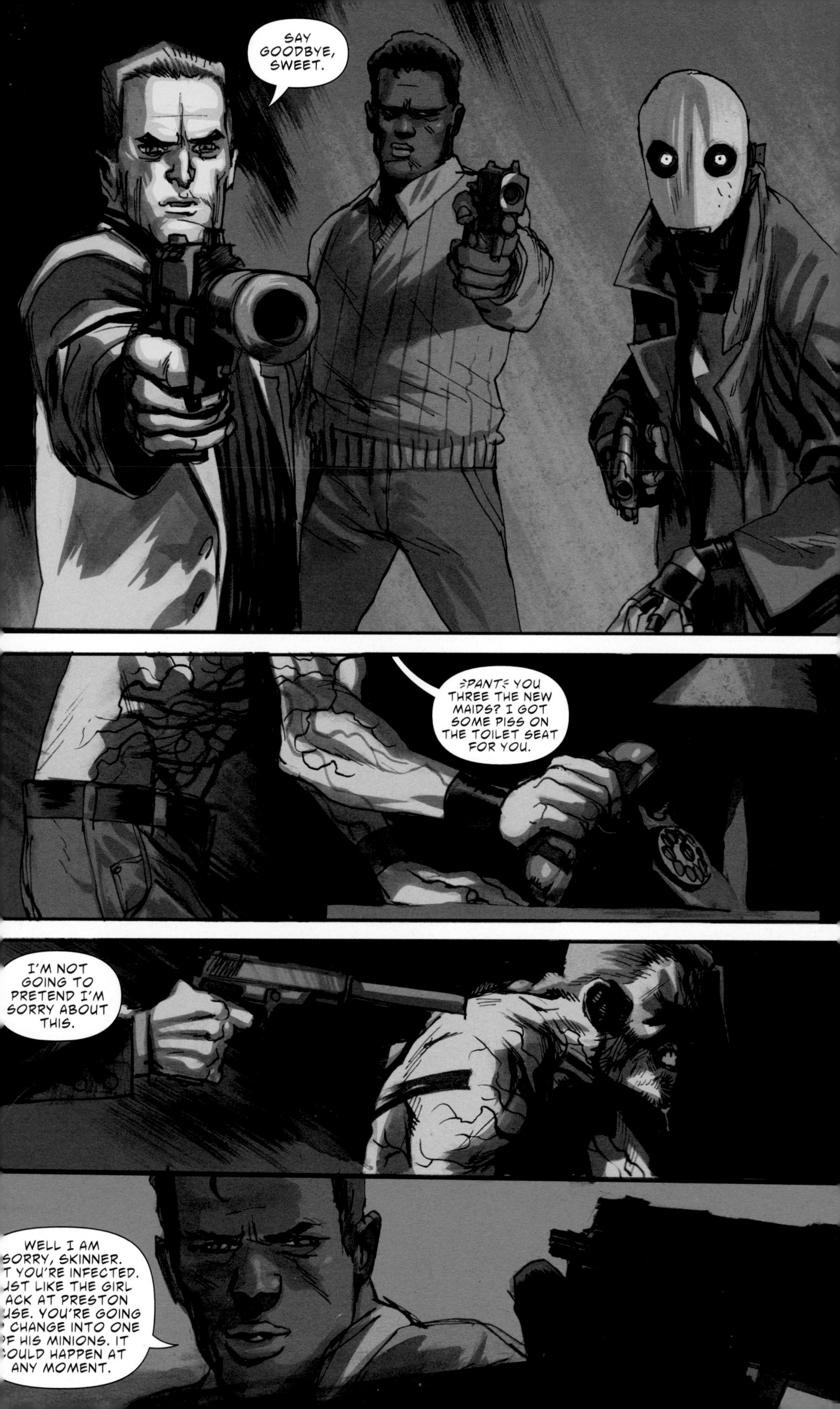
SAY GOODBYE, SWEET.
=PANT= YOU THREE THE NEW MAIDS? I GOT SOME PISS ON THE TOILET SEAT FOR YOU.
I'M NOT GOING TO PRETEND I'M SORRY ABOUT THIS.
WELL I AM SORRY, SKINNER. T YOU'RE INFECTED. UST LIKE THE GIRL ACK AT PRESTON USE. YOU'RE GOING CHANGE INTO ONE F HIS MINIONS. IT OULD HAPPEN AT ANY MOMENT.

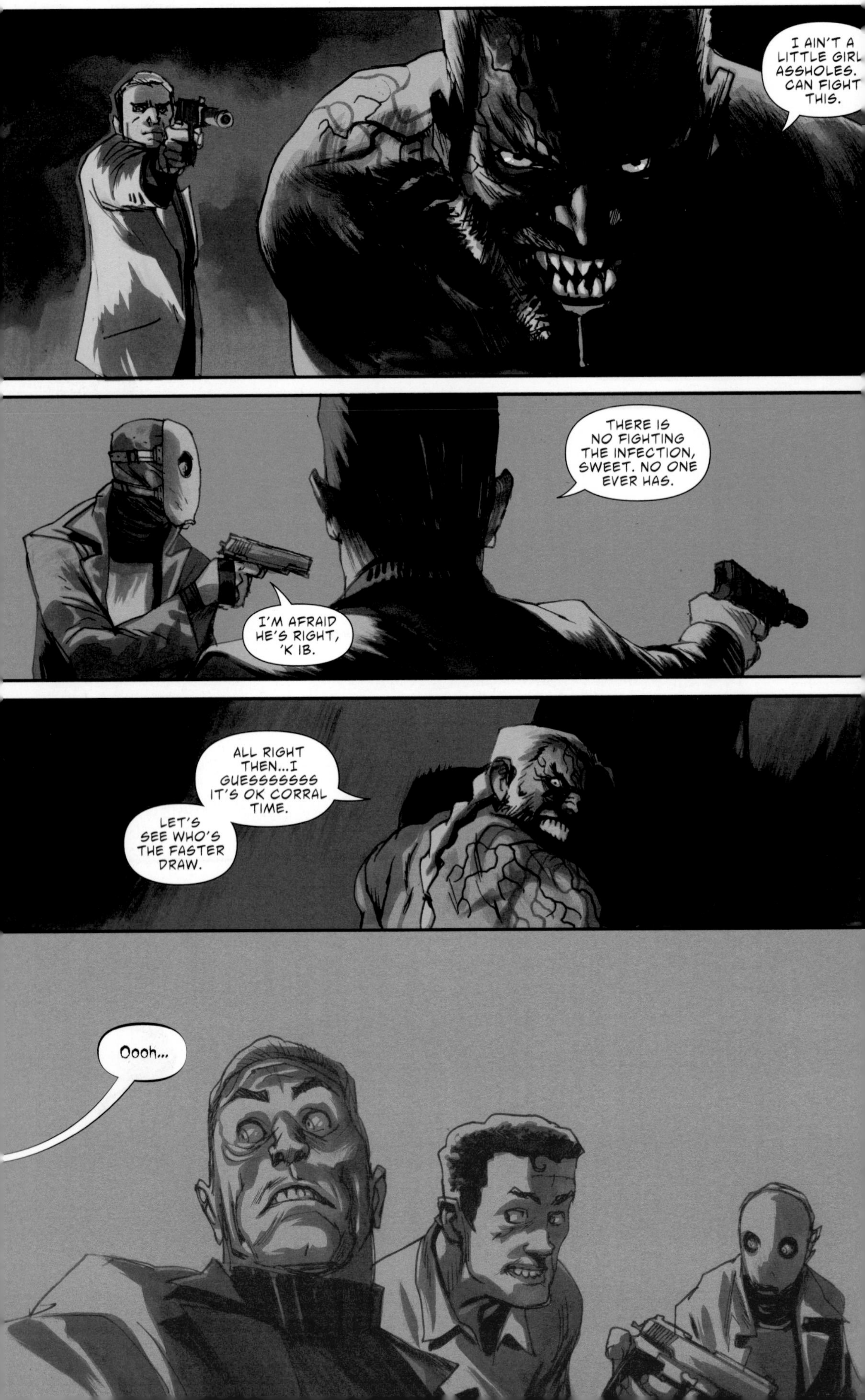
I AIN'T A LITTLE GIRL ASSHOLES. CAN FIGHT THIS.
THERE IS NO FIGHTING THE INFECTION, SWEET. NO ONE EVER HAS.
I'M AFRAID HE'S RIGHT, 'K IB.
ALL RIGHT THEN...I GUESSSSSSS IT'S OK CORRAL TIME.
LET'S SEE WHO'S THE FASTER DRAW.
Oooh...

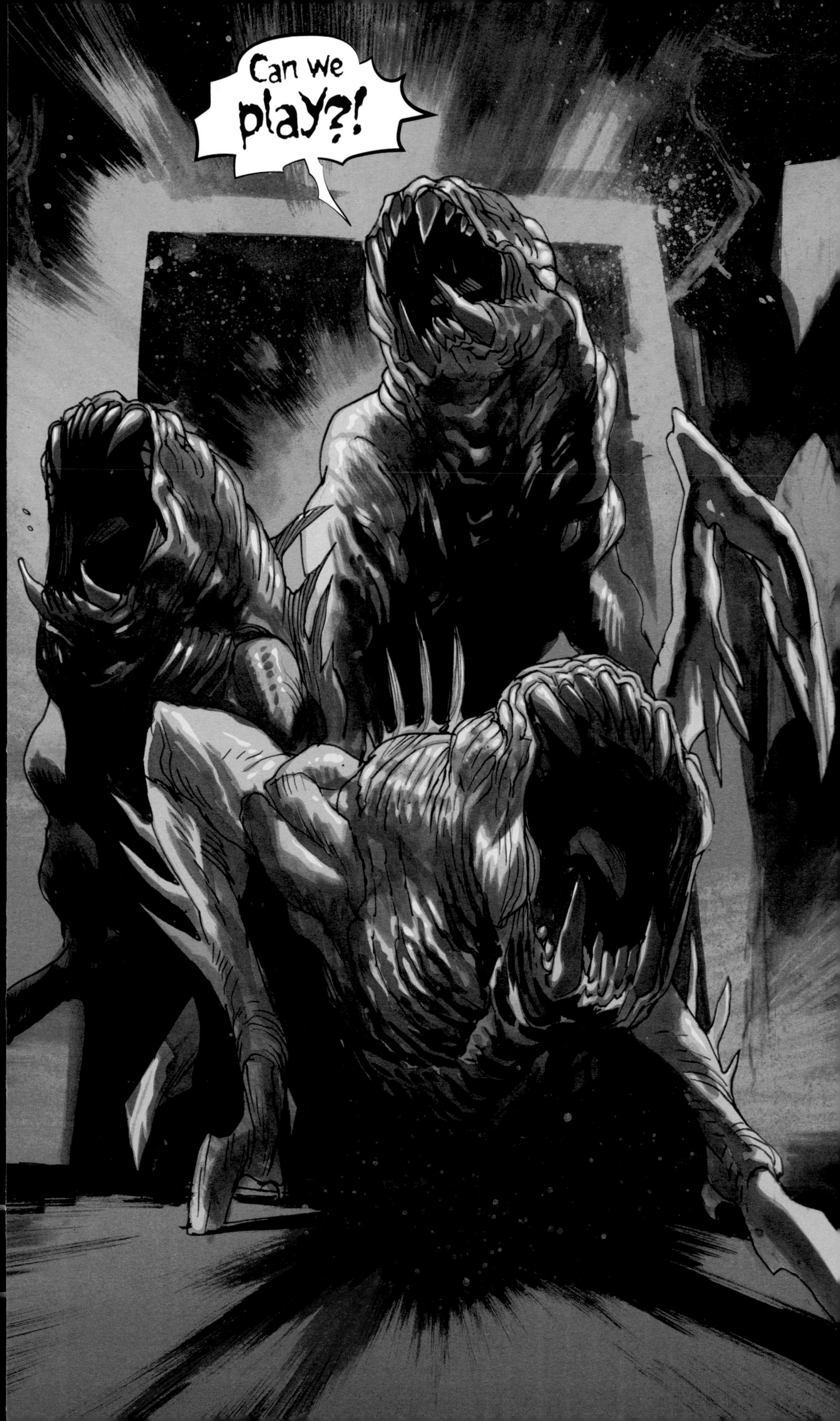
Can we play?!

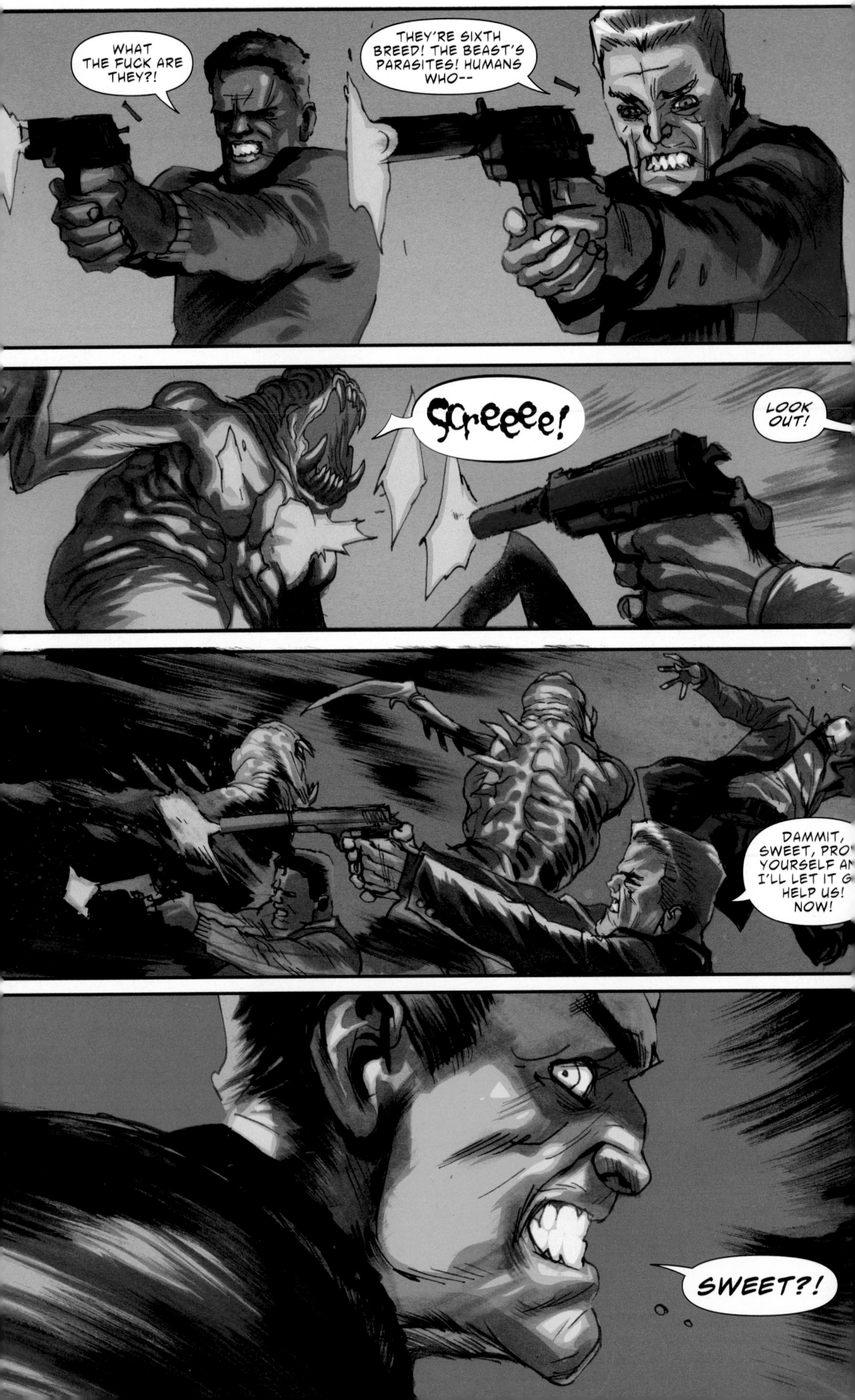
WHAT THE FUCK ARE THEY?!
THEY'RE SIXTH BREED! THE BEAST'S PARASITES! HUMANS WHO--
SCREEEE!
LOOK OUT!
DAMMIT, SWEET, PRO YOURSELF AN I'LL LET IT G HELP US! NOW!
SWEET?!

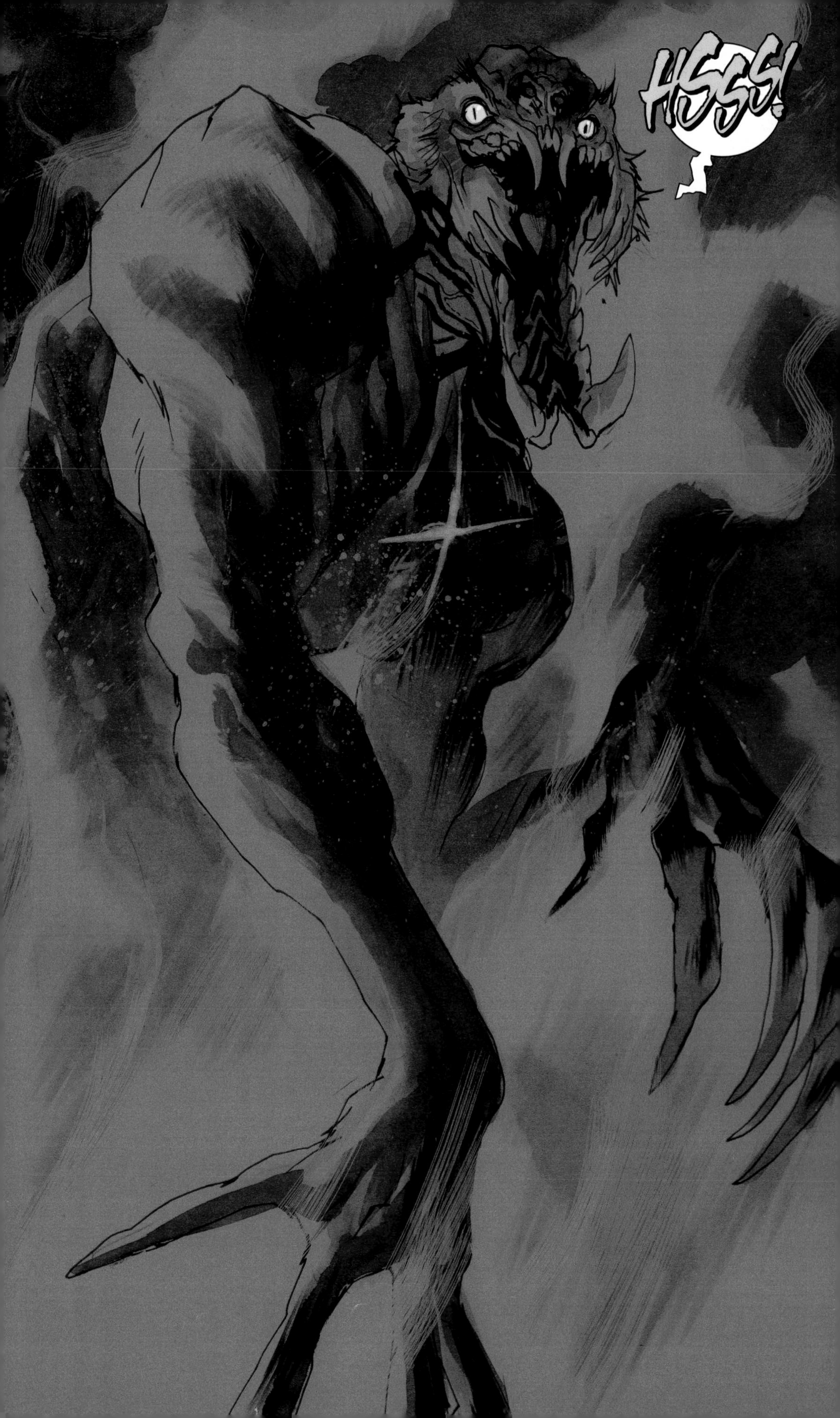
HSSS!

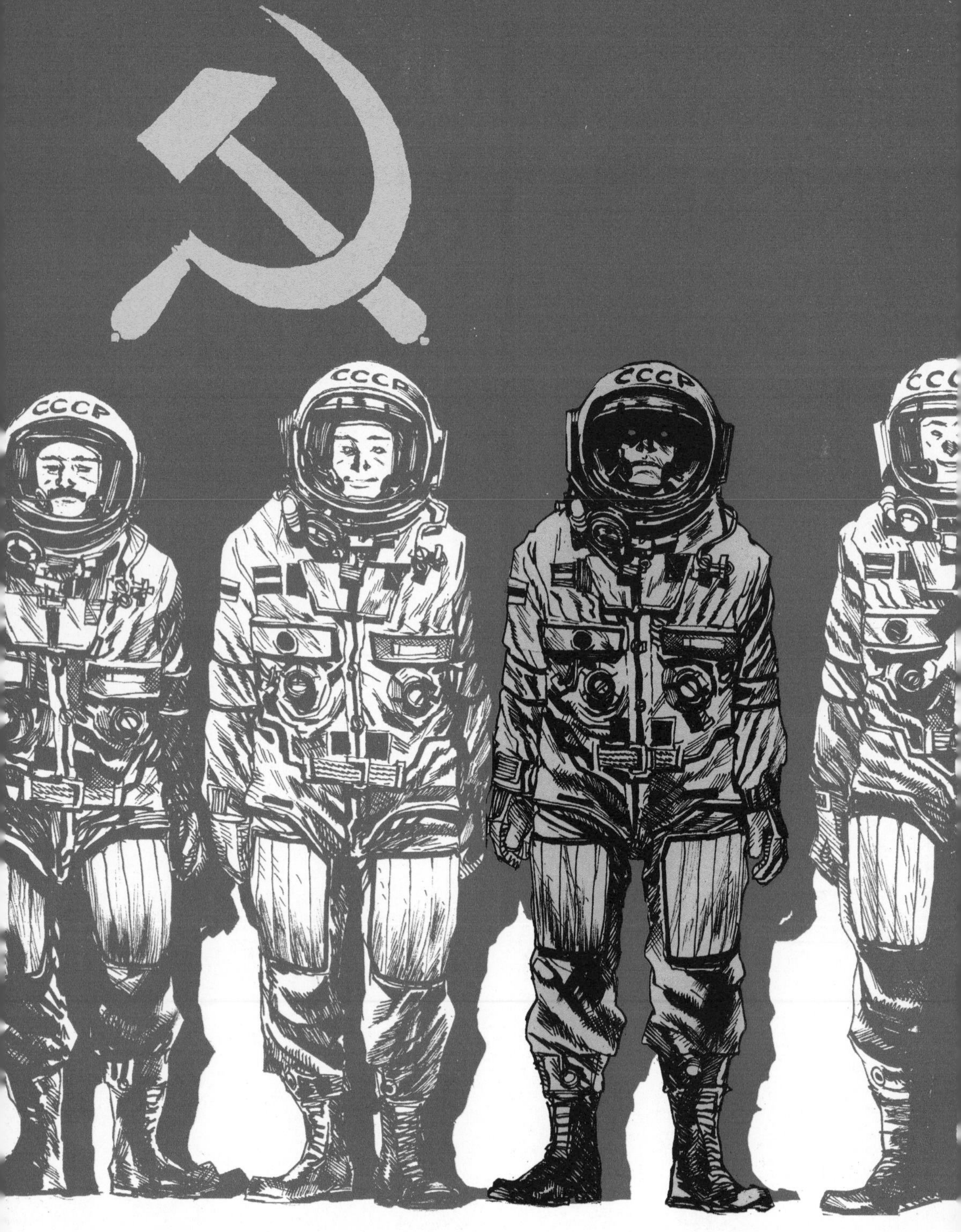
CCCP
CCCP
CCCP
CCCP

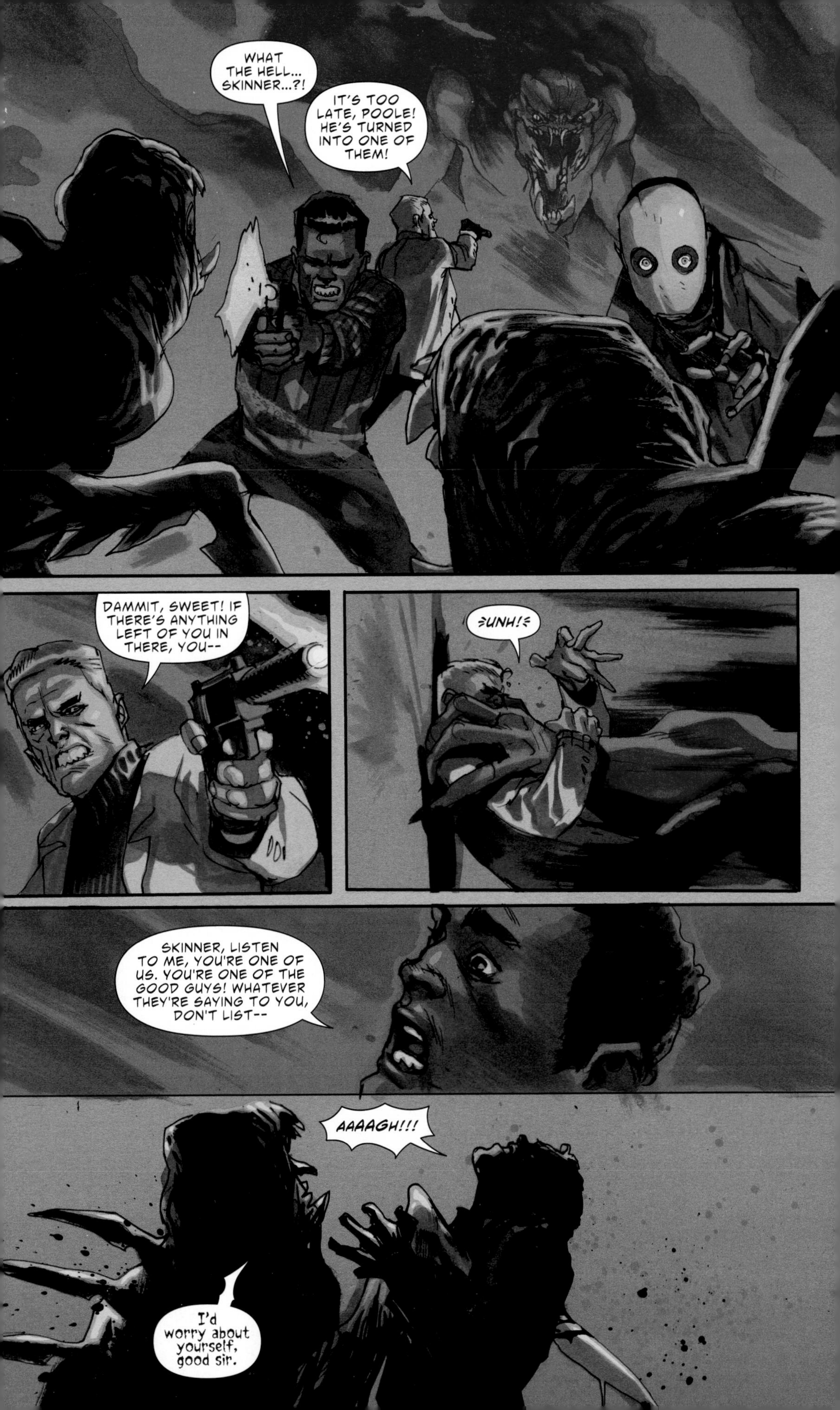
WHAT THE HELL... SKINNER...?!
IT'S TOO LATE, POOLE! HE'S TURNED INTO ONE OF THEM!
DAMMIT, SWEET! IF THERE'S ANYTHING LEFT OF YOU IN THERE, YOU--
UNH!
SKINNER, LISTEN TO ME, YOU'RE ONE OF US. YOU'RE ONE OF THE GOOD GUYS! WHATEVER THEY'RE SAYING TO YOU, DON'T LIST--
AAAAGH!!!
I'd worry about yourself, good sir.

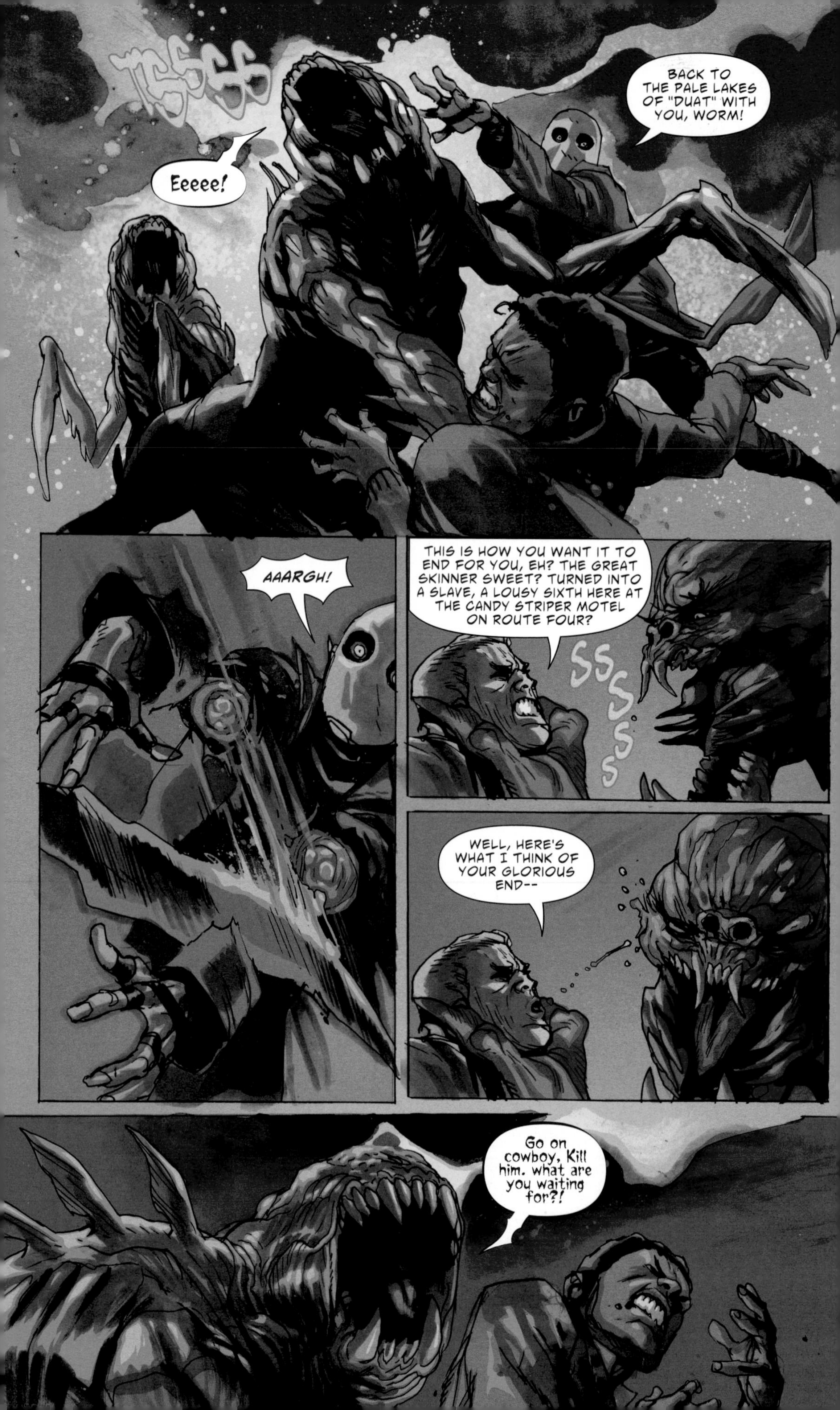

TSSSS
Eeeee!
BACK TO THE PALE LAKES OF "DUAT" WITH YOU, WORM!
AAARGH!
THIS IS HOW YOU WANT IT TO END FOR YOU, EH? THE GREAT SKINNER SWEET? TURNED INTO A SLAVE, A LOUSY SIXTH HERE AT THE CANDY STRIPER MOTEL ON ROUTE FOUR?
SSSSS
WELL, HERE'S WHAT I THINK OF YOUR GLORIOUS END--
Go on cowboy, Kill him. what are you waiting for?!

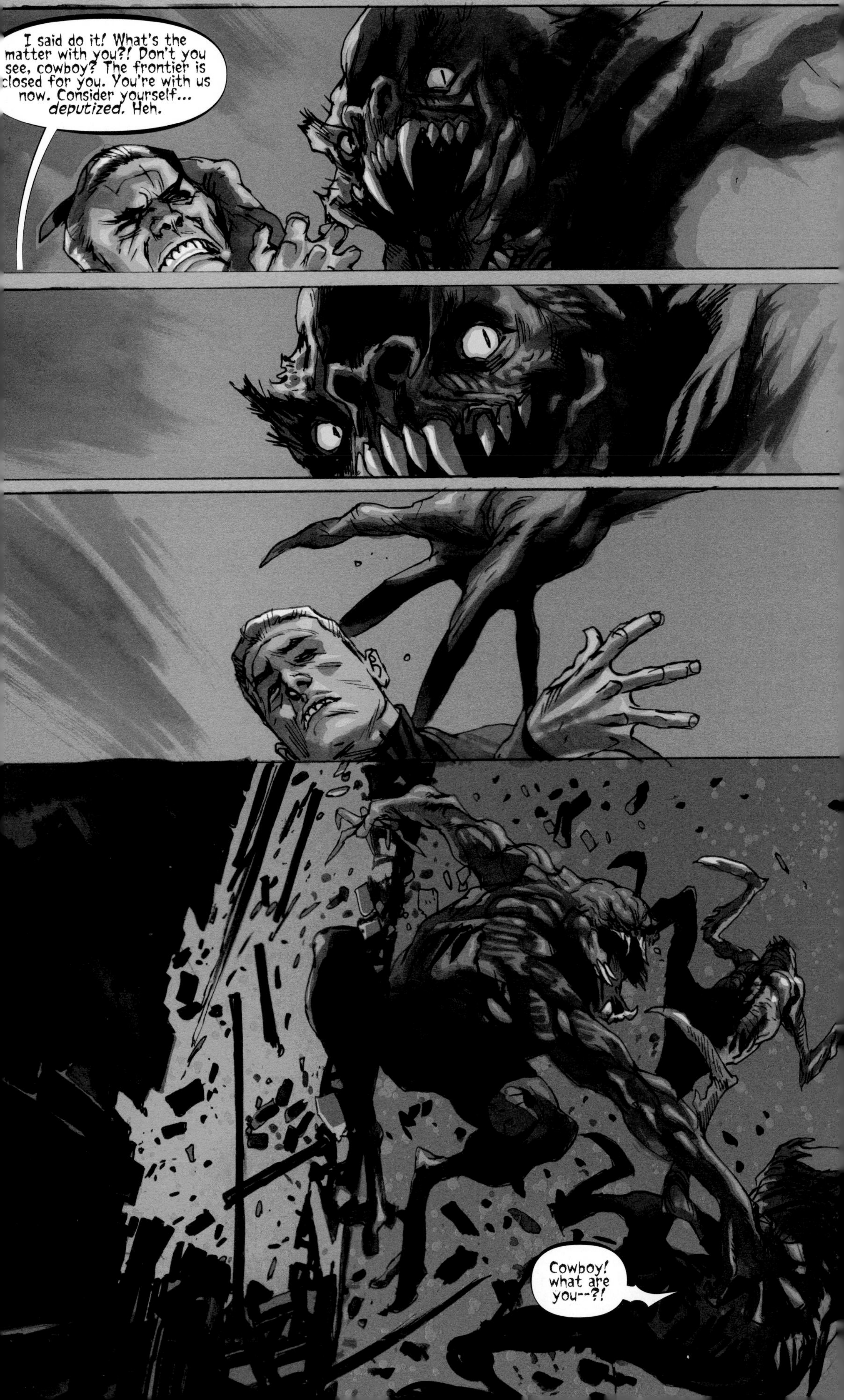
I said do it! What's the matter with you?! Don't you see, cowboy? The frontier is closed for you. You're with us now. Consider yourself... *deputized.* Heh.
Cowboy! what are you--?!

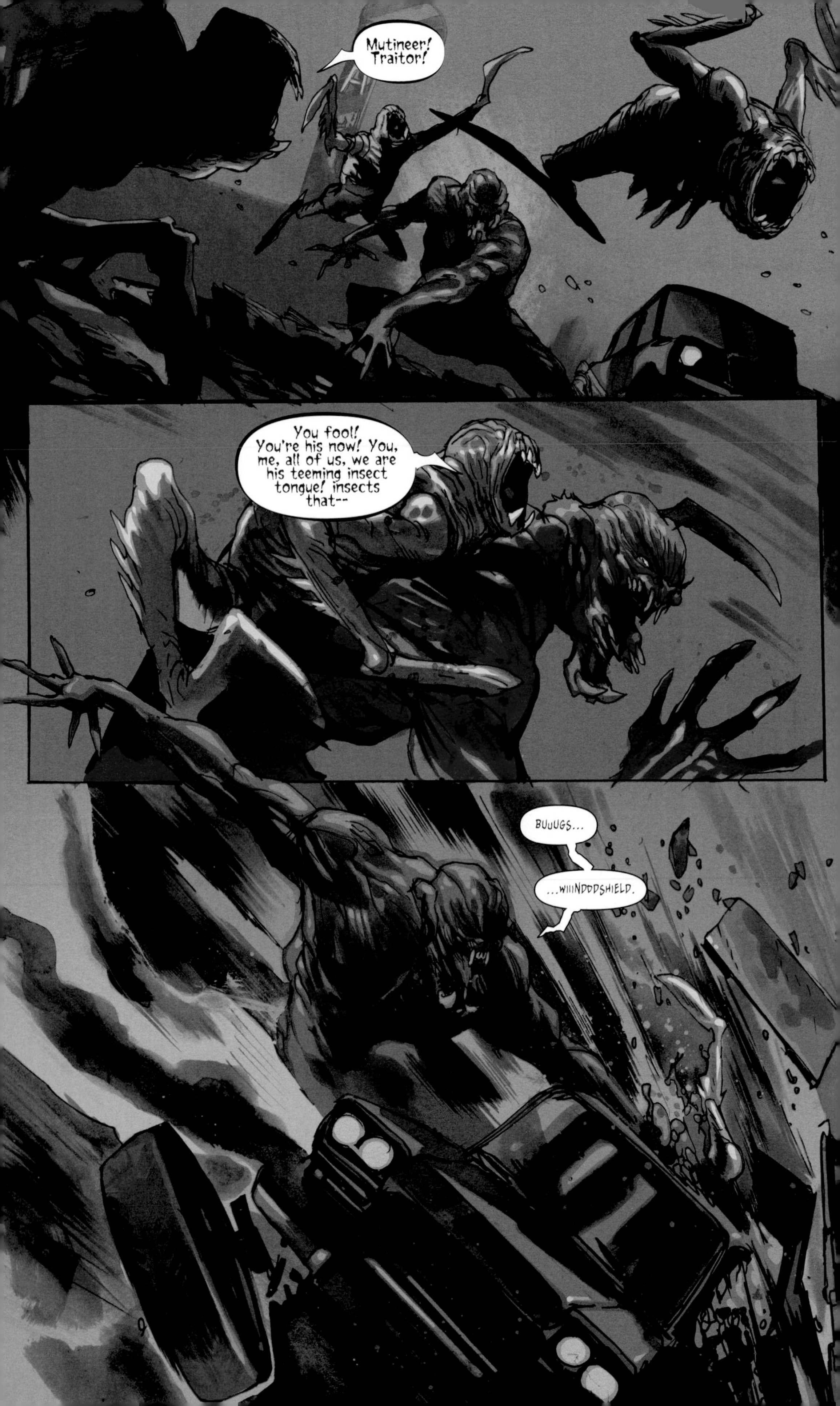
Mutineer! Traitor!
You fool! You're his now! You, me, all of us, we are his teeming insect tongue! insects that--
BUUUGS...
...WIIINDDDSHIELD.

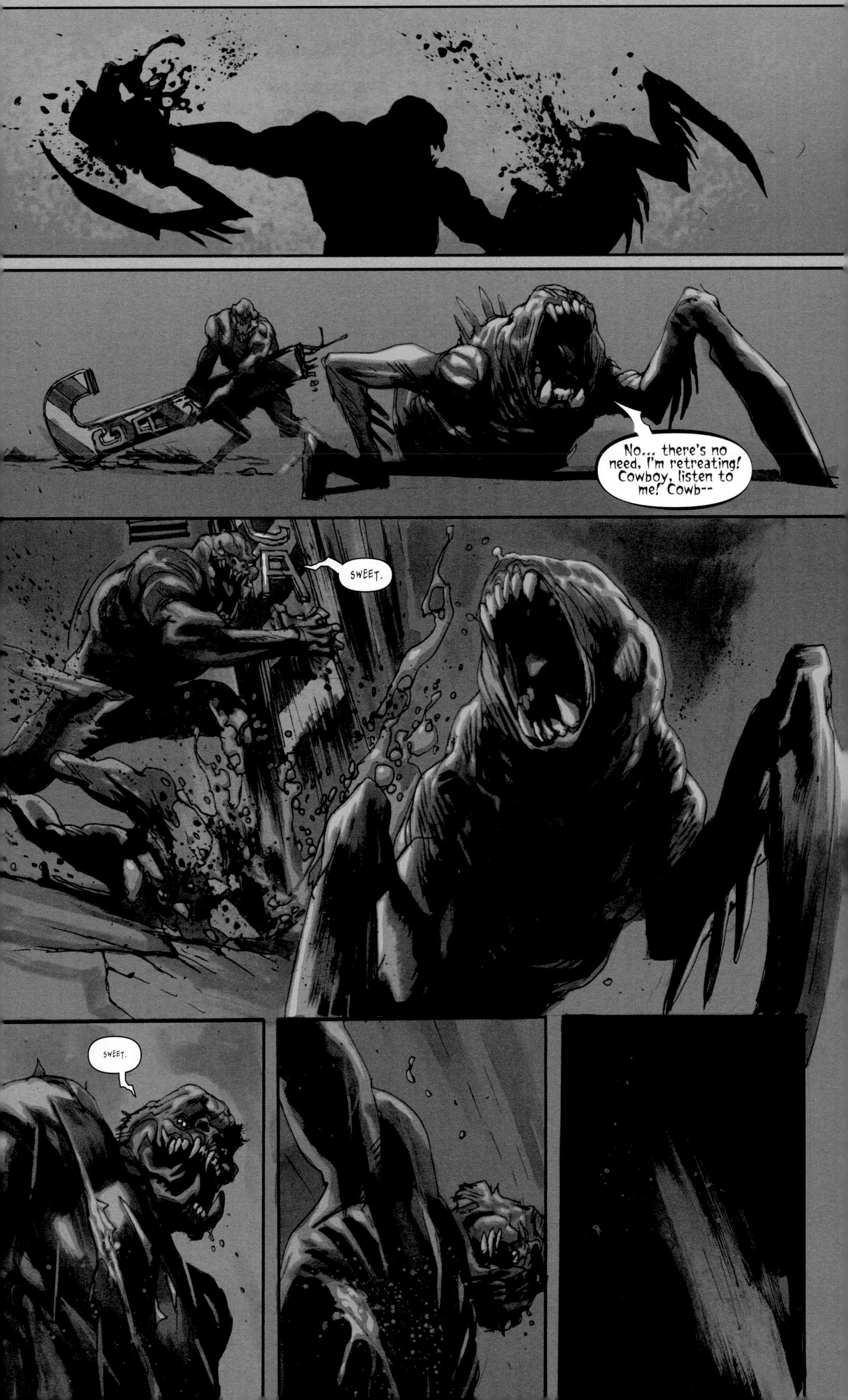
No... there's no need, I'm retreating! Cowboy, listen to me! Cowb--
SWEET.
SWEET.

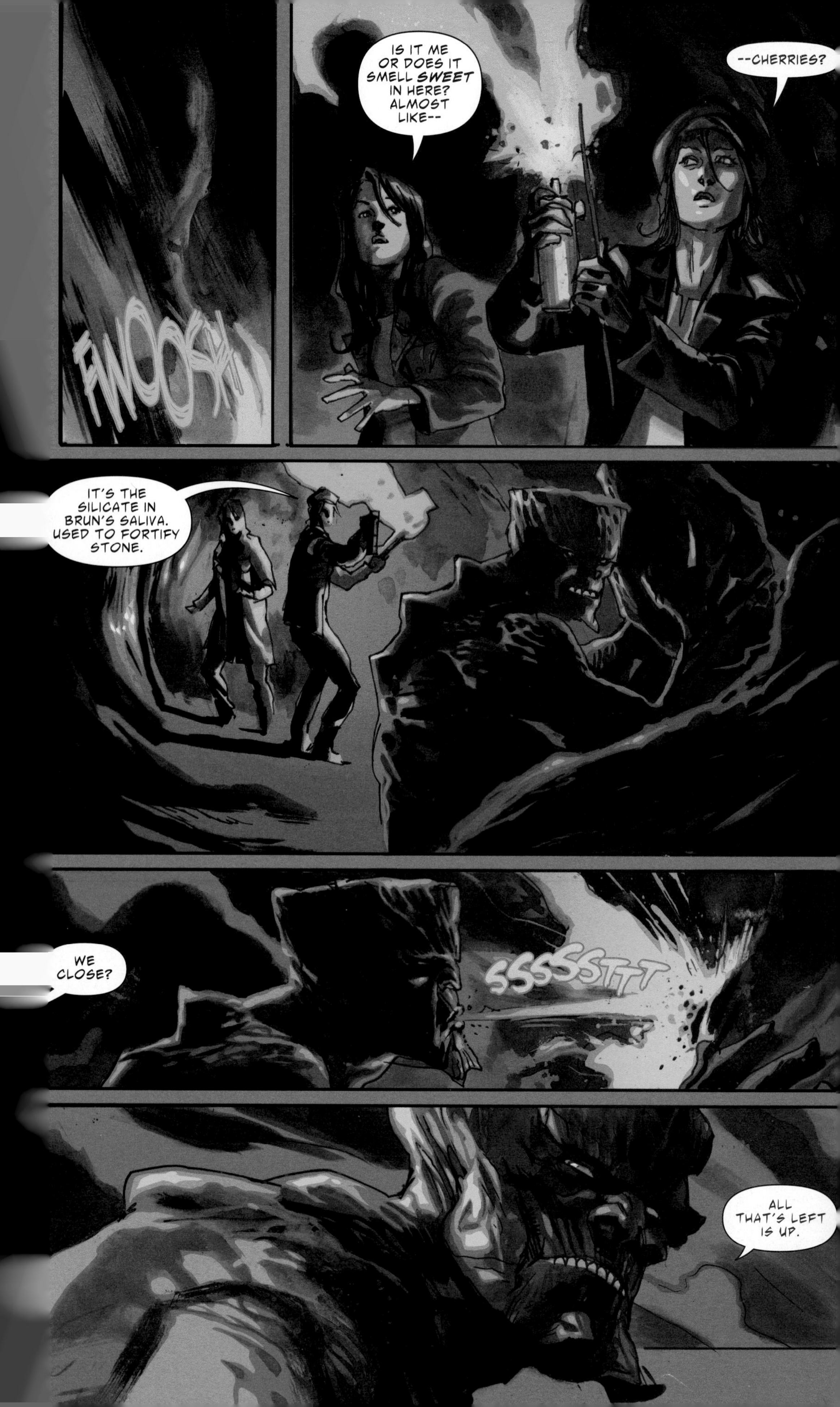
FWOOSH
IS IT ME OR DOES IT SMELL SWEET IN HERE? ALMOST LIKE--
--CHERRIES?
IT'S THE SILICATE IN BRUN'S SALIVA. USED TO FORTIFY STONE.
WE CLOSE?
SSSSSTTT
ALL THAT'S LEFT IS UP.

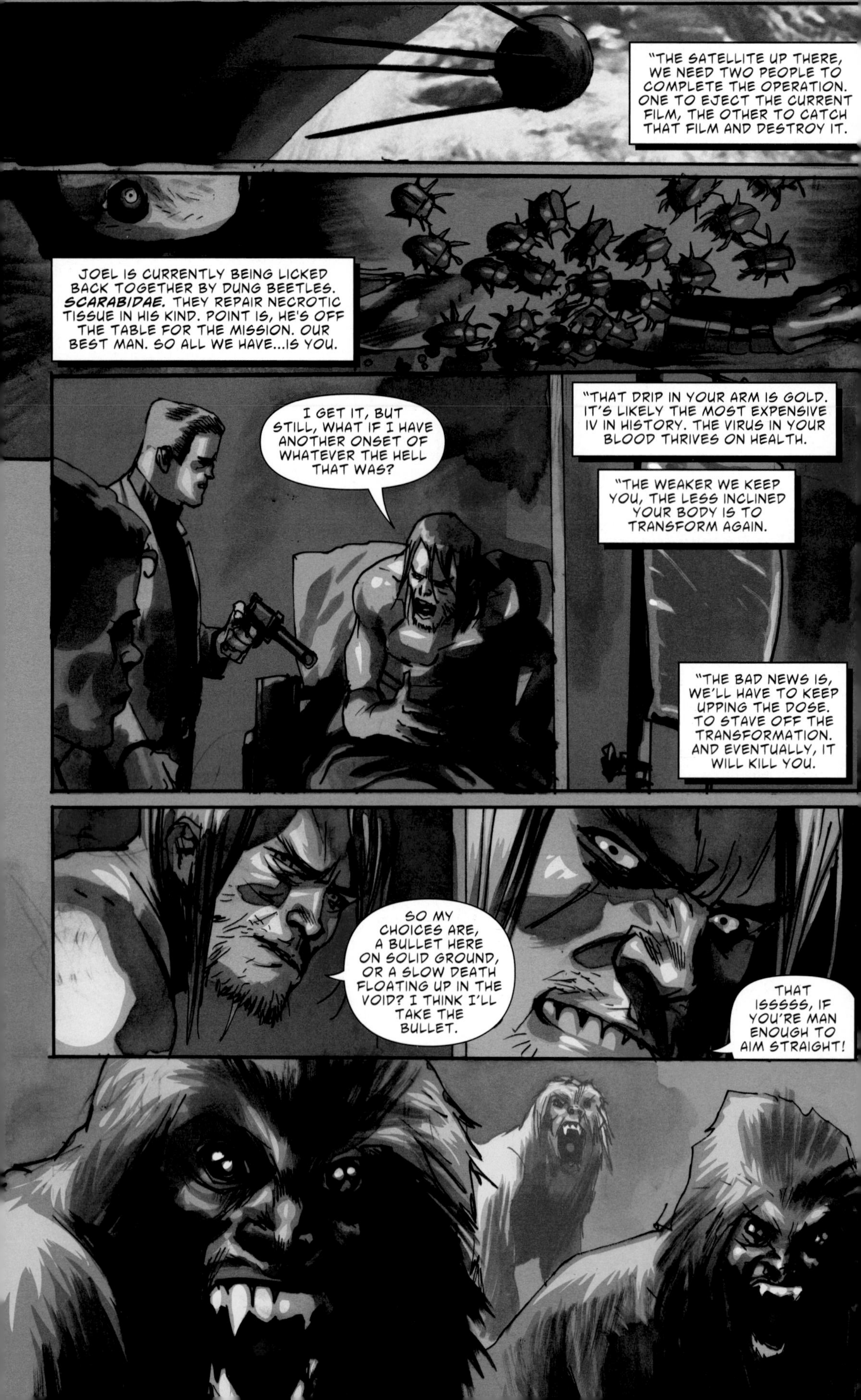
"THE SATELLITE UP THERE, WE NEED TWO PEOPLE TO COMPLETE THE OPERATION. ONE TO EJECT THE CURRENT FILM, THE OTHER TO CATCH THAT FILM AND DESTROY IT.
JOEL IS CURRENTLY BEING LICKED BACK TOGETHER BY DUNG BEETLES. SCARABIDAE. THEY REPAIR NECROTIC TISSUE IN HIS KIND. POINT IS, HE'S OFF THE TABLE FOR THE MISSION. OUR BEST MAN. SO ALL WE HAVE...IS YOU.
I GET IT, BUT STILL, WHAT IF I HAVE ANOTHER ONSET OF WHATEVER THE HELL THAT WAS?
"THAT DRIP IN YOUR ARM IS GOLD. IT'S LIKELY THE MOST EXPENSIVE IV IN HISTORY. THE VIRUS IN YOUR BLOOD THRIVES ON HEALTH.
"THE WEAKER WE KEEP YOU, THE LESS INCLINED YOUR BODY IS TO TRANSFORM AGAIN.
"THE BAD NEWS IS, WE'LL HAVE TO KEEP UPPING THE DOSE. TO STAVE OFF THE TRANSFORMATION. AND EVENTUALLY, IT WILL KILL YOU.
SO MY CHOICES ARE, A BULLET HERE ON SOLID GROUND, OR A SLOW DEATH FLOATING UP IN THE VOID? I THINK I'LL TAKE THE BULLET.
THAT ISSSSS, IF YOU'RE MAN ENOUGH TO AIM STRAIGHT!

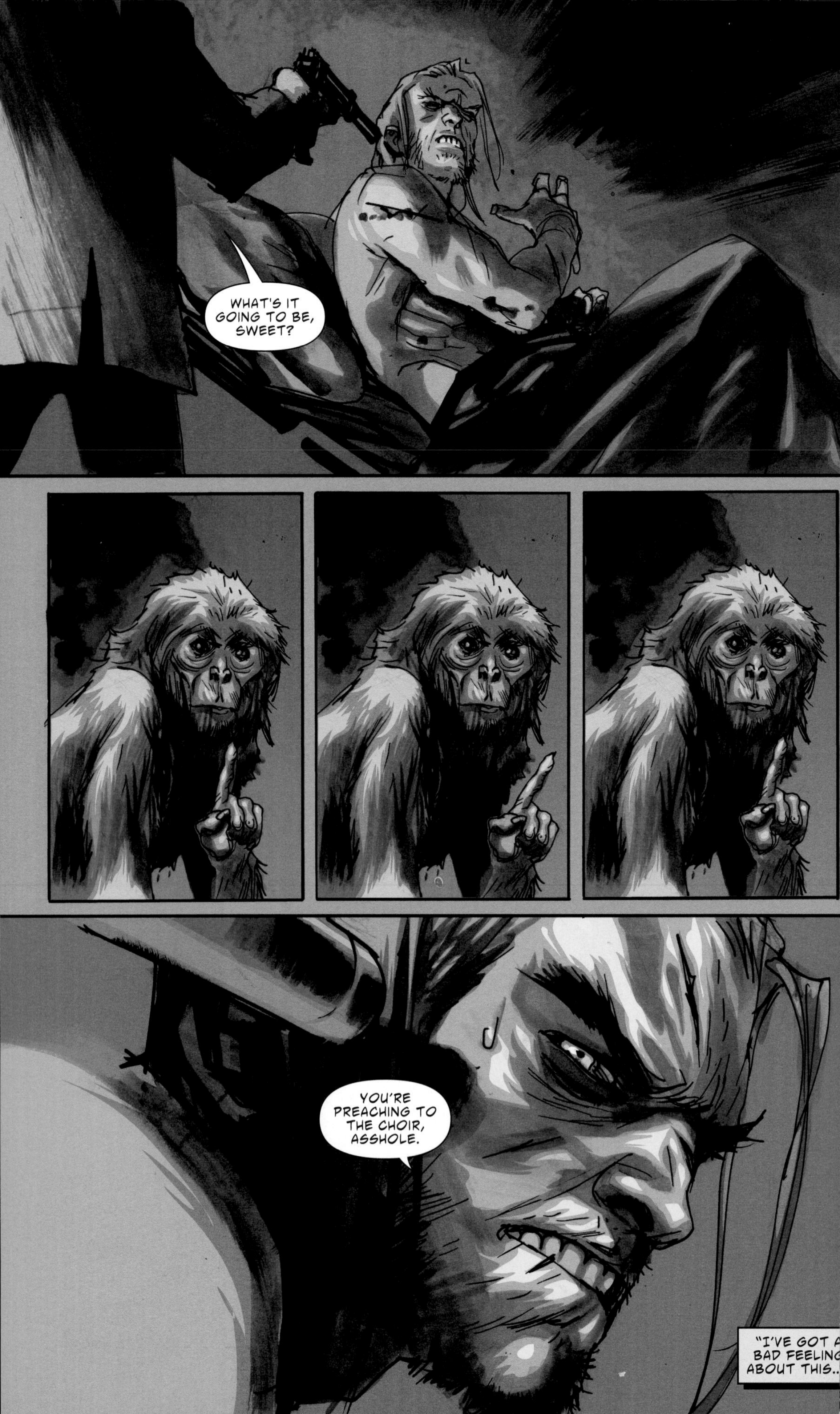
WHAT'S IT GOING TO BE, SWEET?
YOU'RE PREACHING TO THE CHOIR, ASSHOLE.
"I'VE GOT A BAD FEELING ABOUT THIS...

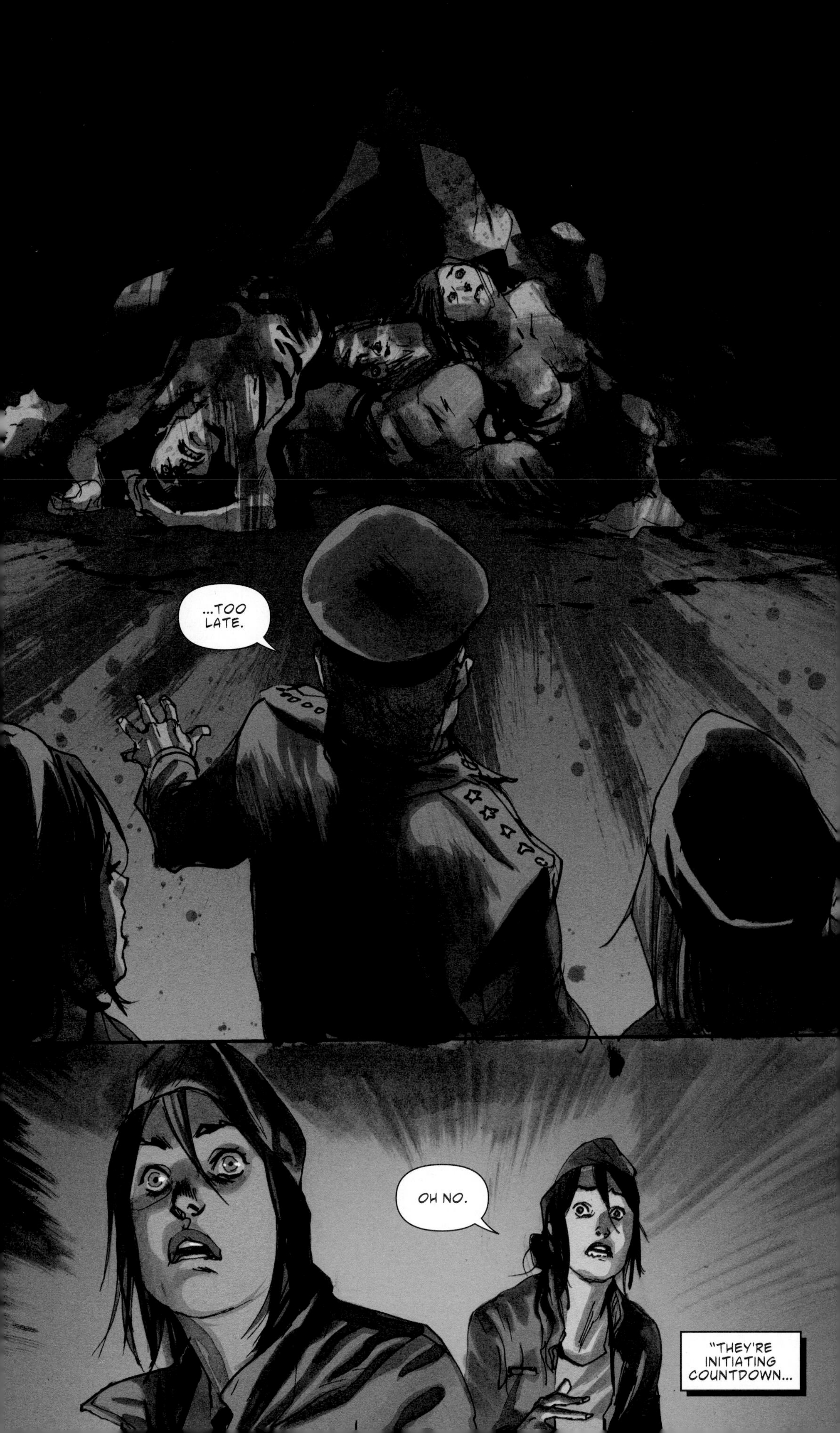
...TOO LATE.
OH NO.
"THEY'RE INITIATING COUNTDOWN...

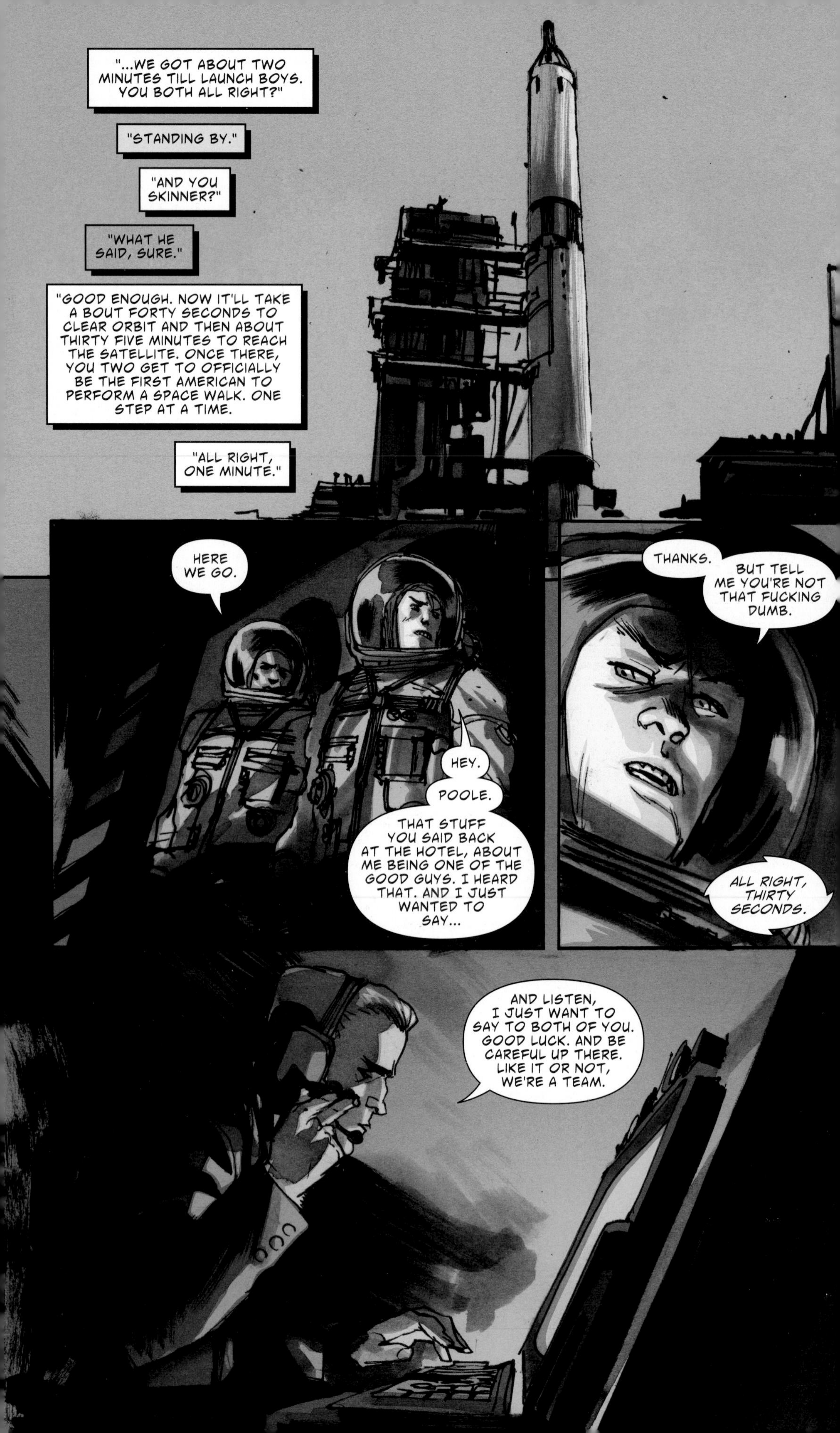
"...WE GOT ABOUT TWO MINUTES TILL LAUNCH BOYS. YOU BOTH ALL RIGHT?"
"STANDING BY."
"AND YOU SKINNER?"
"WHAT HE SAID, SURE."
"GOOD ENOUGH. NOW IT'LL TAKE A BOUT FORTY SECONDS TO CLEAR ORBIT AND THEN ABOUT THIRTY FIVE MINUTES TO REACH THE SATELLITE. ONCE THERE, YOU TWO GET TO OFFICIALLY BE THE FIRST AMERICAN TO PERFORM A SPACE WALK. ONE STEP AT A TIME.
"ALL RIGHT, ONE MINUTE."
HERE WE GO.
HEY.
POOLE.
THAT STUFF YOU SAID BACK AT THE HOTEL, ABOUT ME BEING ONE OF THE GOOD GUYS. I HEARD THAT. AND I JUST WANTED TO SAY...
THANKS.
BUT TELL ME YOU'RE NOT THAT FUCKING DUMB.
ALL RIGHT, THIRTY SECONDS.
AND LISTEN, I JUST WANT TO SAY TO BOTH OF YOU. GOOD LUCK. AND BE CAREFUL UP THERE. LIKE IT OR NOT, WE'RE A TEAM.

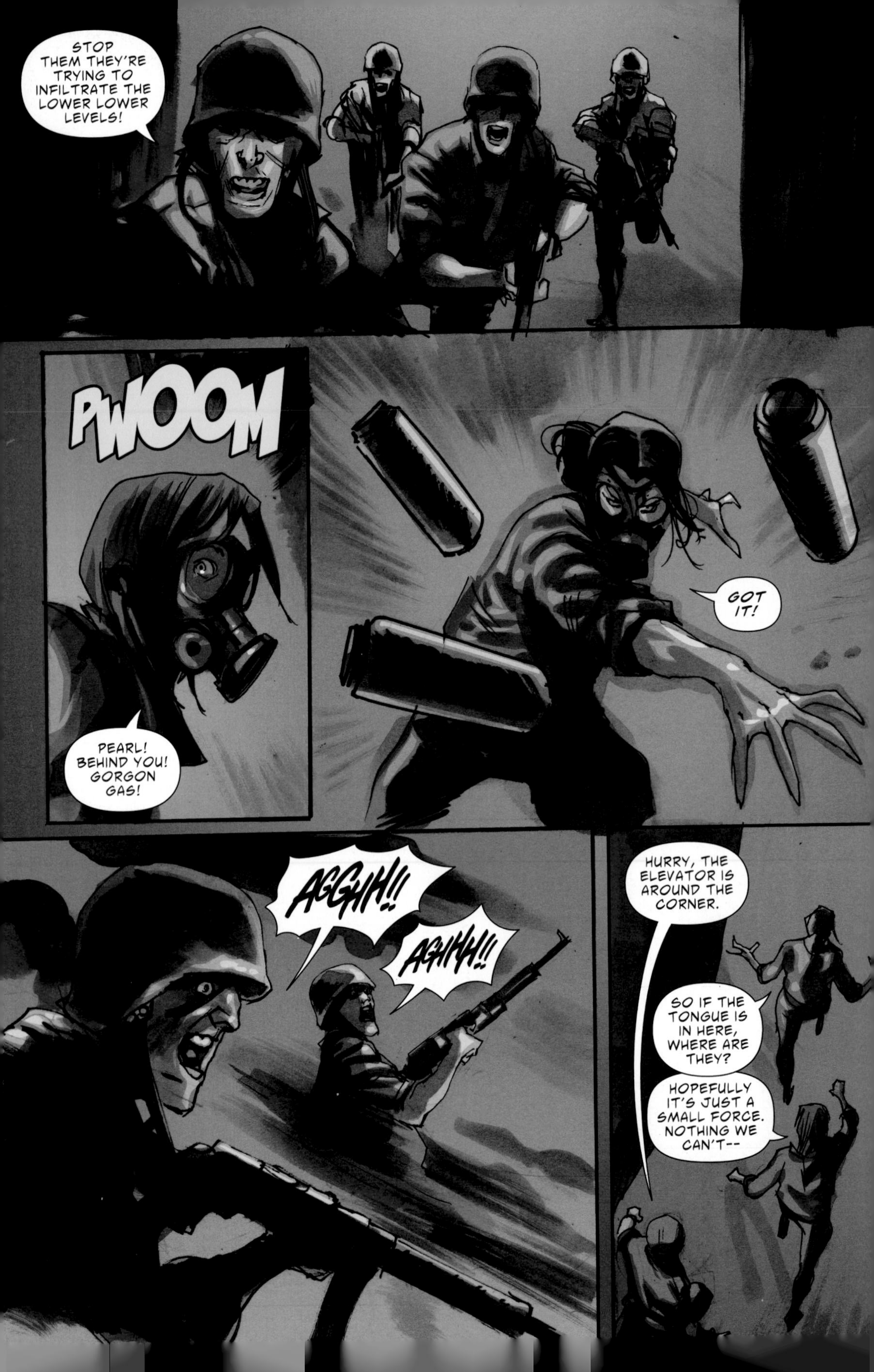
STOP THEM THEY'RE TRYING TO INFILTRATE THE LOWER LOWER LEVELS!
PWOOM
PEARL! BEHIND YOU! GORGON GAS!
GOT IT!
AGGHH!!
AGHHH!!
HURRY, THE ELEVATOR IS AROUND THE CORNER.
SO IF THE TONGUE IS IN HERE, WHERE ARE THEY?
HOPEFULLY IT'S JUST A SMALL FORCE. NOTHING WE CAN'T--

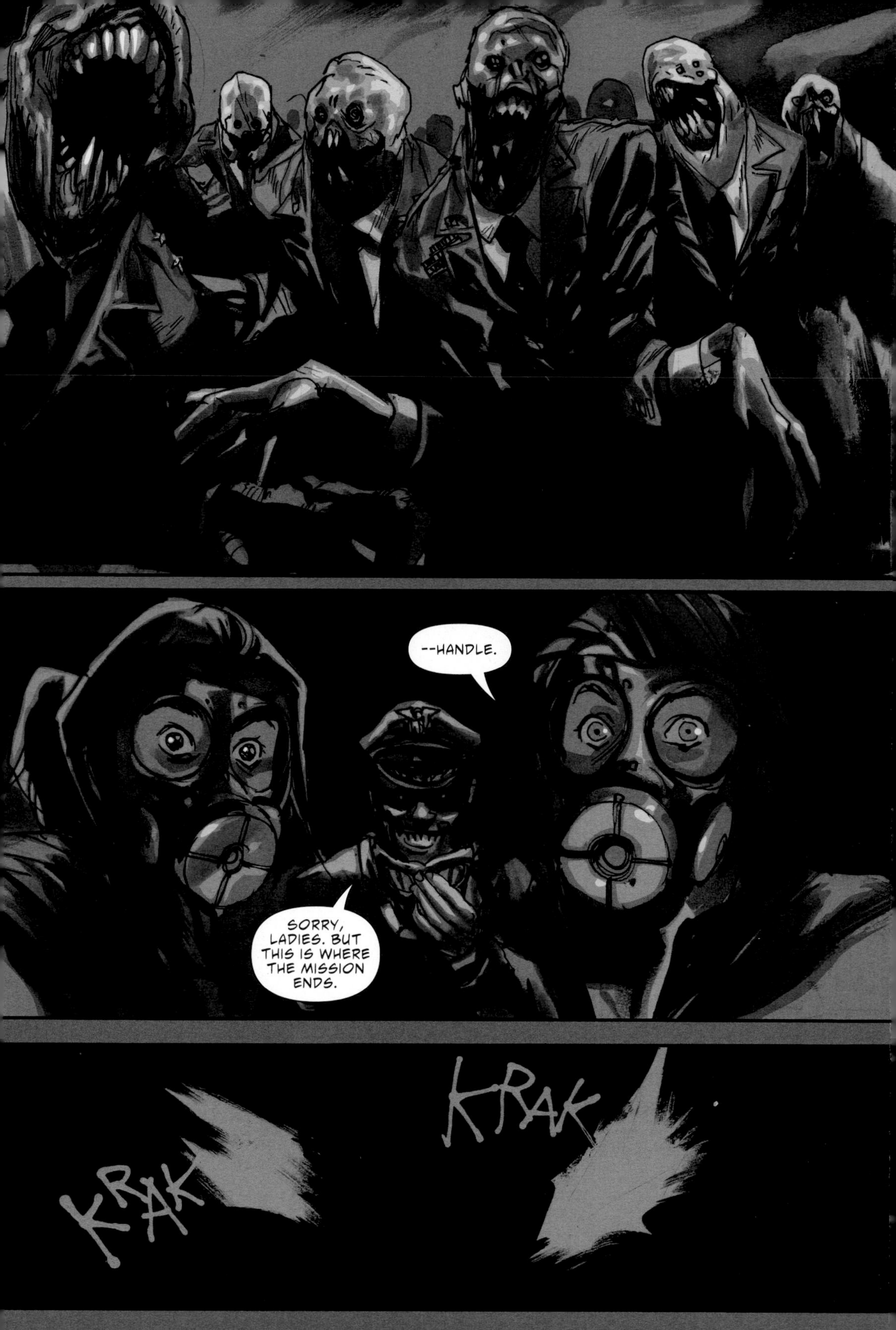
--HANDLE.
SORRY, LADIES. BUT THIS IS WHERE THE MISSION ENDS.
KRAK
KRAK

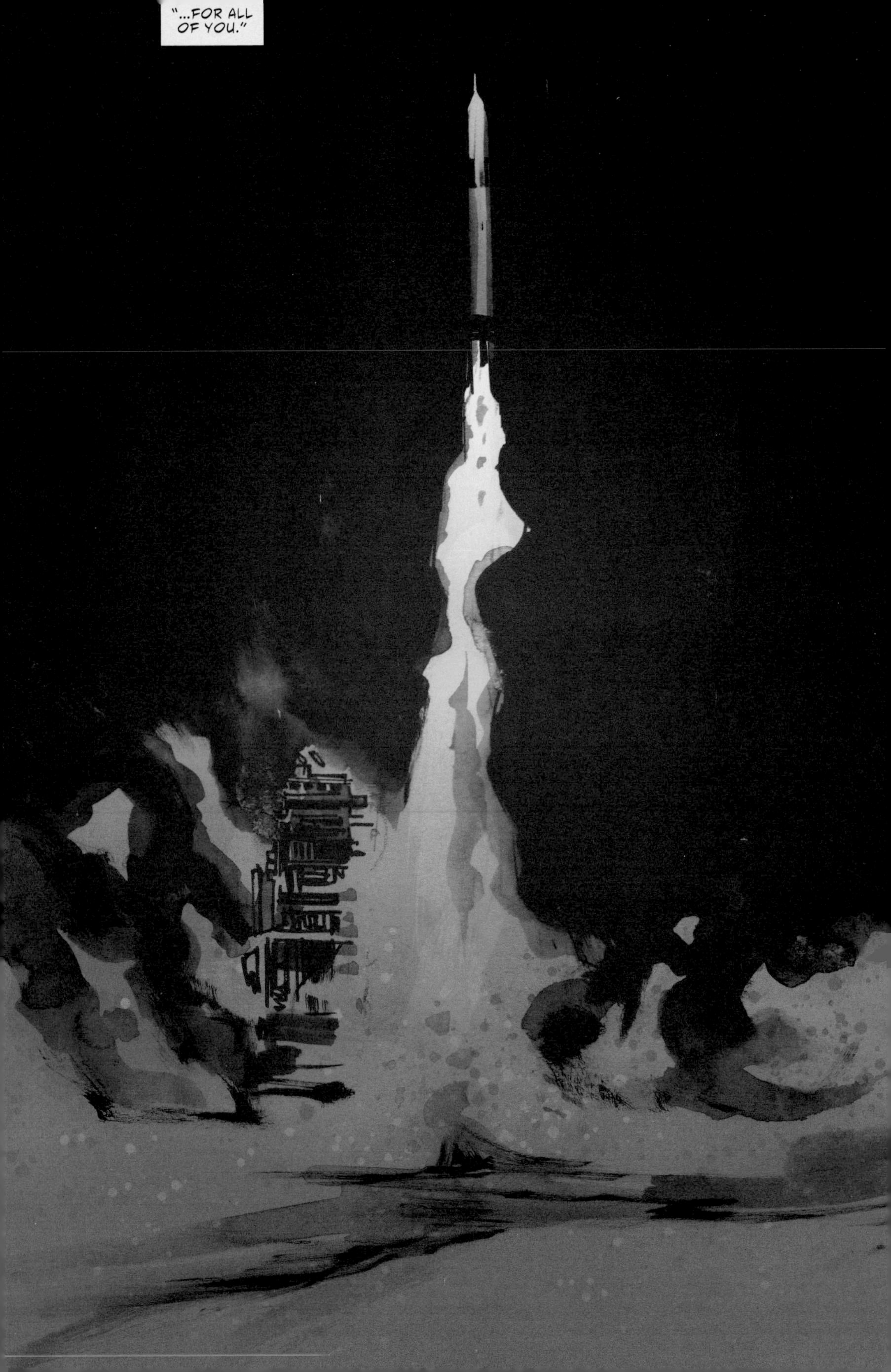
"...FOR ALL
OF YOU."

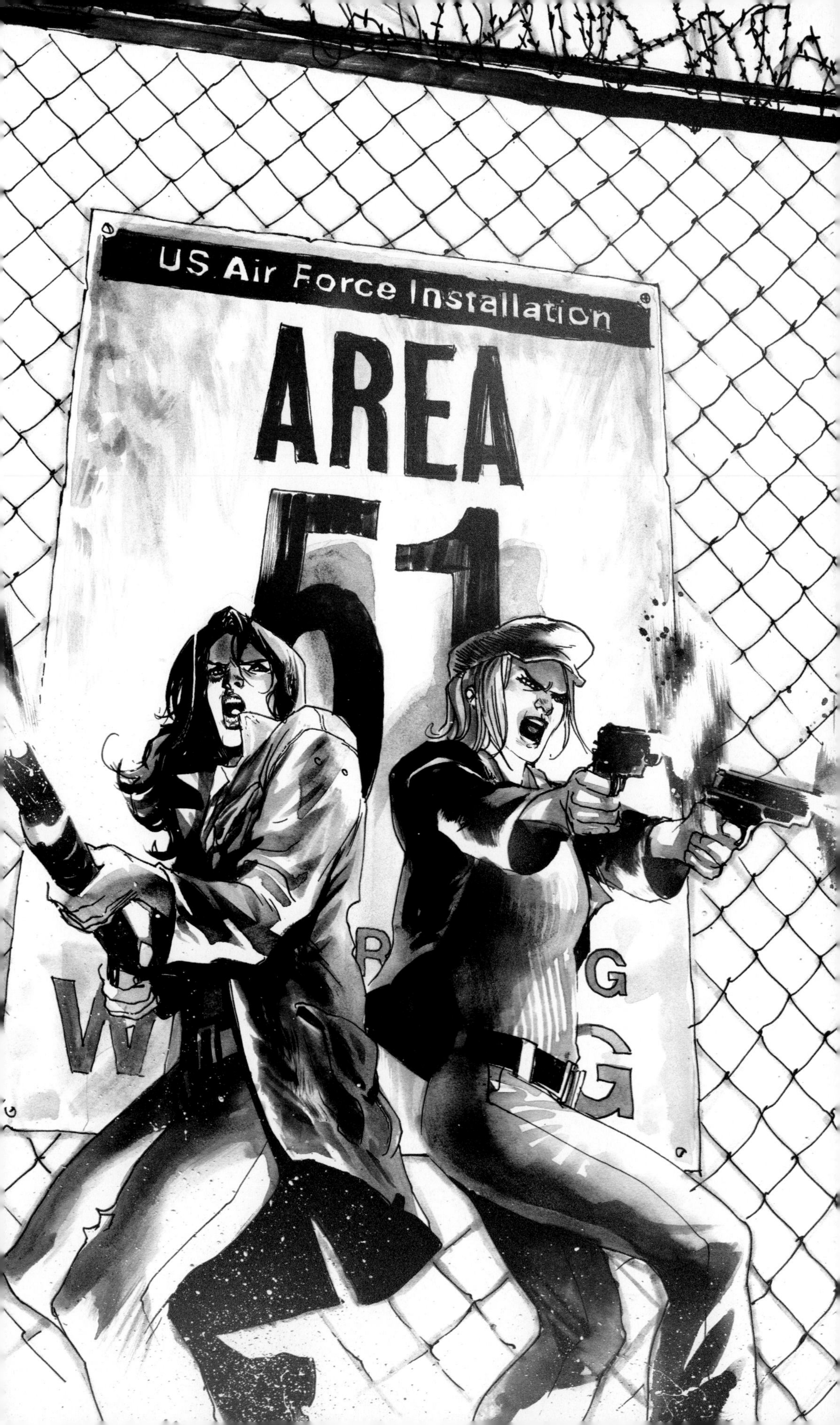
US Air Force Installation
AREA
51

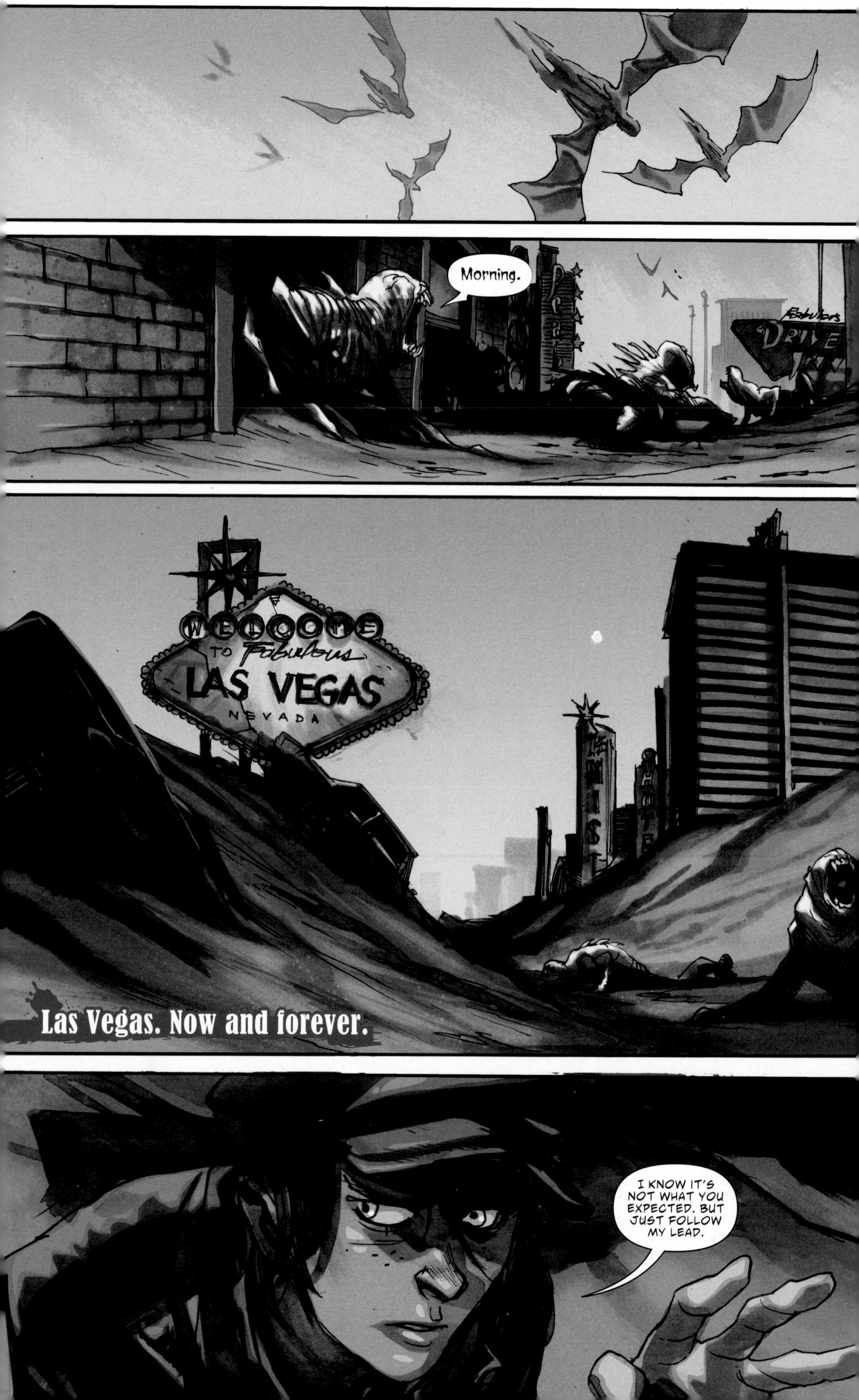
Morning.
WELCOME TO Fabulous LAS VEGAS NEVADA
Las Vegas. Now and forever.
I KNOW IT'S NOT WHAT YOU EXPECTED. BUT JUST FOLLOW MY LEAD.

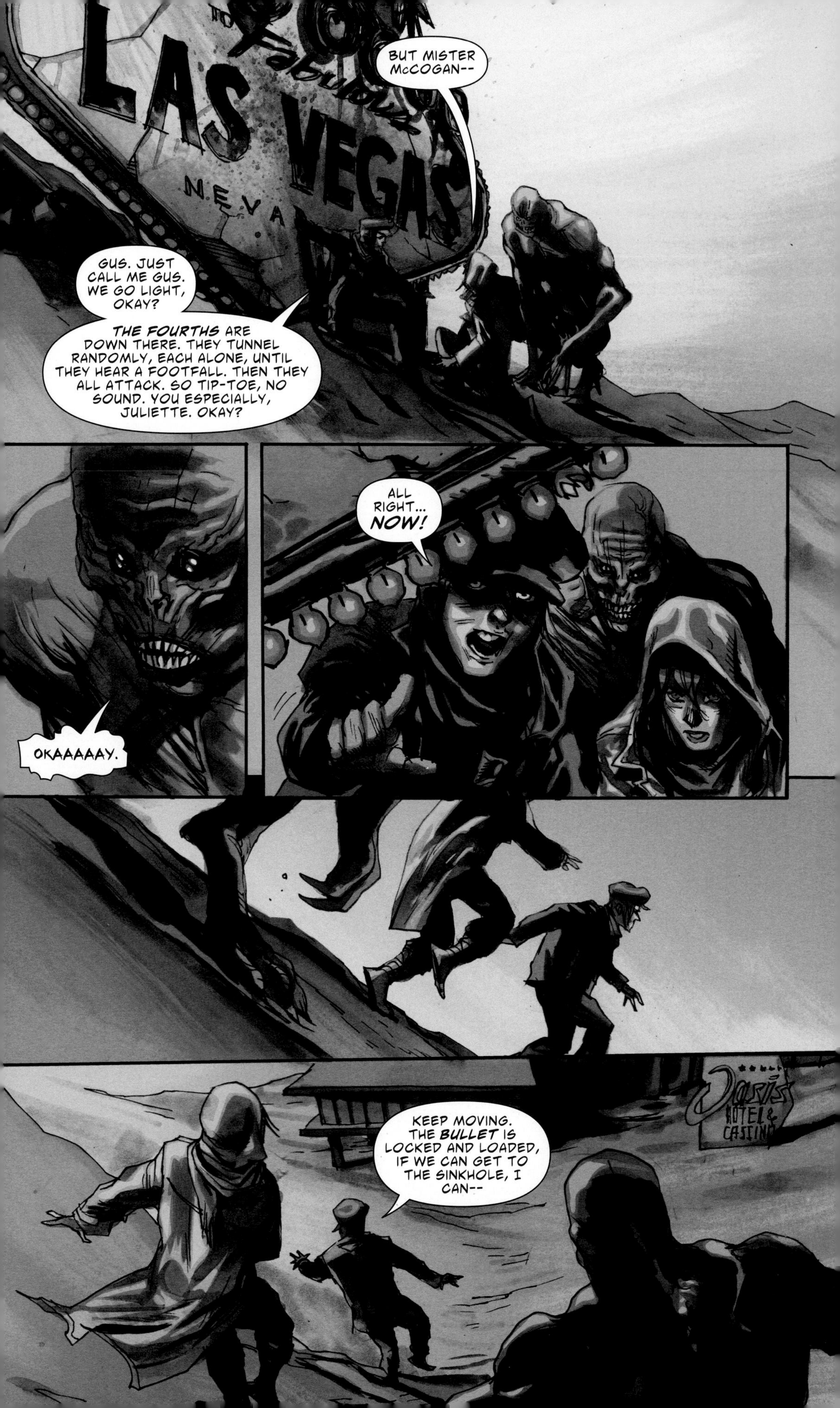
BUT MISTER McCOGAN--
GUS. JUST CALL ME GUS. WE GO LIGHT, OKAY?
THE FOURTHS ARE DOWN THERE. THEY TUNNEL RANDOMLY, EACH ALONE, UNTIL THEY HEAR A FOOTFALL. THEN THEY ALL ATTACK. SO TIP-TOE, NO SOUND. YOU ESPECIALLY, JULIETTE. OKAY?
OKAAAAAY.
ALL RIGHT... NOW!
KEEP MOVING. THE BULLET IS LOCKED AND LOADED, IF WE CAN GET TO THE SINKHOLE, I CAN--

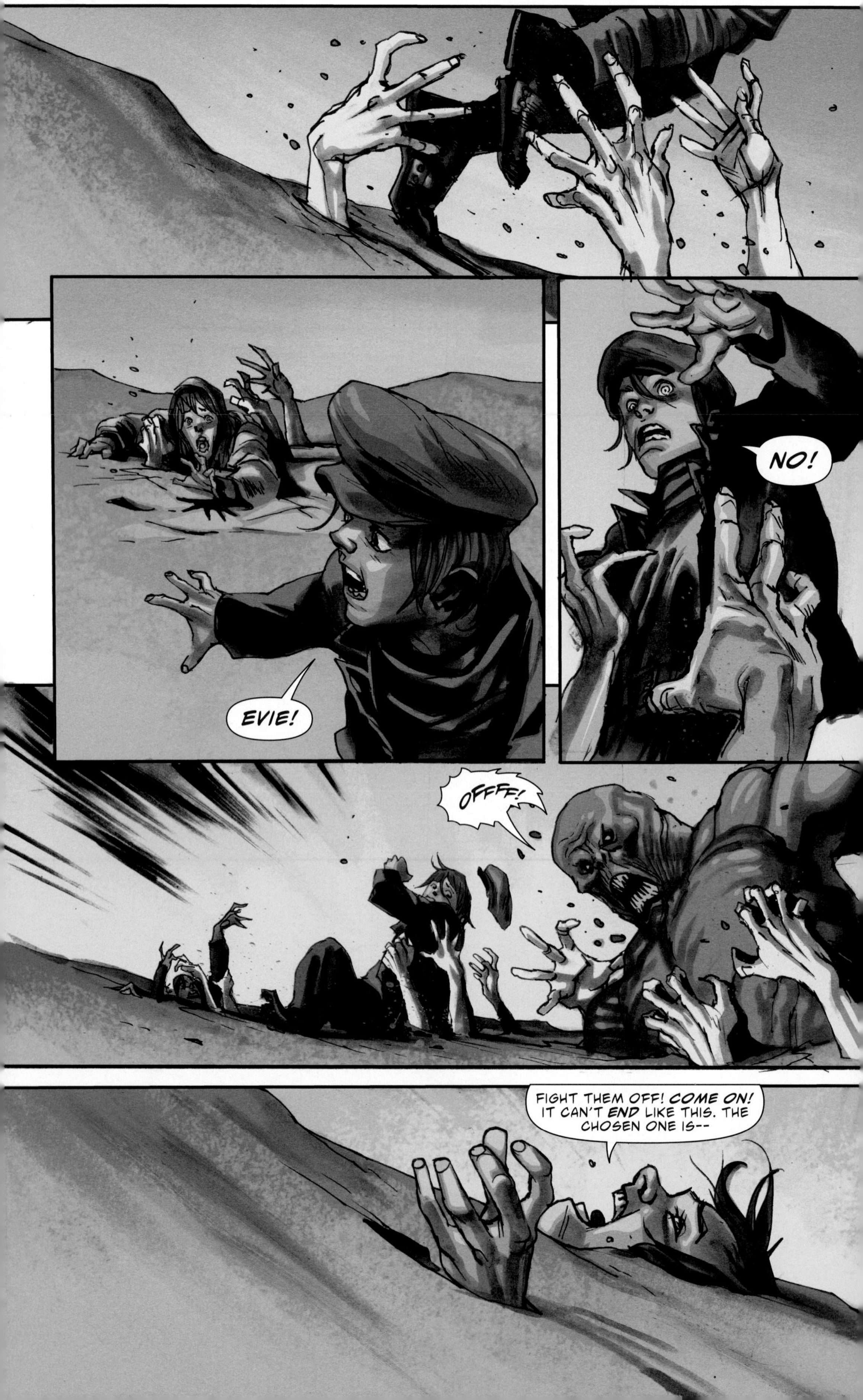
EVIE!
NO!
OFFFF!
FIGHT THEM OFF! COME ON! IT CAN'T END LIKE THIS. THE CHOSEN ONE IS--

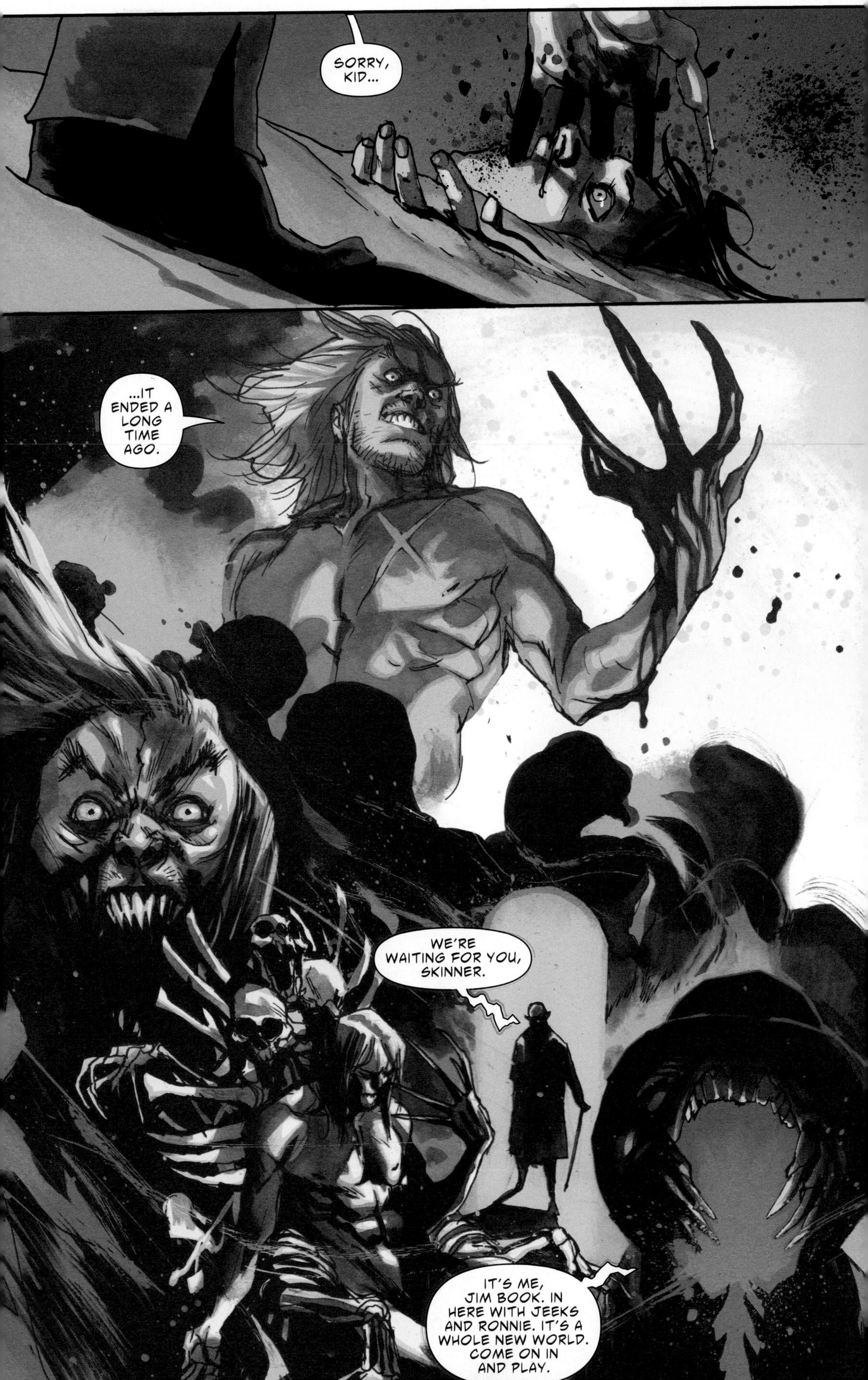
SORRY, KID...
...IT ENDED A LONG TIME AGO.
WE'RE WAITING FOR YOU, SKINNER.
IT'S ME, JIM BOOK. IN HERE WITH JEEKS AND RONNIE. IT'S A WHOLE NEW WORLD. COME ON IN AND PLAY.

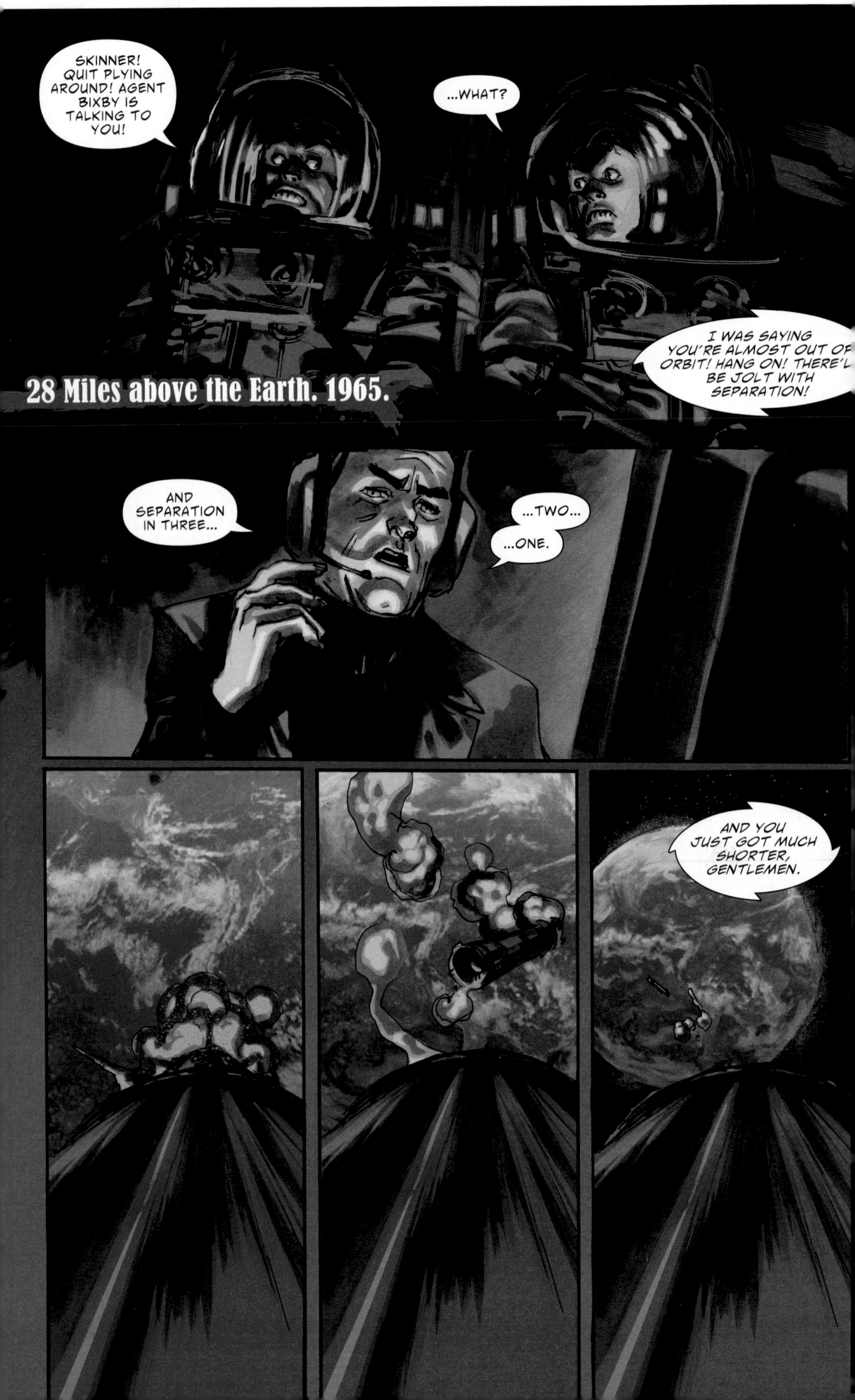
SKINNER! QUIT PLYING AROUND! AGENT BIXBY IS TALKING TO YOU!
...WHAT?
28 Miles above the Earth. 1965.
I WAS SAYING YOU'RE ALMOST OUT OF ORBIT! HANG ON! THERE'LL BE JOLT WITH SEPARATION!
AND SEPARATION IN THREE...
...TWO...
...ONE.
AND YOU JUST GOT MUCH SHORTER, GENTLEMEN.

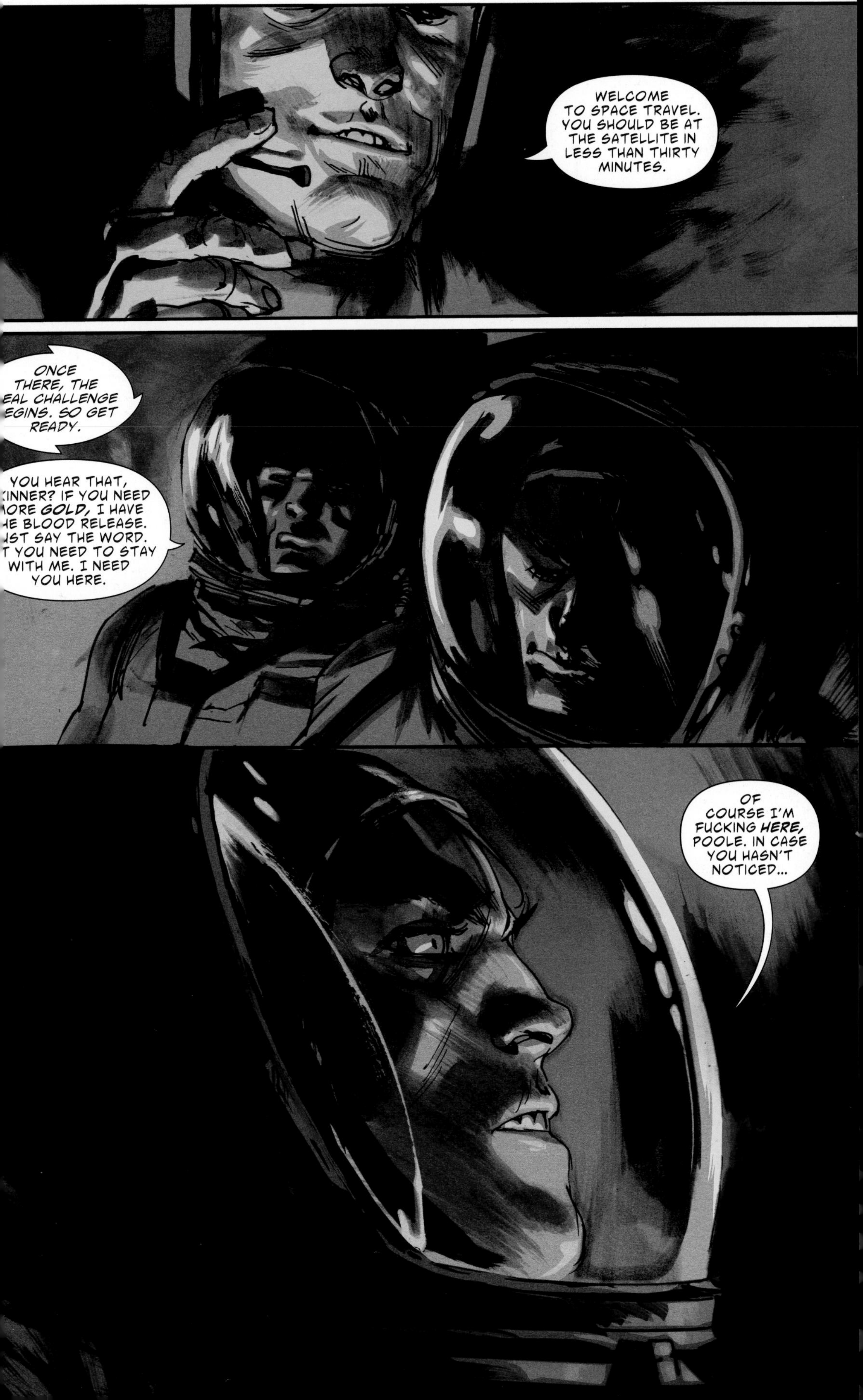
WELCOME TO SPACE TRAVEL. YOU SHOULD BE AT THE SATELLITE IN LESS THAN THIRTY MINUTES.
ONCE THERE, THE EAL CHALLENGE EGINS. SO GET READY.
YOU HEAR THAT, KINNER? IF YOU NEED ORE GOLD, I HAVE HE BLOOD RELEASE. JST SAY THE WORD. T YOU NEED TO STAY WITH ME. I NEED YOU HERE.
OF COURSE I'M FUCKING HERE, POOLE. IN CASE YOU HASN'T NOTICED...

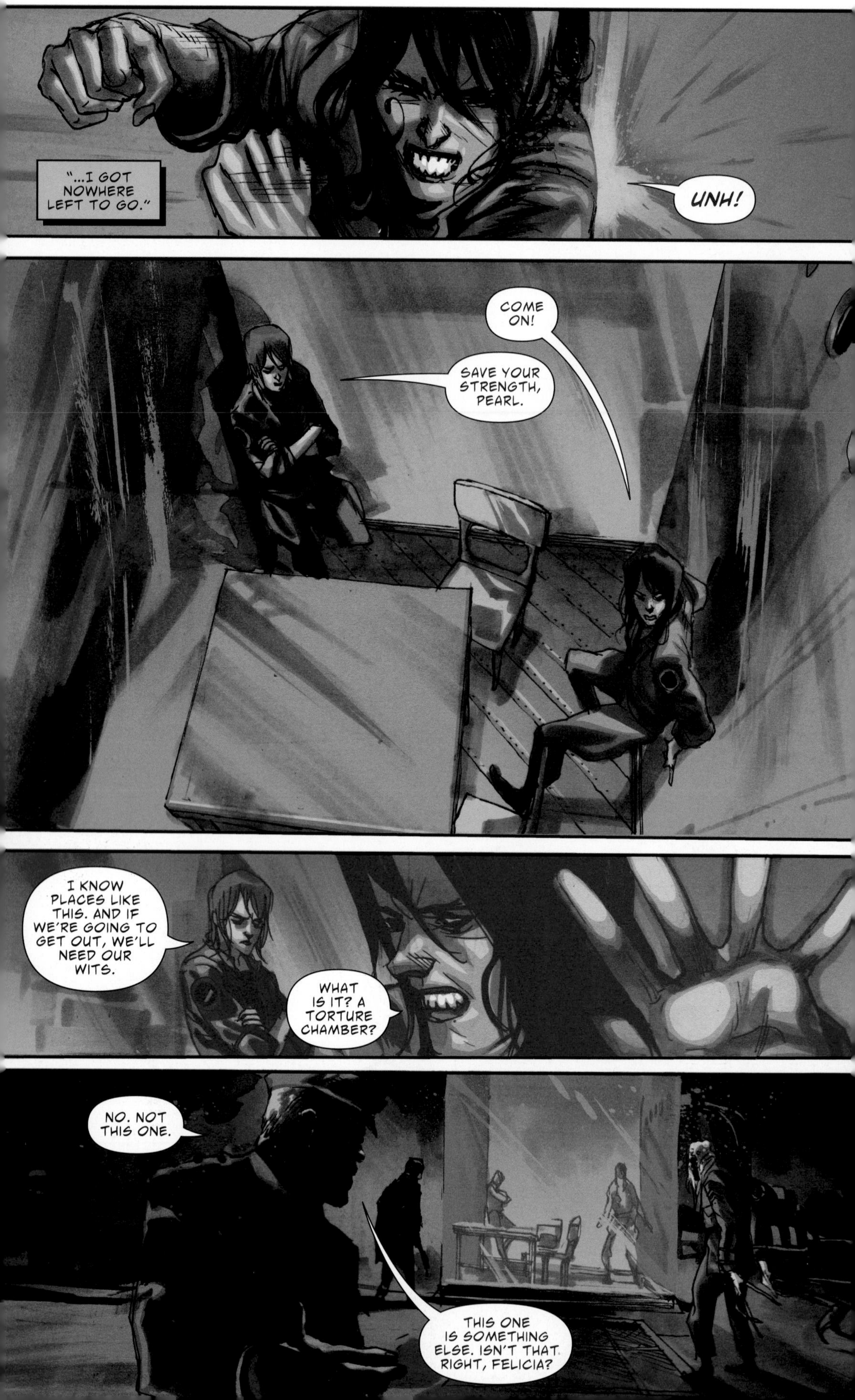
"...I GOT NOWHERE LEFT TO GO."
UNH!
COME ON!
SAVE YOUR STRENGTH, PEARL.
I KNOW PLACES LIKE THIS. AND IF WE'RE GOING TO GET OUT, WE'LL NEED OUR WITS.
WHAT IS IT? A TORTURE CHAMBER?
NO. NOT THIS ONE.
THIS ONE IS SOMETHING ELSE. ISN'T THAT RIGHT, FELICIA?

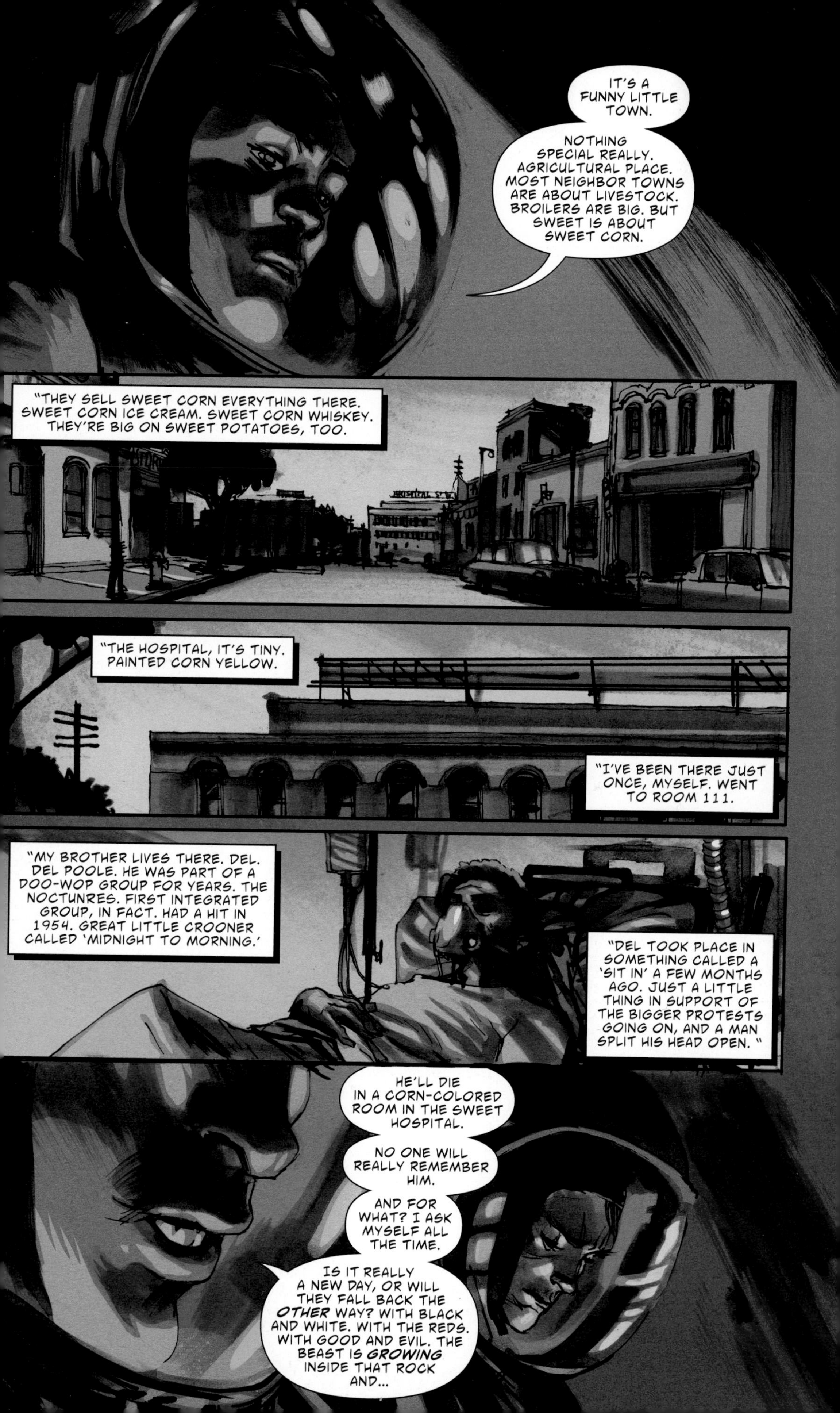
IT'S A FUNNY LITTLE TOWN.
NOTHING SPECIAL REALLY. AGRICULTURAL PLACE. MOST NEIGHBOR TOWNS ARE ABOUT LIVESTOCK. BROILERS ARE BIG. BUT SWEET IS ABOUT SWEET CORN.
"THEY SELL SWEET CORN EVERYTHING THERE. SWEET CORN ICE CREAM. SWEET CORN WHISKEY. THEY'RE BIG ON SWEET POTATOES, TOO.
"THE HOSPITAL, IT'S TINY. PAINTED CORN YELLOW.
"I'VE BEEN THERE JUST ONCE, MYSELF. WENT TO ROOM 111.
"MY BROTHER LIVES THERE. DEL. DEL POOLE. HE WAS PART OF A DOO-WOP GROUP FOR YEARS. THE NOCTUNRES. FIRST INTEGRATED GROUP, IN FACT. HAD A HIT IN 1954. GREAT LITTLE CROONER CALLED 'MIDNIGHT TO MORNING.'
"DEL TOOK PLACE IN SOMETHING CALLED A 'SIT IN' A FEW MONTHS AGO. JUST A LITTLE THING IN SUPPORT OF THE BIGGER PROTESTS GOING ON, AND A MAN SPLIT HIS HEAD OPEN."
HE'LL DIE IN A CORN-COLORED ROOM IN THE SWEET HOSPITAL.
NO ONE WILL REALLY REMEMBER HIM.
AND FOR WHAT? I ASK MYSELF ALL THE TIME.
IS IT REALLY A NEW DAY, OR WILL THEY FALL BACK THE *OTHER* WAY? WITH BLACK AND WHITE. WITH THE REDS. WITH GOOD AND EVIL. THE BEAST IS *GROWING* INSIDE THAT ROCK AND...

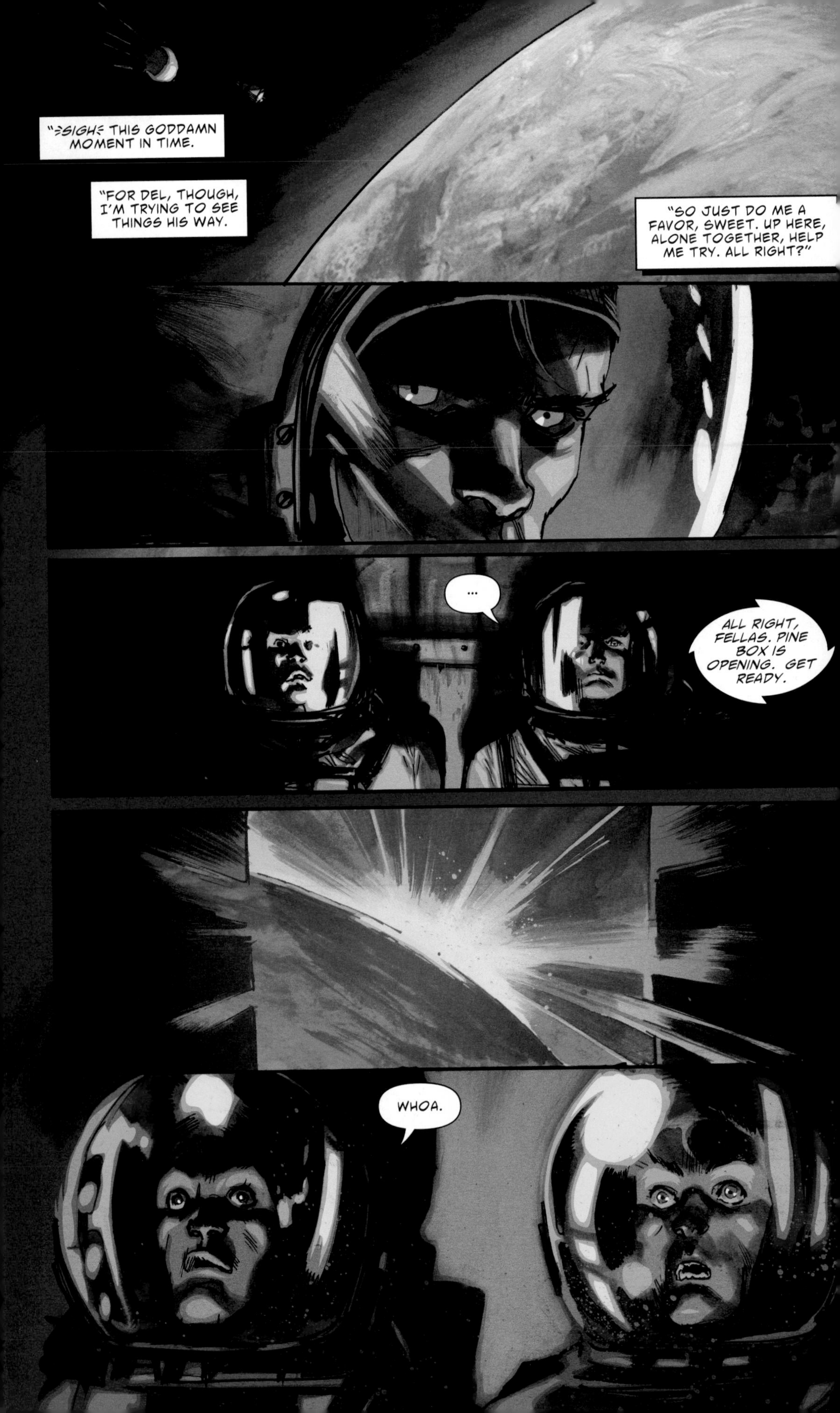
"=SIGH= THIS GODDAMN MOMENT IN TIME.
"FOR DEL, THOUGH, I'M TRYING TO SEE THINGS HIS WAY.
"SO JUST DO ME A FAVOR, SWEET. UP HERE, ALONE TOGETHER, HELP ME TRY. ALL RIGHT?"
...
ALL RIGHT, FELLAS. PINE BOX IS OPENING. GET READY.
WHOA.

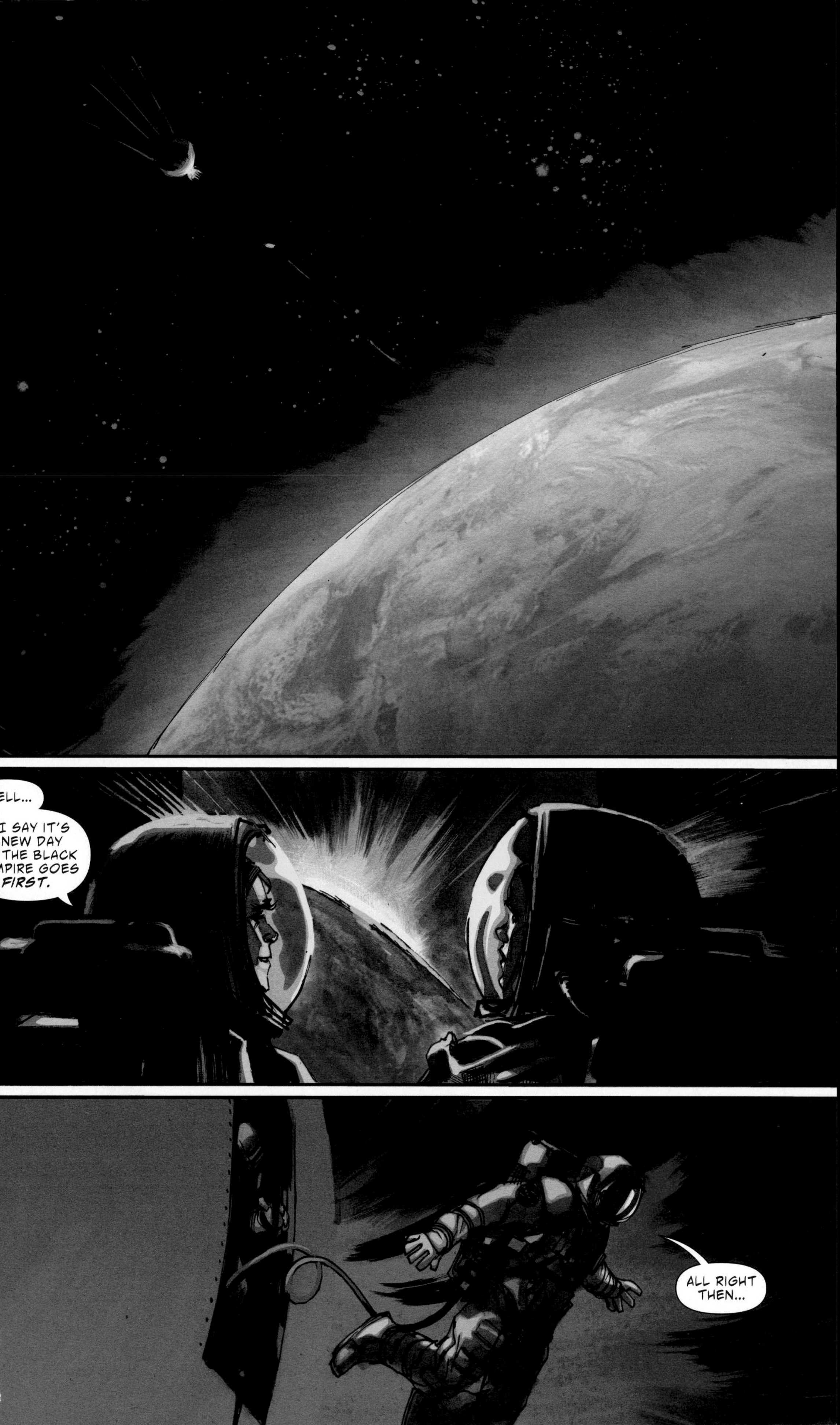
ELL...
I SAY IT'S NEW DAY THE BLACK MPIRE GOES FIRST.
ALL RIGHT THEN...

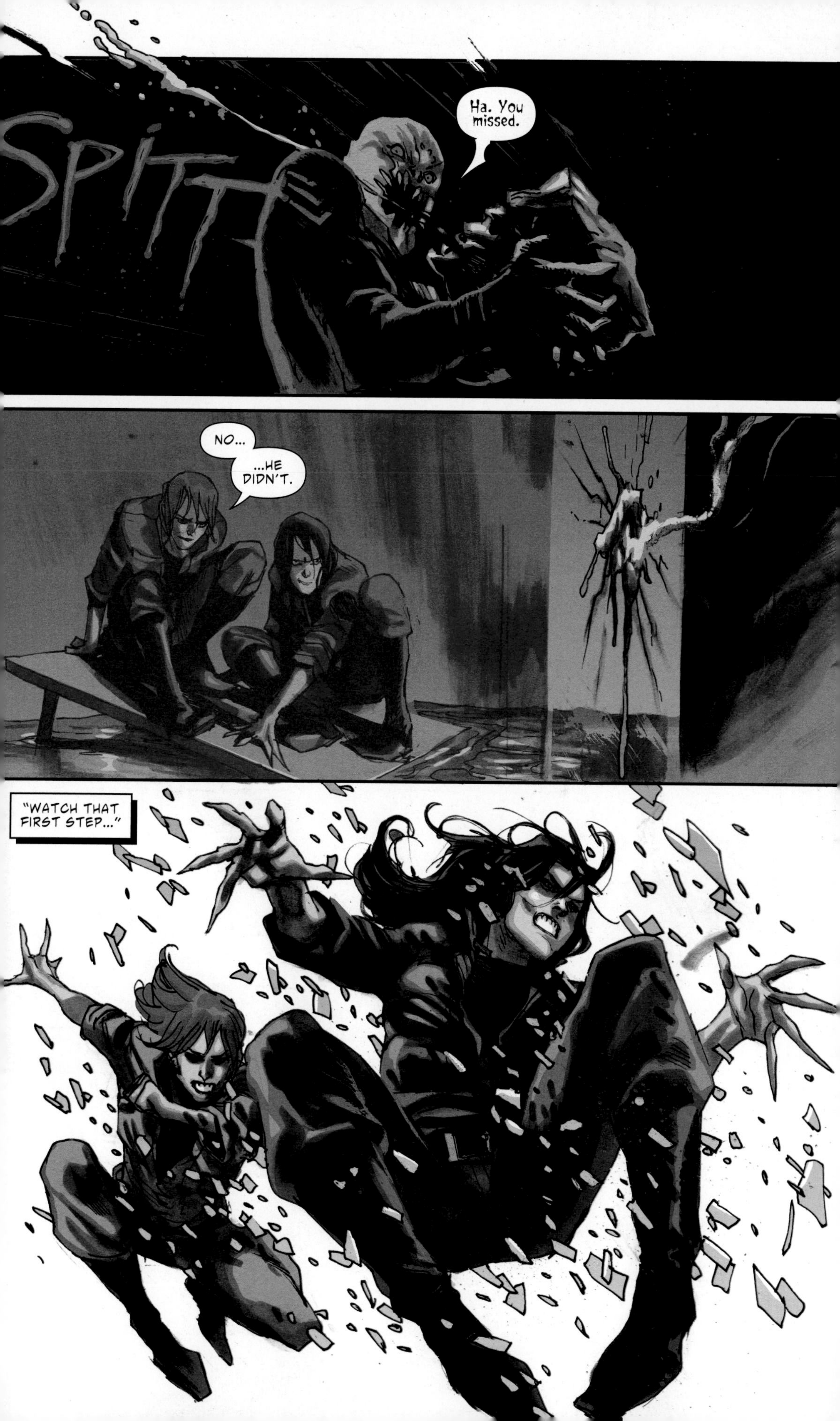
SPITT
Ha. You missed.
NO...
...HE DIDN'T.
"WATCH THAT FIRST STEP..."

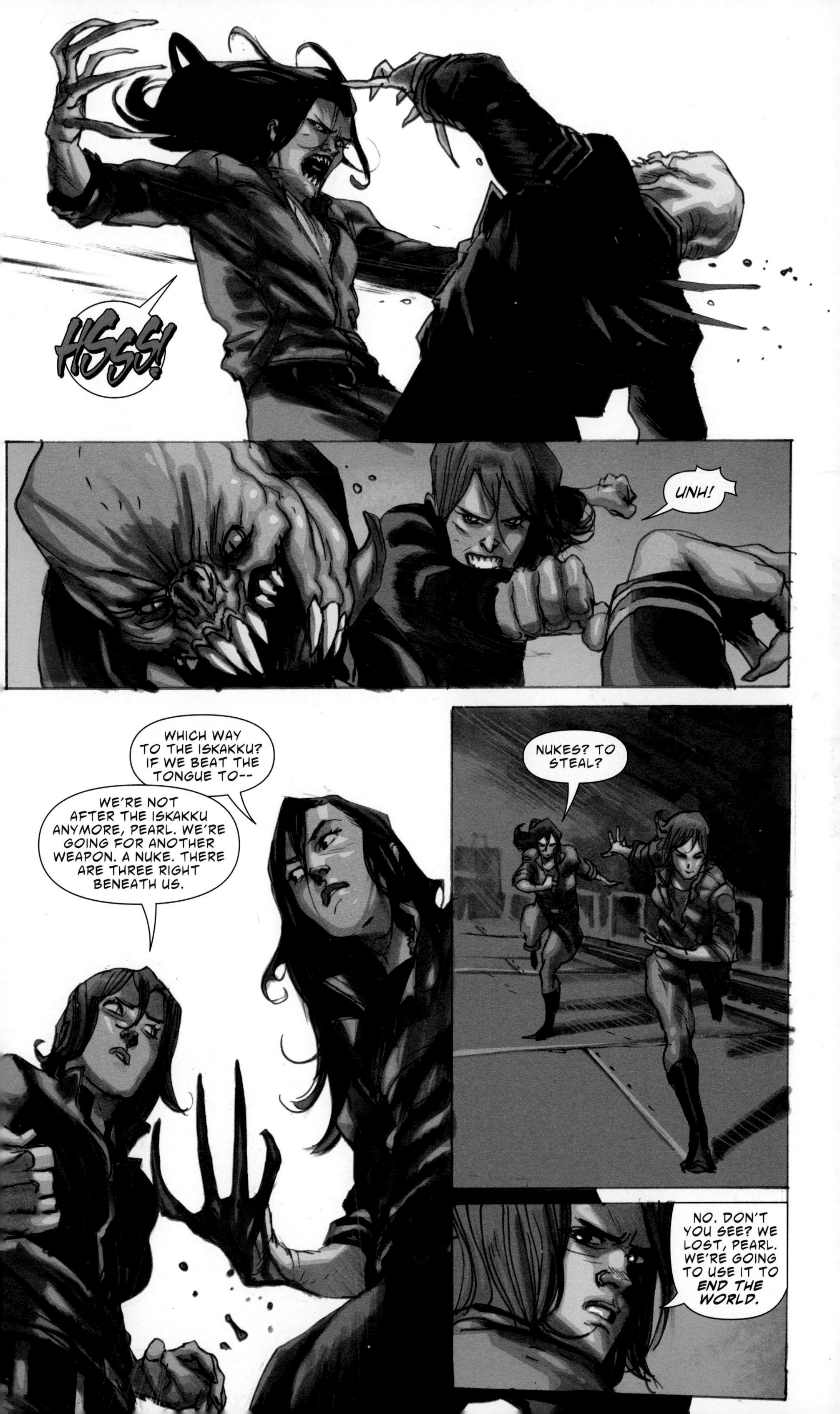
HSSS!
UNH!
WHICH WAY TO THE ISKAKKU? IF WE BEAT THE TONGUE TO--
WE'RE NOT AFTER THE ISKAKKU ANYMORE, PEARL. WE'RE GOING FOR ANOTHER WEAPON. A NUKE. THERE ARE THREE RIGHT BENEATH US.
NUKES? TO STEAL?
NO. DON'T YOU SEE? WE LOST, PEARL. WE'RE GOING TO USE IT TO *END THE WORLD.*

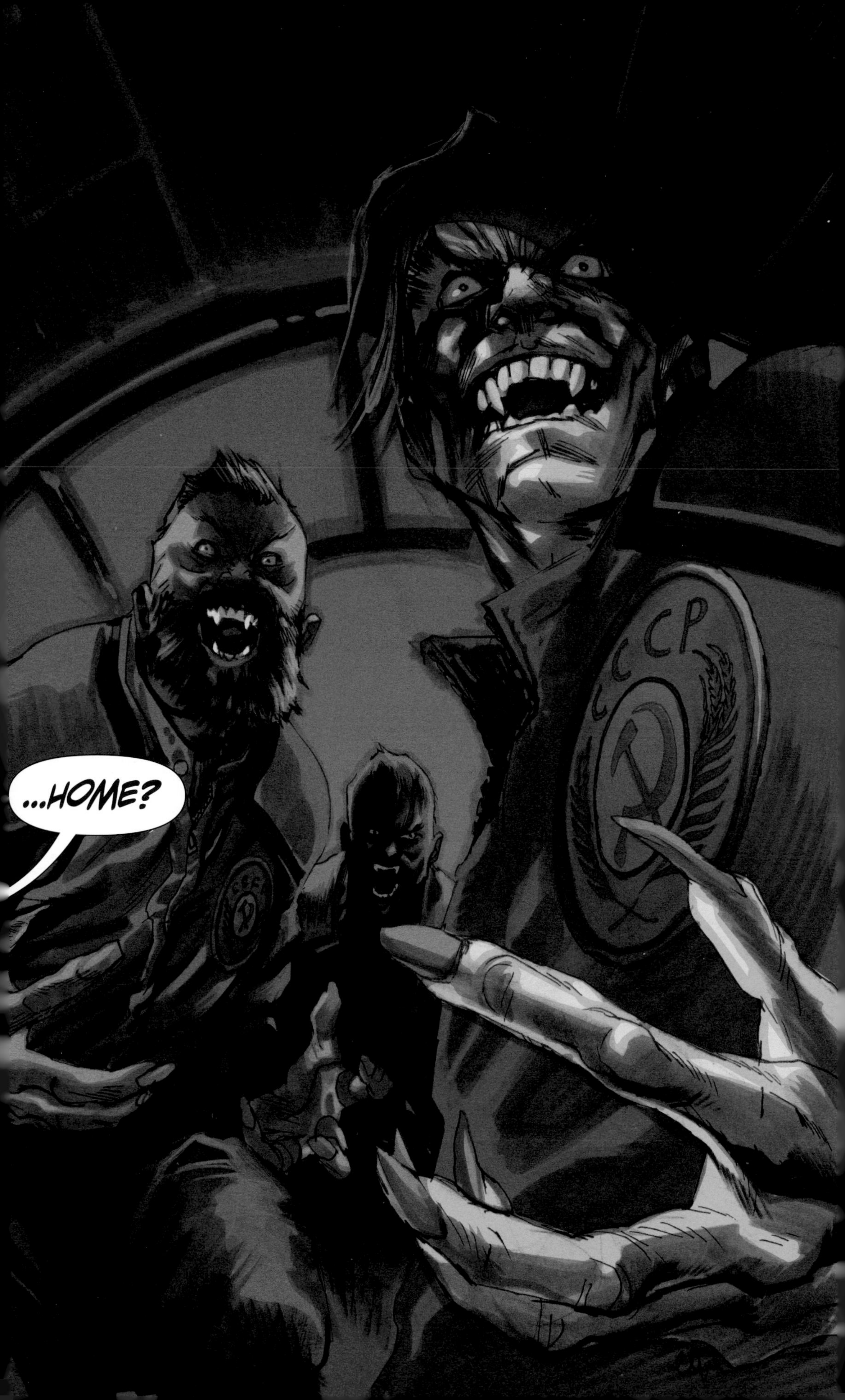
...HOME?
CCCP

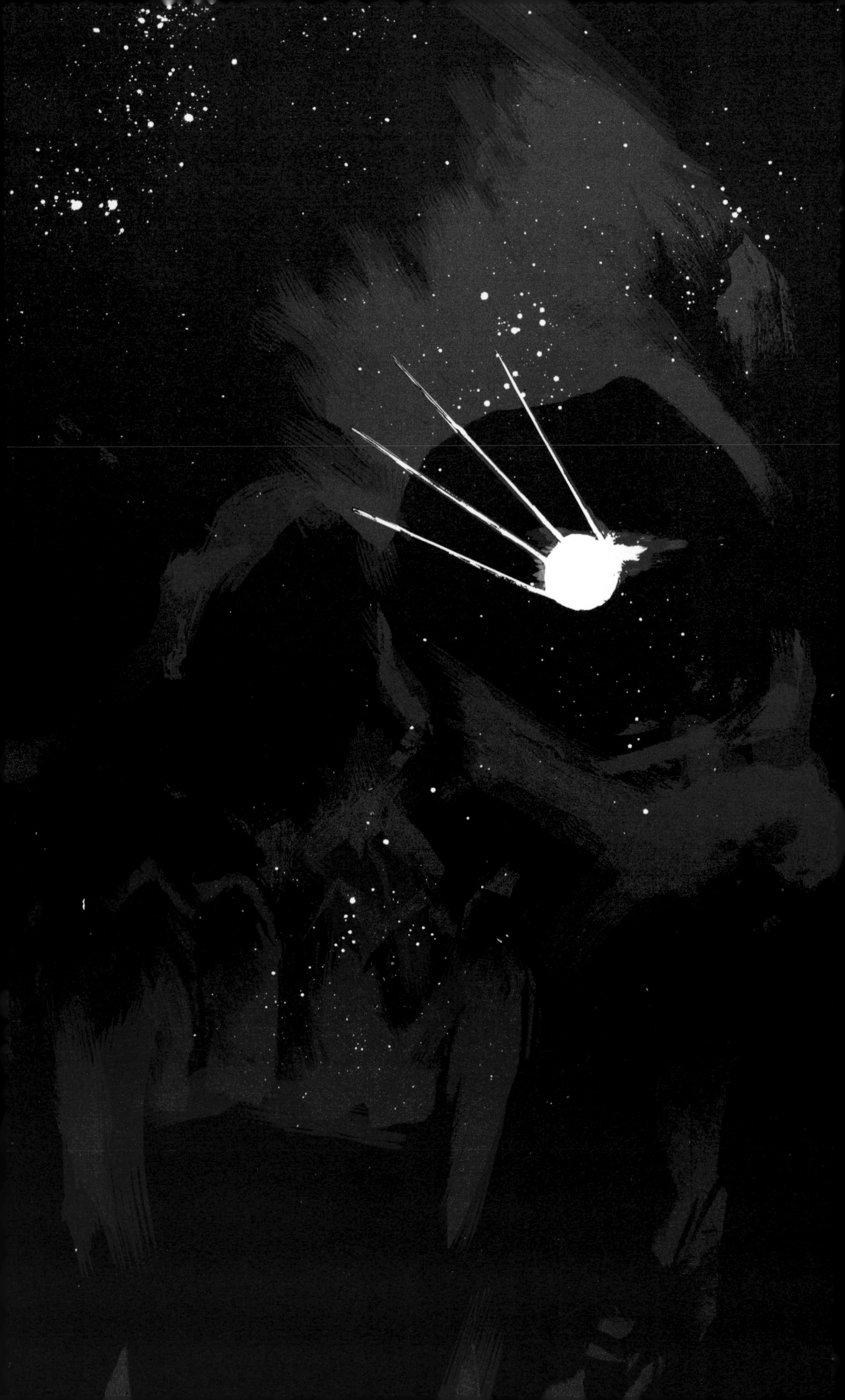

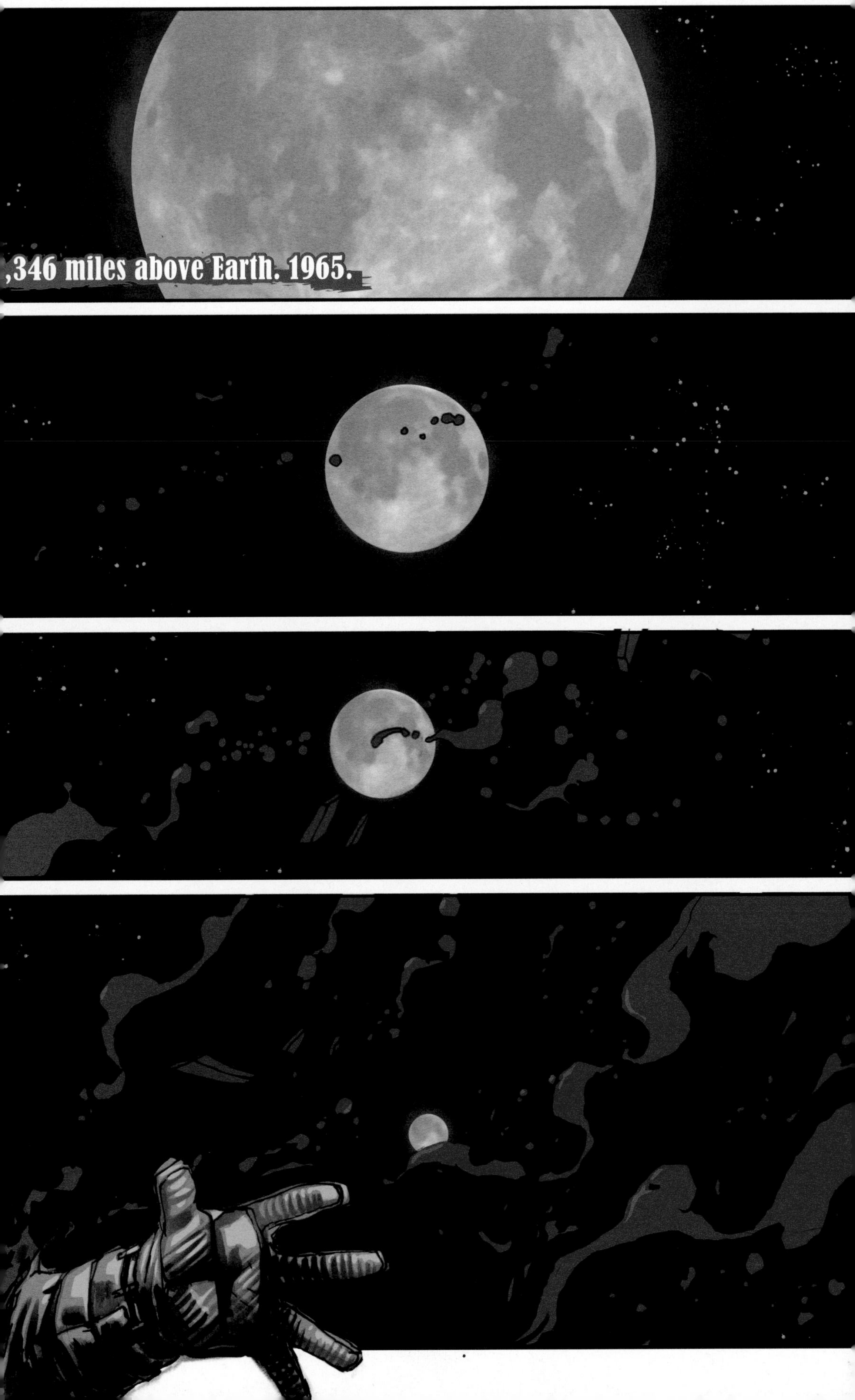
,346 miles above Earth. 1965.

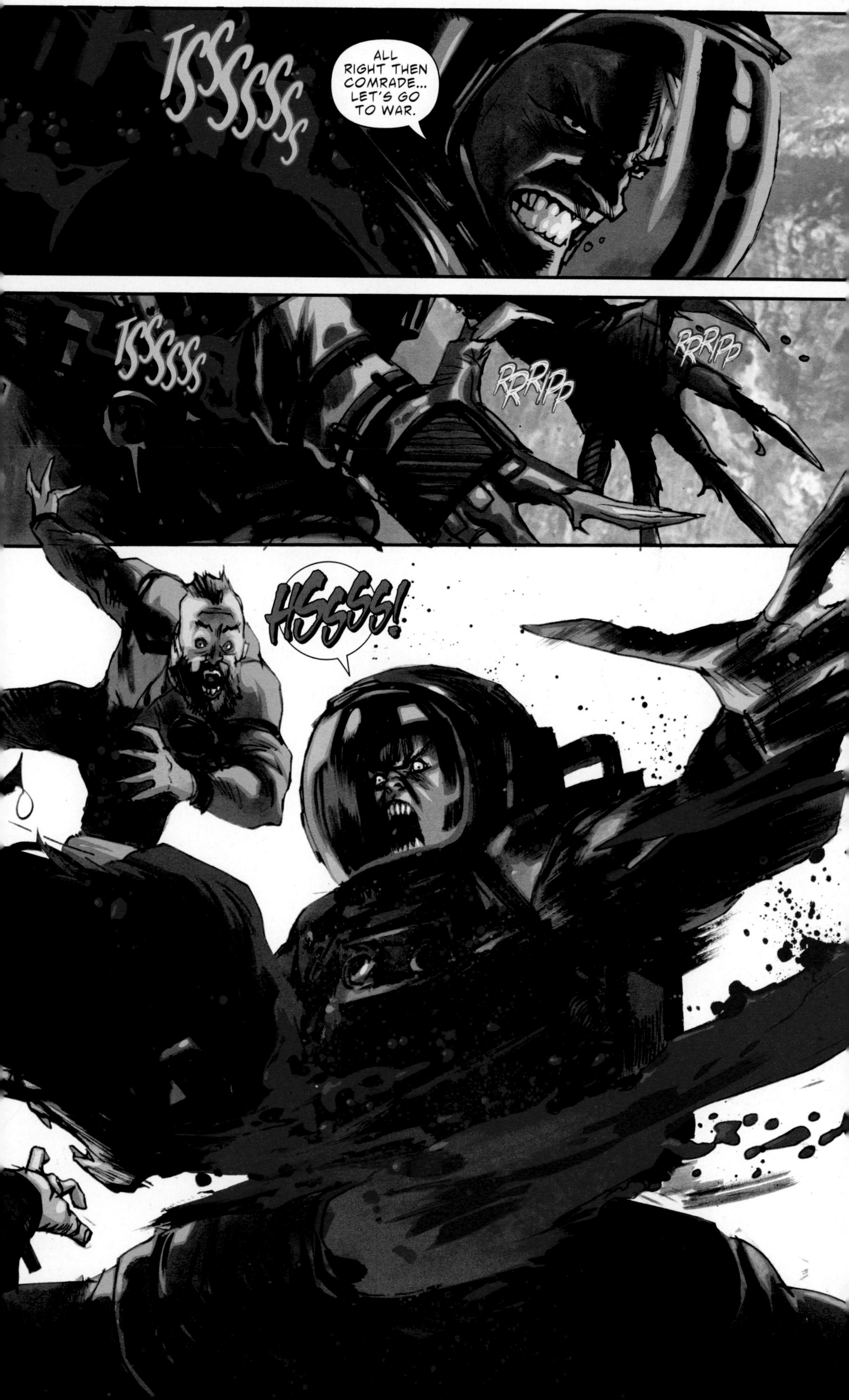
TSSSSSSS
ALL RIGHT THEN COMRADE... LET'S GO TO WAR.
TSSSSS
RRRIPP
RRRIPP
HSSSS!

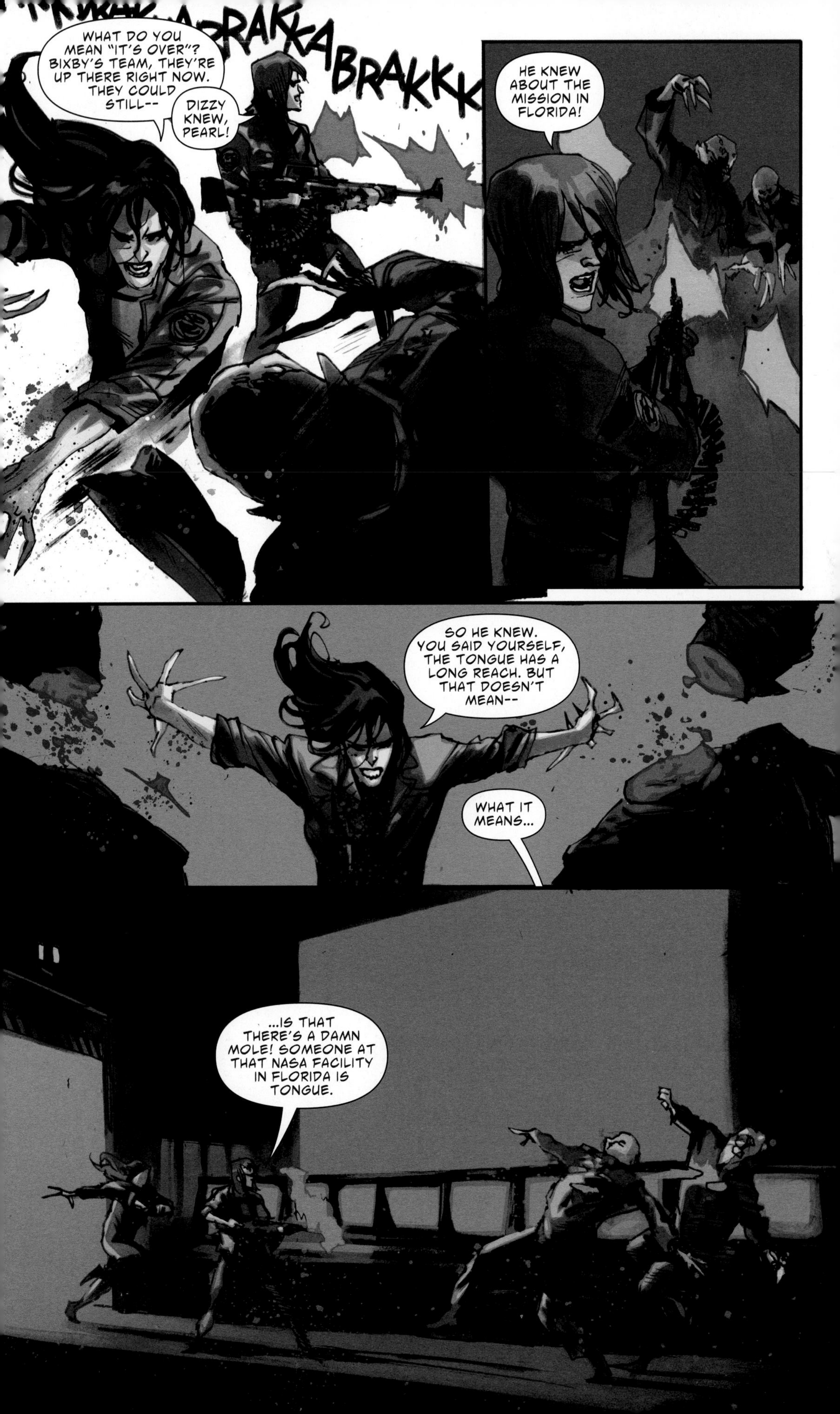
BRAKKA BRAKKA BRAKKK
WHAT DO YOU MEAN "IT'S OVER"? BIXBY'S TEAM, THEY'RE UP THERE RIGHT NOW. THEY COULD STILL--
DIZZY KNEW, PEARL!
HE KNEW ABOUT THE MISSION IN FLORIDA!
SO HE KNEW. YOU SAID YOURSELF, THE TONGUE HAS A LONG REACH. BUT THAT DOESN'T MEAN--
WHAT IT MEANS...
...IS THAT THERE'S A DAMN MOLE! SOMEONE AT THAT NASA FACILITY IN FLORIDA IS TONGUE.

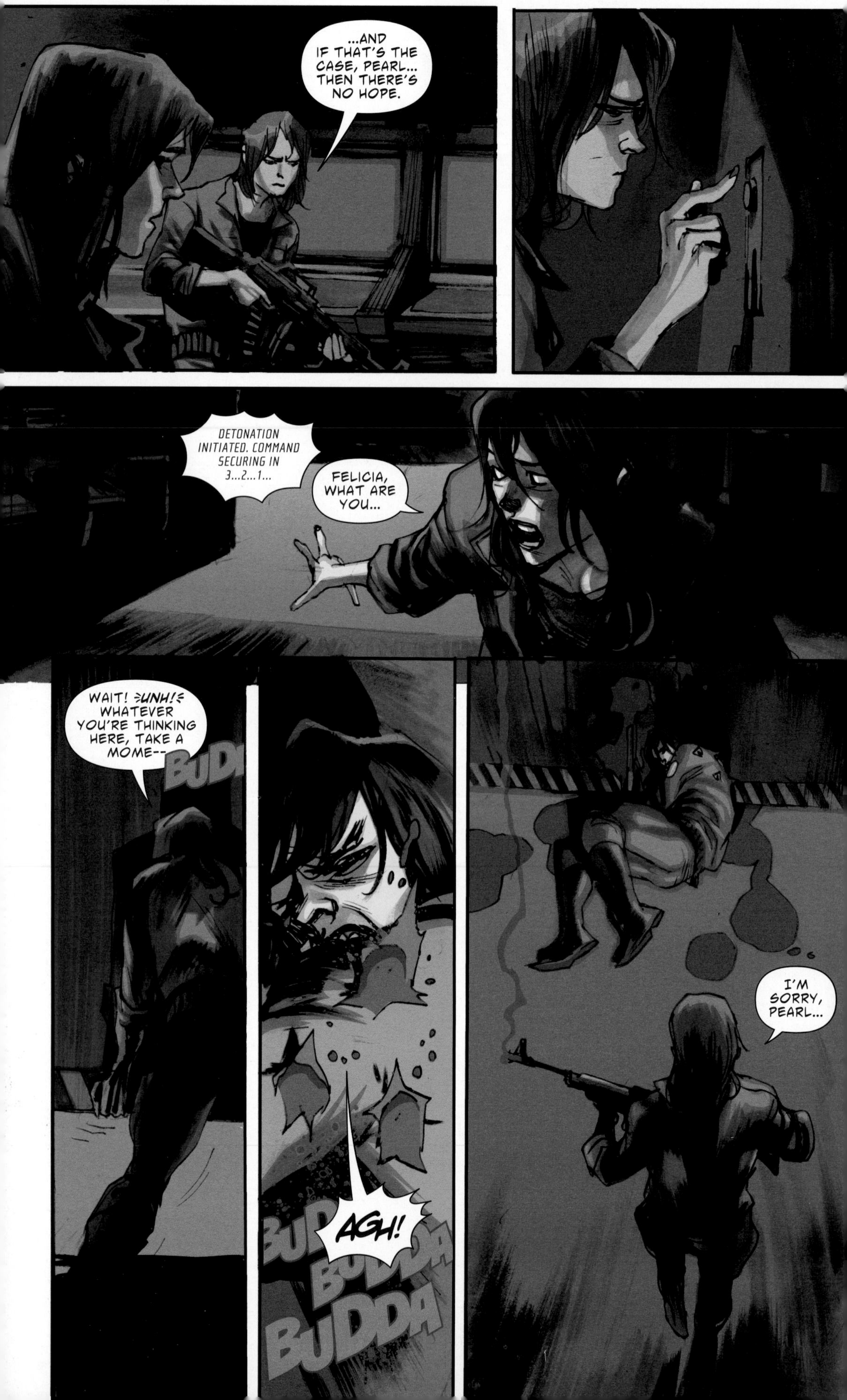
...AND IF THAT'S THE CASE, PEARL... THEN THERE'S NO HOPE.
DETONATION INITIATED. COMMAND SECURING IN 3...2...1...
FELICIA, WHAT ARE YOU...
WAIT! UNH! WHATEVER YOU'RE THINKING HERE, TAKE A MOME--
BUDD
AGH!
BUDDA BUDDA BUDDA
I'M SORRY, PEARL...

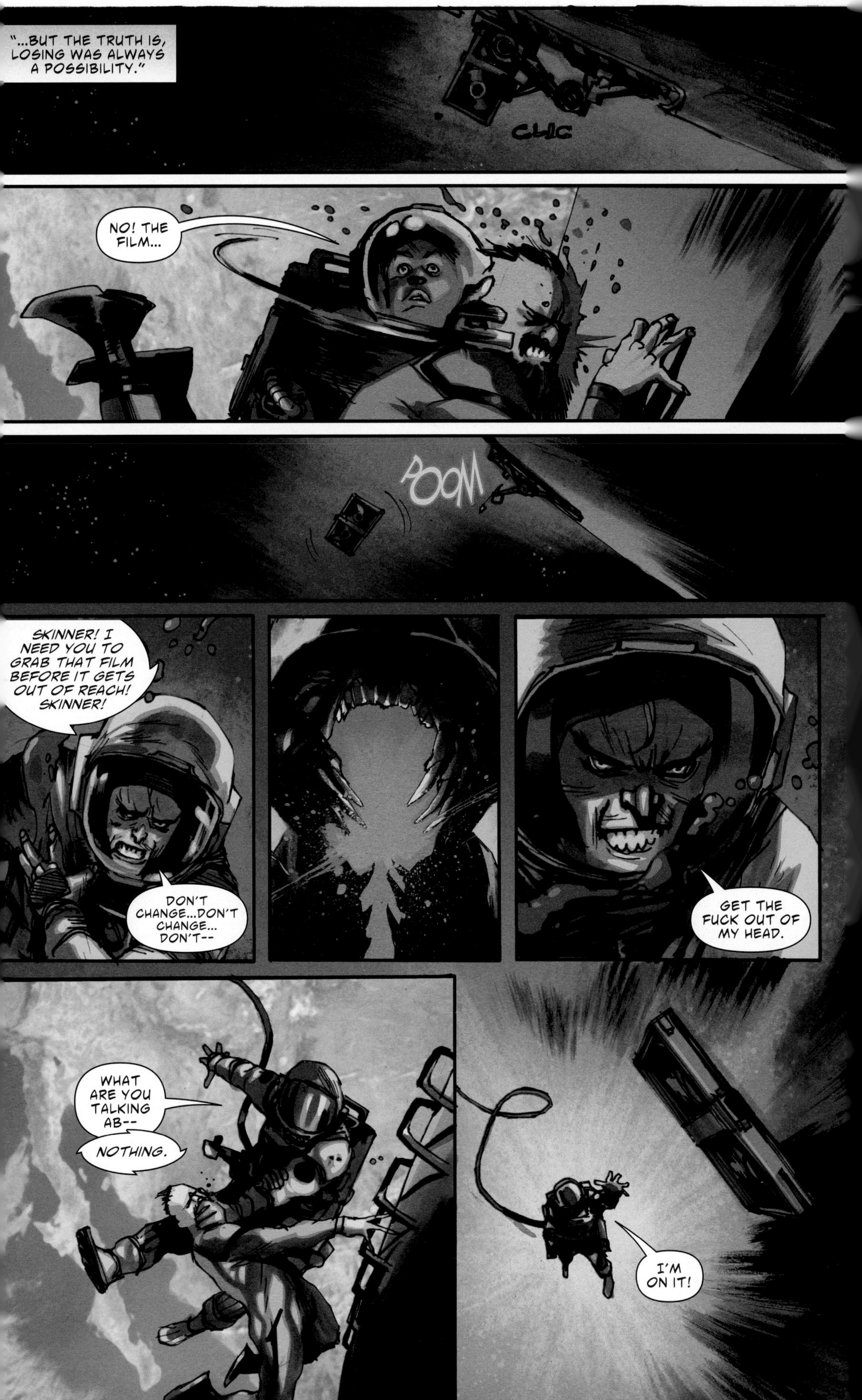
"...BUT THE TRUTH IS, LOSING WAS ALWAYS A POSSIBILITY."
CLIIC
NO! THE FILM...
POOM
SKINNER! I NEED YOU TO GRAB THAT FILM BEFORE IT GETS OUT OF REACH! SKINNER!
DON'T CHANGE...DON'T CHANGE... DON'T--
GET THE FUCK OUT OF MY HEAD.
WHAT ARE YOU TALKING AB--
NOTHING.
I'M ON IT!

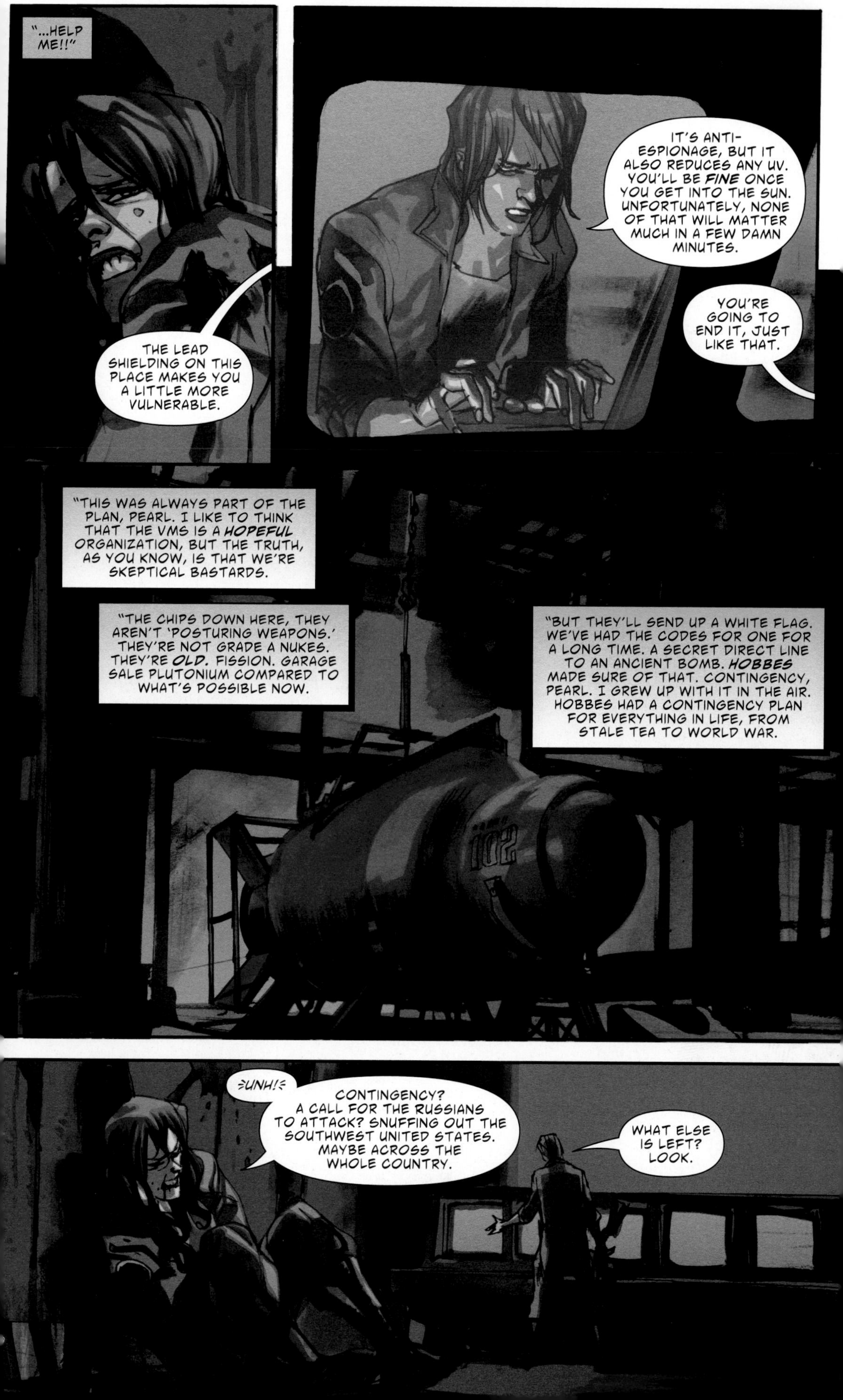
"...HELP ME!!"
THE LEAD SHIELDING ON THIS PLACE MAKES YOU A LITTLE MORE VULNERABLE.
IT'S ANTI-ESPIONAGE, BUT IT ALSO REDUCES ANY UV. YOU'LL BE *FINE* ONCE YOU GET INTO THE SUN. UNFORTUNATELY, NONE OF THAT WILL MATTER MUCH IN A FEW DAMN MINUTES.
YOU'RE GOING TO END IT, JUST LIKE THAT.
"THIS WAS ALWAYS PART OF THE PLAN, PEARL. I LIKE TO THINK THAT THE VMS IS A *HOPEFUL* ORGANIZATION, BUT THE TRUTH, AS YOU KNOW, IS THAT WE'RE SKEPTICAL BASTARDS.
"THE CHIPS DOWN HERE, THEY AREN'T 'POSTURING WEAPONS.' THEY'RE NOT GRADE A NUKES. THEY'RE *OLD.* FISSION. GARAGE SALE PLUTONIUM COMPARED TO WHAT'S POSSIBLE NOW.
"BUT THEY'LL SEND UP A WHITE FLAG. WE'VE HAD THE CODES FOR ONE FOR A LONG TIME. A SECRET DIRECT LINE TO AN ANCIENT BOMB. *HOBBES* MADE SURE OF THAT. CONTINGENCY, PEARL. I GREW UP WITH IT IN THE AIR. HOBBES HAD A CONTINGENCY PLAN FOR EVERYTHING IN LIFE, FROM STALE TEA TO WORLD WAR.
UNH!
CONTINGENCY? A CALL FOR THE RUSSIANS TO ATTACK? SNUFFING OUT THE SOUTHWEST UNITED STATES. MAYBE ACROSS THE WHOLE COUNTRY.
WHAT ELSE IS LEFT? LOOK.

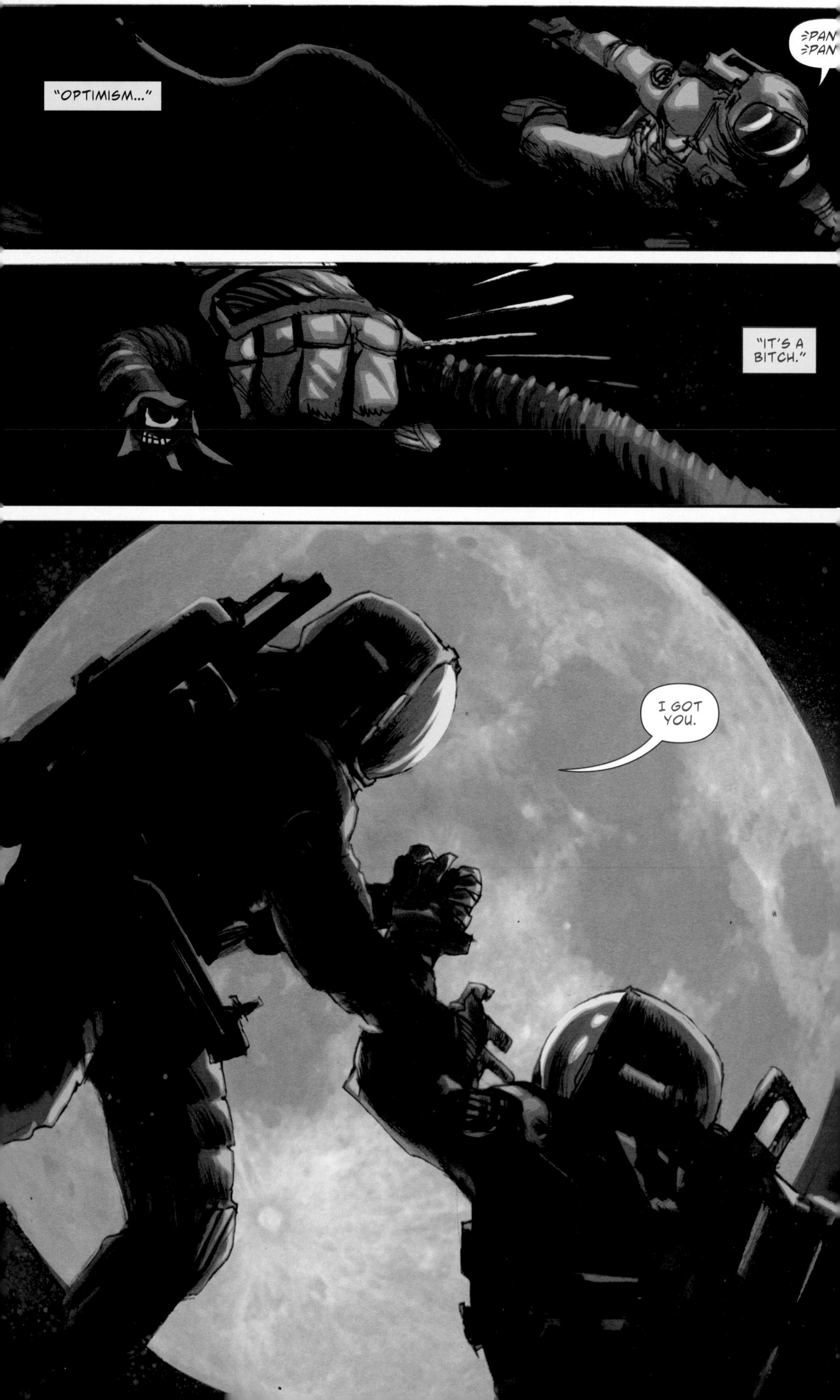
"OPTIMISM..."
PAN
PAN
"IT'S A BITCH."
I GOT YOU.

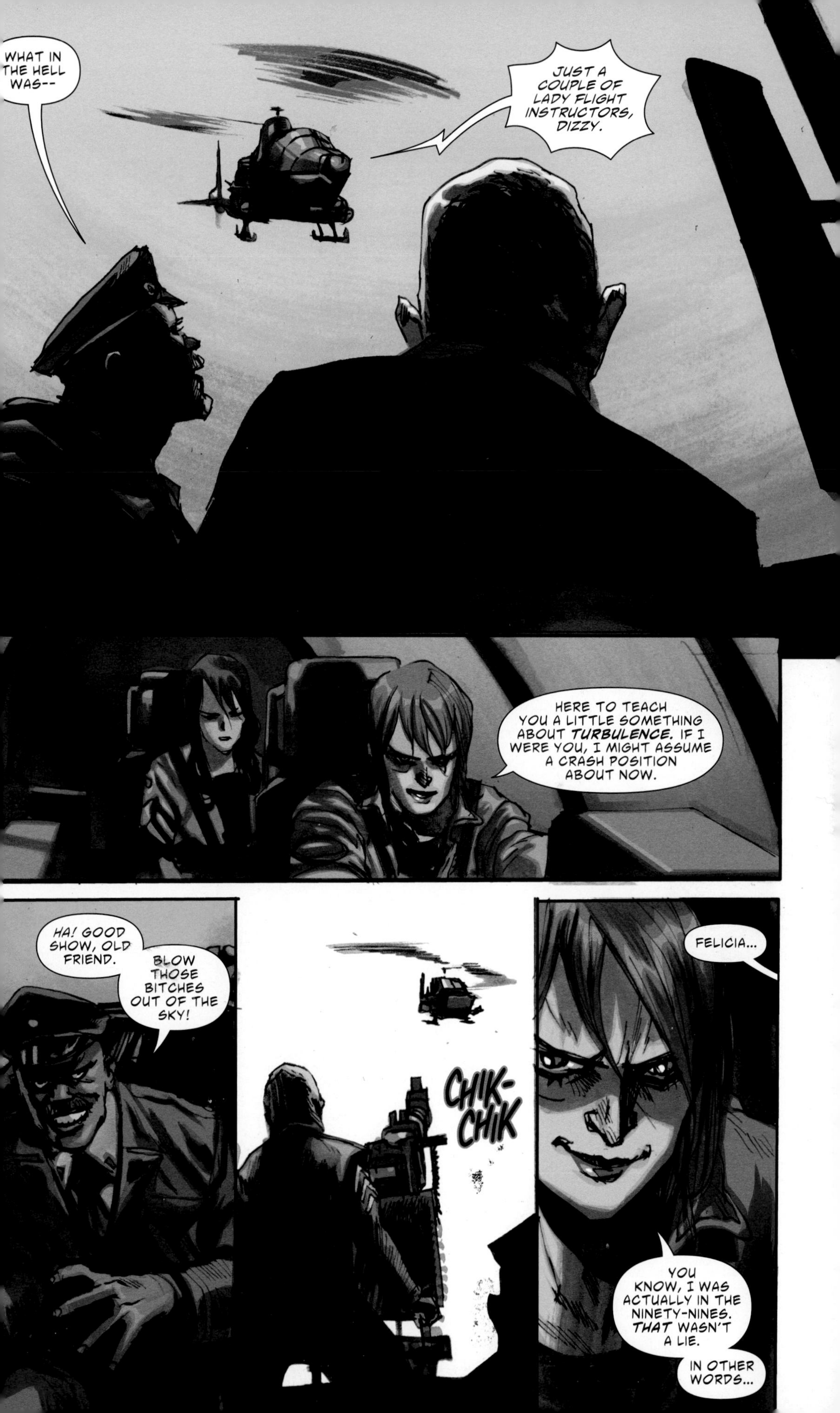
WHAT IN THE HELL WAS--
JUST A COUPLE OF LADY FLIGHT INSTRUCTORS, DIZZY.
HERE TO TEACH YOU A LITTLE SOMETHING ABOUT TURBULENCE. IF I WERE YOU, I MIGHT ASSUME A CRASH POSITION ABOUT NOW.
HA! GOOD SHOW, OLD FRIEND.
BLOW THOSE BITCHES OUT OF THE SKY!
CHIK-CHIK
FELICIA...
YOU KNOW, I WAS ACTUALLY IN THE NINETY-NINES. THAT WASN'T A LIE.
IN OTHER WORDS...

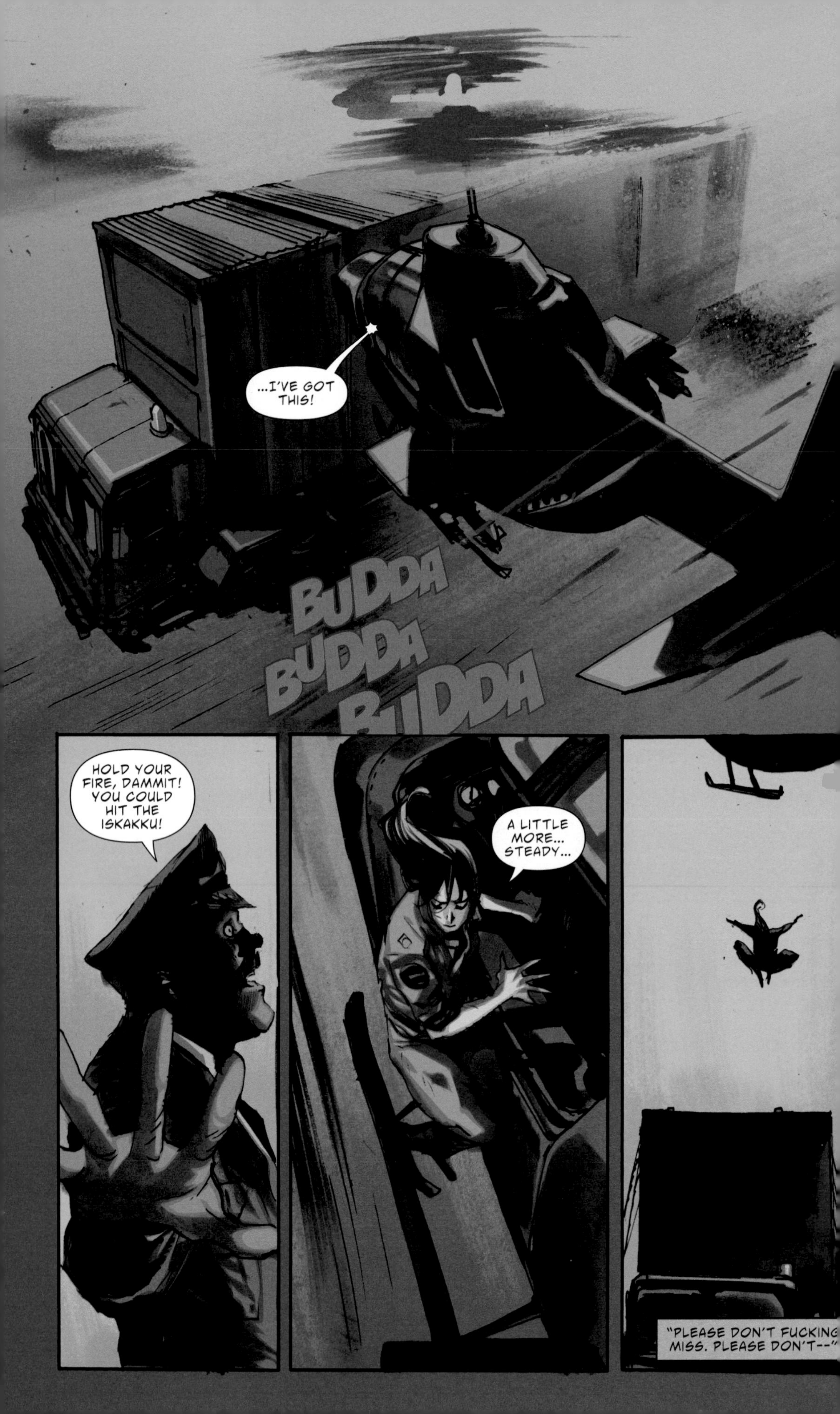
...I'VE GOT THIS!
BUDDA BUDDA BUDDA
HOLD YOUR FIRE, DAMMIT! YOU COULD HIT THE ISKAKKU!
A LITTLE MORE... STEADY...
"PLEASE DON'T FUCKING MISS. PLEASE DON'T--"

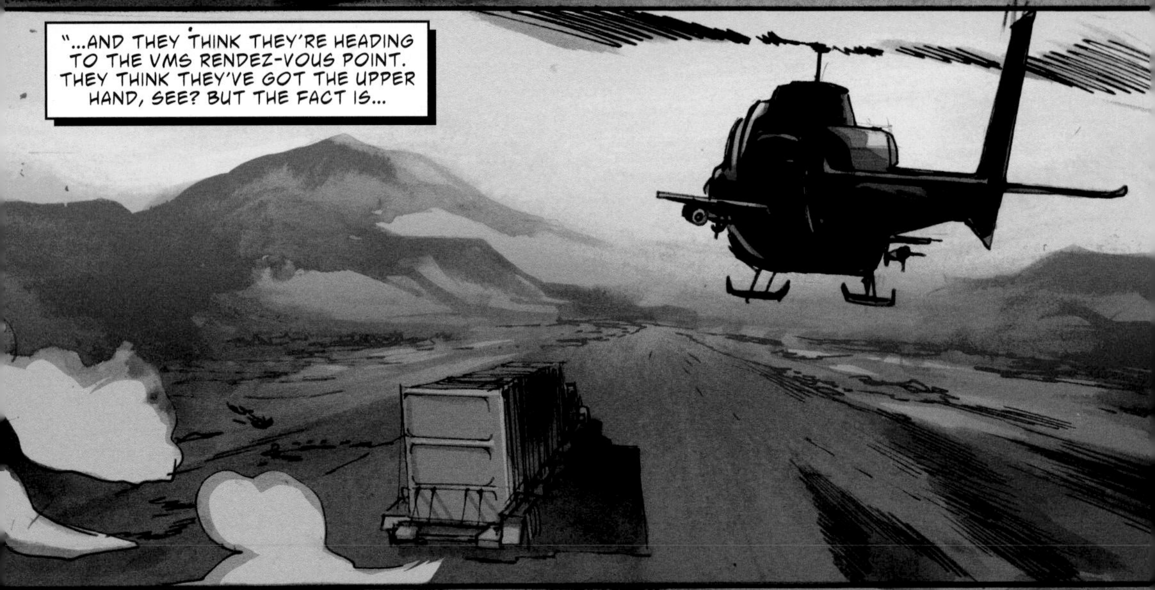
"...AND THEY THINK THEY'RE HEADING TO THE VMS RENDEZ-VOUS POINT. THEY THINK THEY'VE GOT THE UPPER HAND, SEE? BUT THE FACT IS...

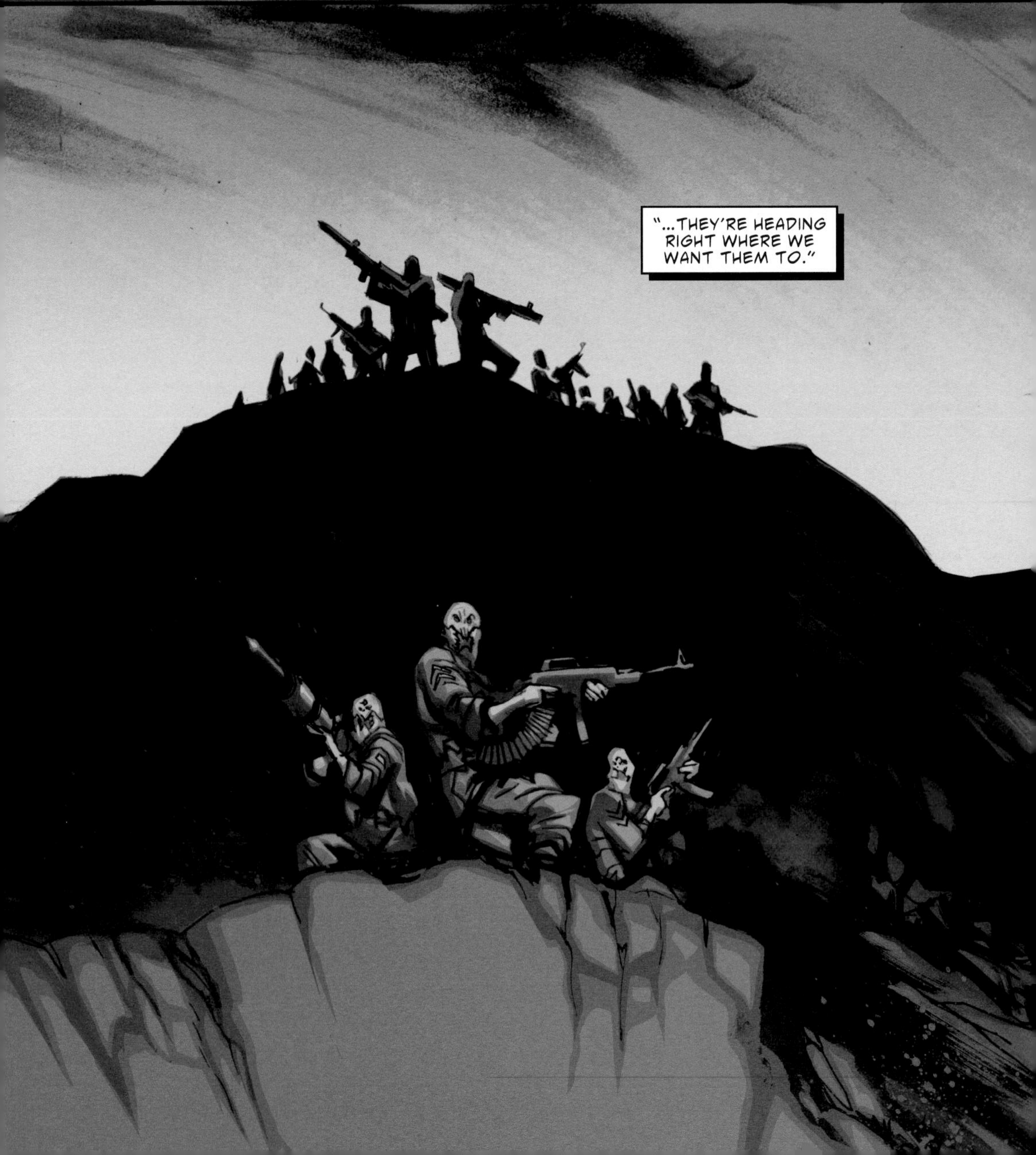
"...THEY'RE HEADING RIGHT WHERE WE WANT THEM TO."

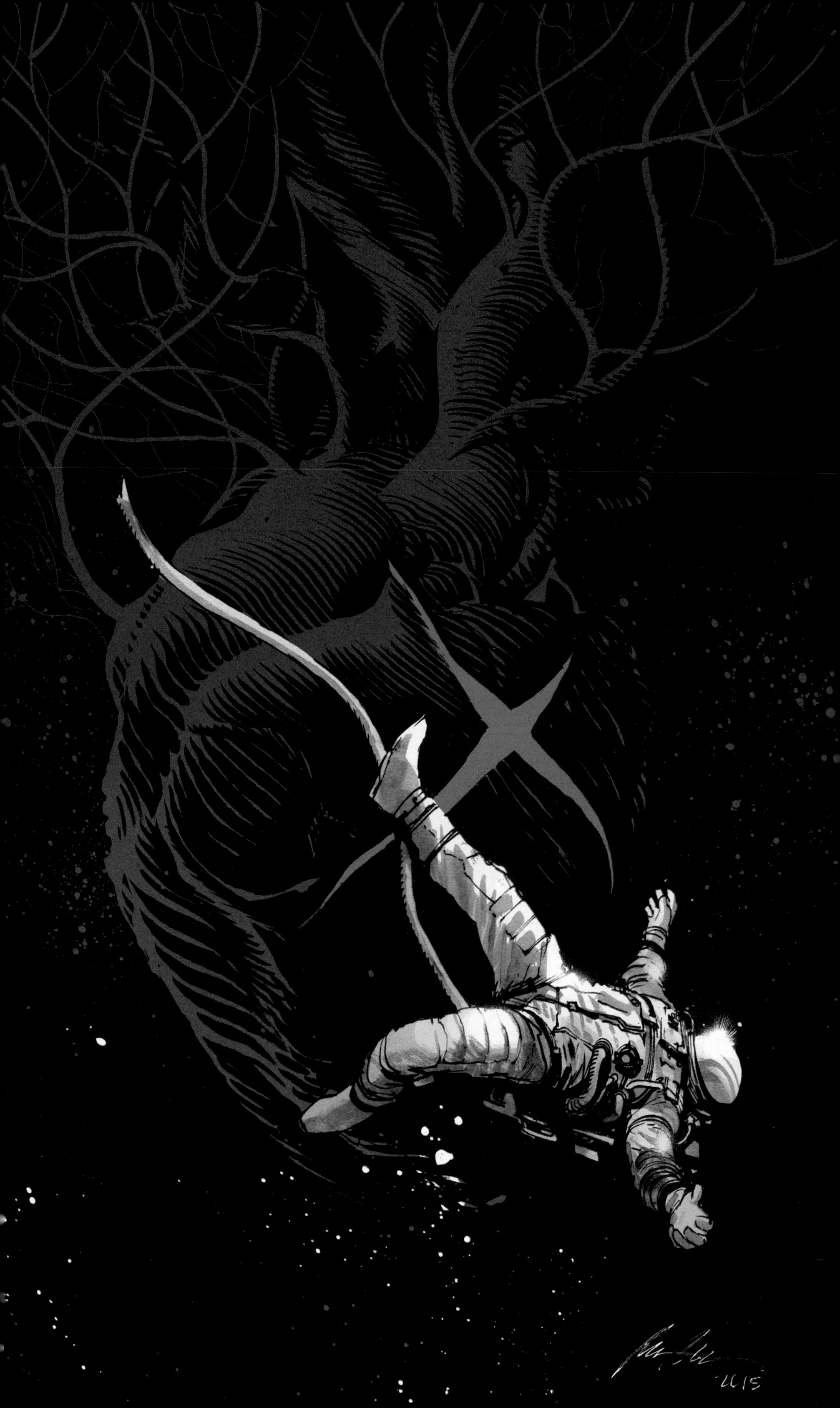

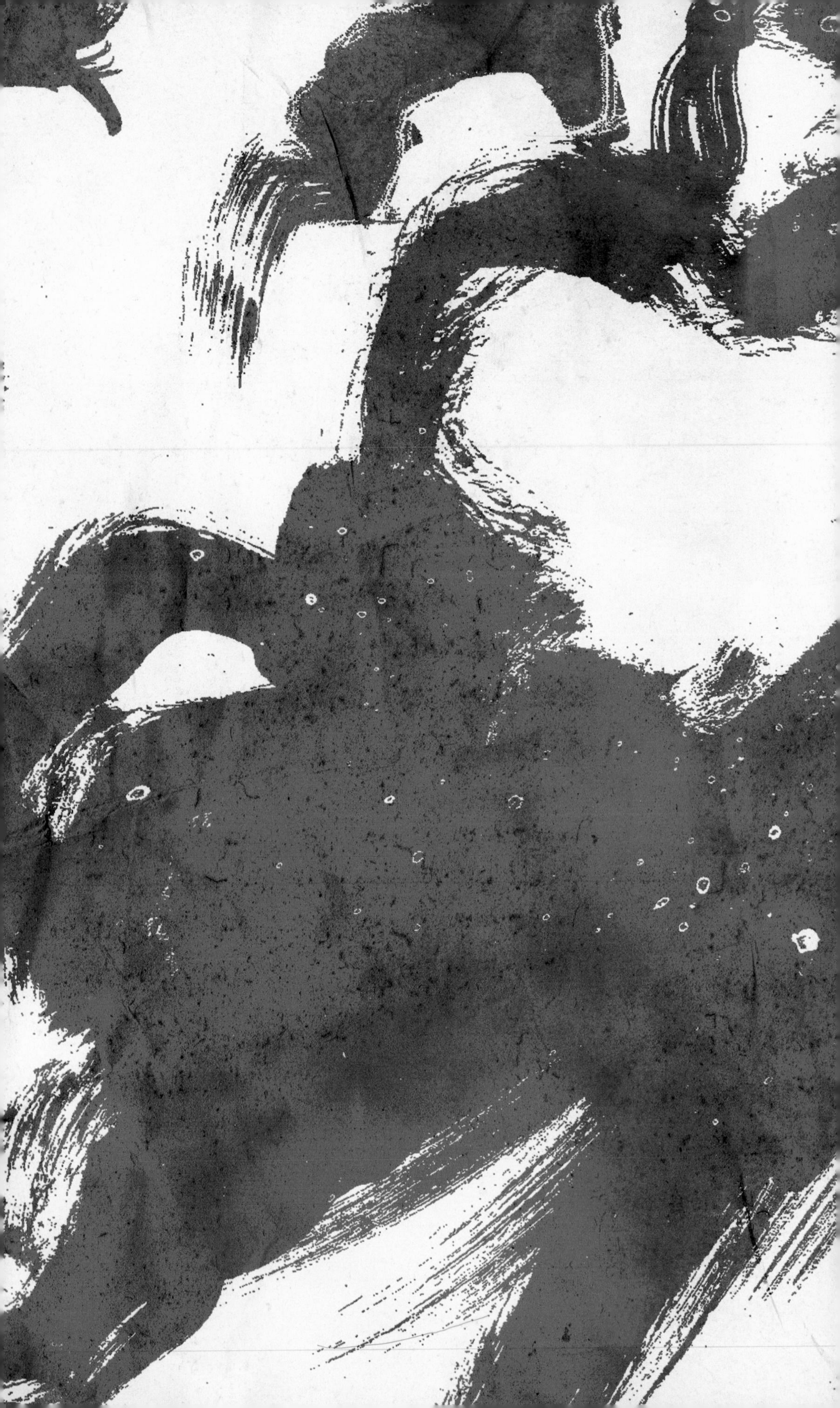

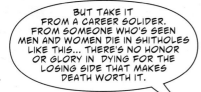

BUT TAKE IT FROM A CAREER SOLIDER. FROM SOMEONE WHO'S SEEN MEN AND WOMEN DIE IN SHITHOLES LIKE THIS... THERE'S NO HONOR OR GLORY IN DYING FOR THE LOSING SIDE THAT MAKES DEATH WORTH IT.

IN THE LAST MOMENTS, THERE'S ONLY PAIN AND FEAR AND REGRET. FOLKS CRYING FOR THEIR OWN BEDS, THEIR FRIENDS HOLDING THEIR *GUTS* AS THEY DIE. A GOOD SOLIDER DIES ALONE IN THE DESERT. A *REAL* SOLIDER SWITCHES SIDES. COME WITH US.

MY HUSBAND WAS A CAREER SOLIDER, TOO, "DIZZY." I TAKE MY LESSONS FROM HIM.

HAHA! LOVE AN FAITH. LC AND FAIT ALL RIG THEN!

"YOU MIGHT NOT WANT TO HEAR IT, BUT IT'S THE TRUTH..."

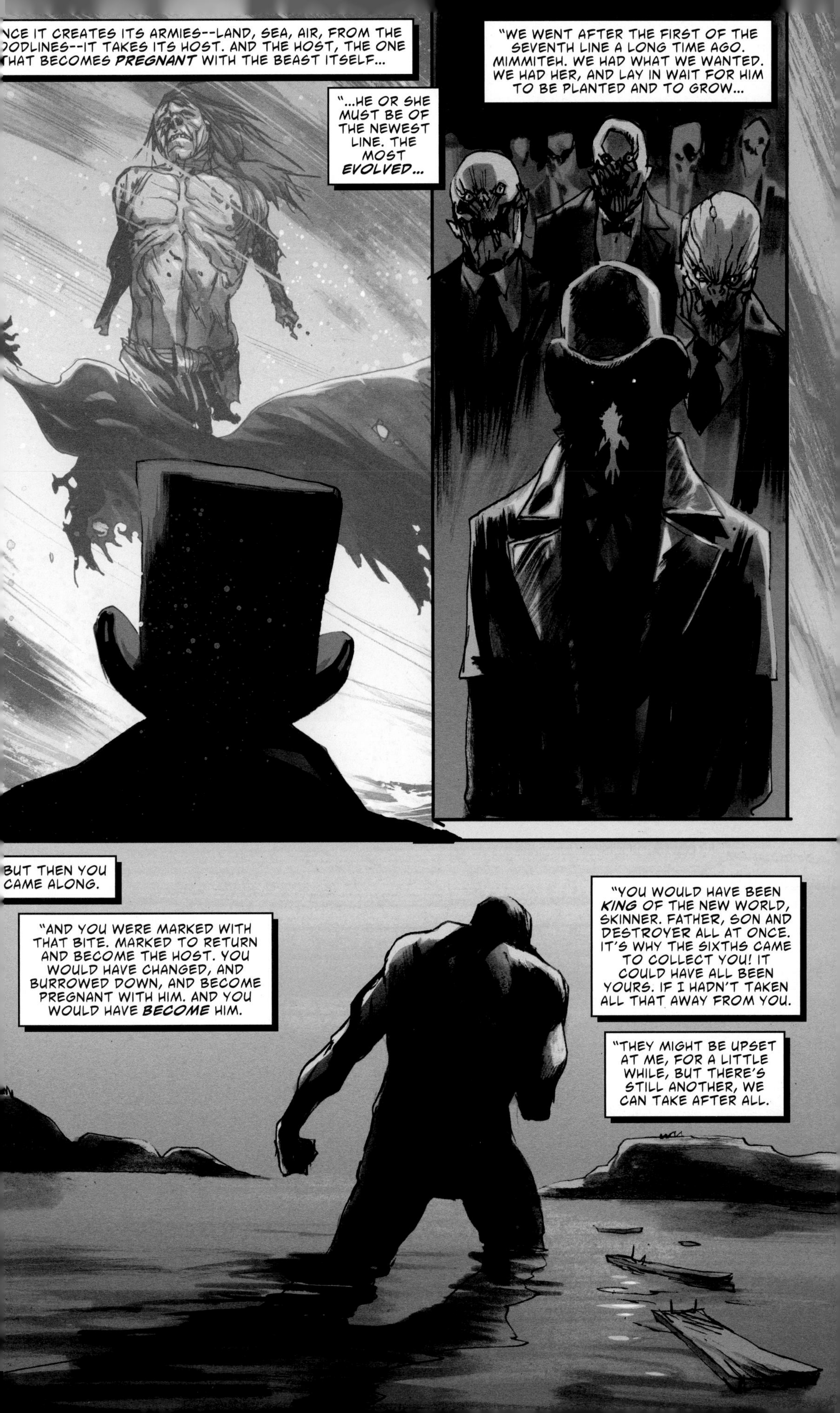
NCE IT CREATES ITS ARMIES--LAND, SEA, AIR, FROM THE ODLINES--IT TAKES ITS HOST. AND THE HOST, THE ONE THAT BECOMES *PREGNANT* WITH THE BEAST ITSELF...
"...HE OR SHE MUST BE OF THE NEWEST LINE. THE MOST *EVOLVED*...
"WE WENT AFTER THE FIRST OF THE SEVENTH LINE A LONG TIME AGO. MIMMITEH. WE HAD WHAT WE WANTED. WE HAD HER, AND LAY IN WAIT FOR HIM TO BE PLANTED AND TO GROW...
BUT THEN YOU CAME ALONG.
"AND YOU WERE MARKED WITH THAT BITE. MARKED TO RETURN AND BECOME THE HOST. YOU WOULD HAVE CHANGED, AND BURROWED DOWN, AND BECOME PREGNANT WITH HIM. AND YOU WOULD HAVE *BECOME* HIM.
"YOU WOULD HAVE BEEN *KING* OF THE NEW WORLD, SKINNER. FATHER, SON AND DESTROYER ALL AT ONCE. IT'S WHY THE SIXTHS CAME TO COLLECT YOU! IT COULD HAVE ALL BEEN YOURS. IF I HADN'T TAKEN ALL THAT AWAY FROM YOU.
"THEY MIGHT BE UPSET AT ME, FOR A LITTLE WHILE, BUT THERE'S STILL ANOTHER, WE CAN TAKE AFTER ALL.

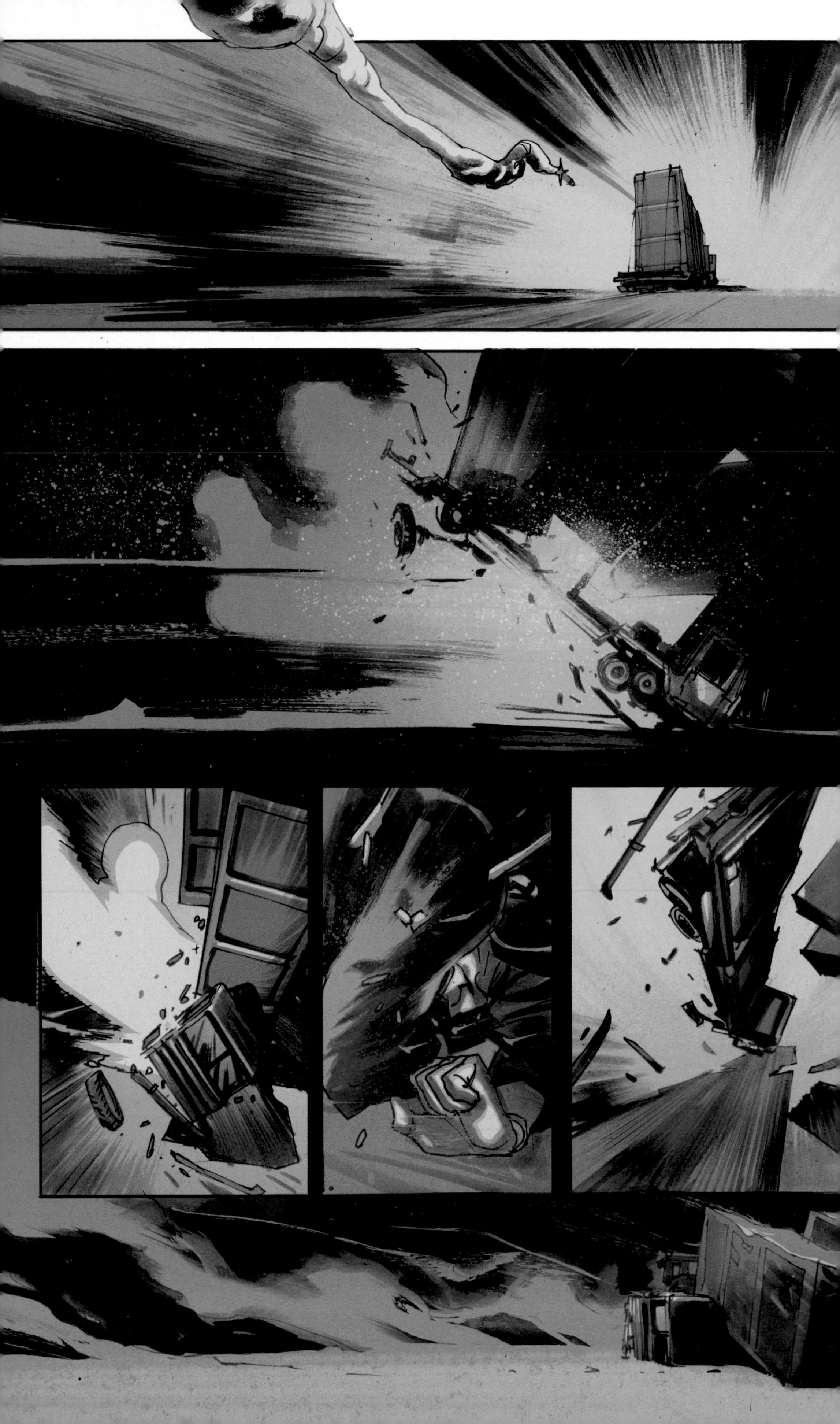

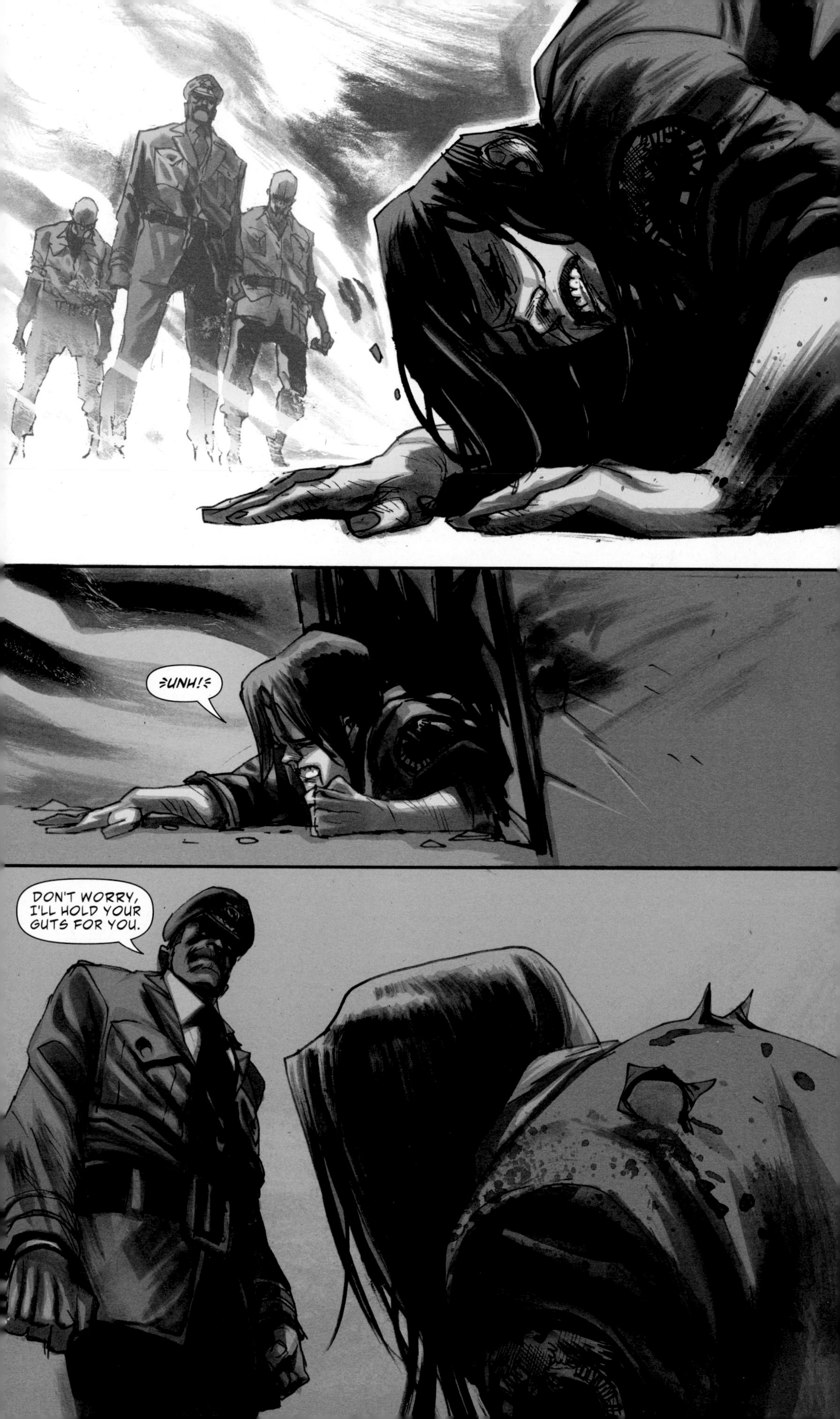

UNH!
DON'T WORRY, I'LL HOLD YOUR GUTS FOR YOU.

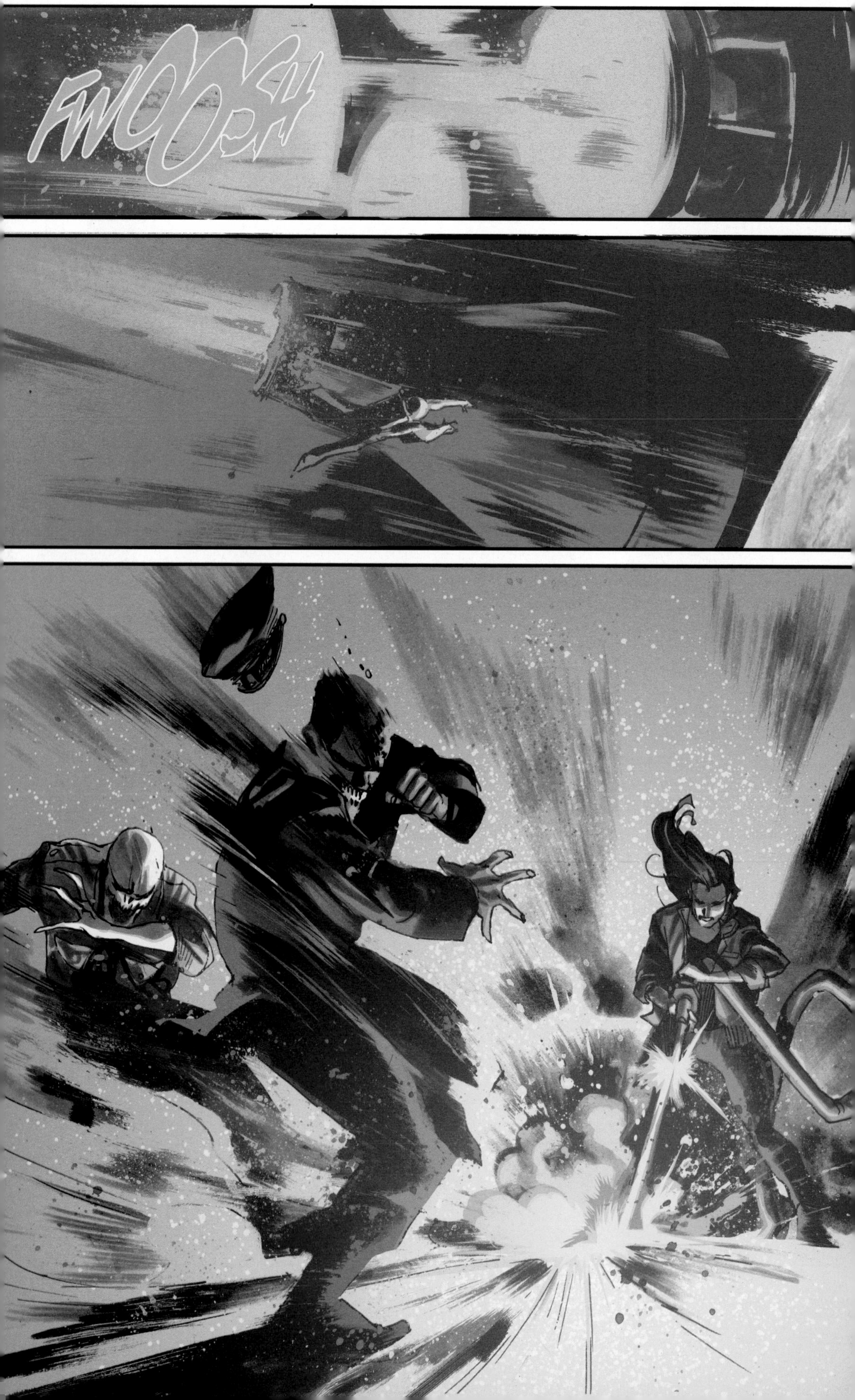
FWOOOSH

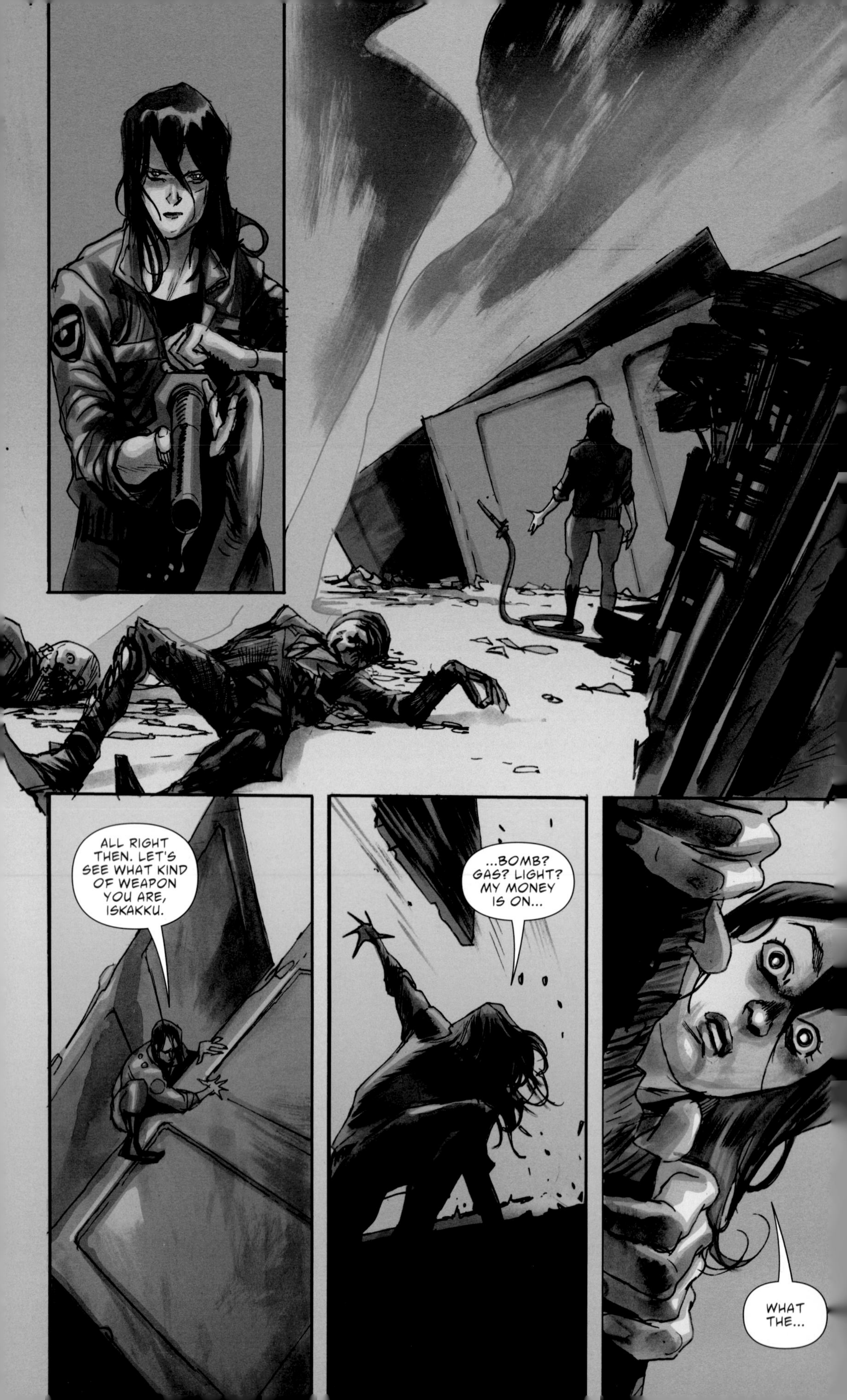
ALL RIGHT THEN. LET'S SEE WHAT KIND OF WEAPON YOU ARE, ISKAKKU.
...BOMB? GAS? LIGHT? MY MONEY IS ON...
WHAT THE...

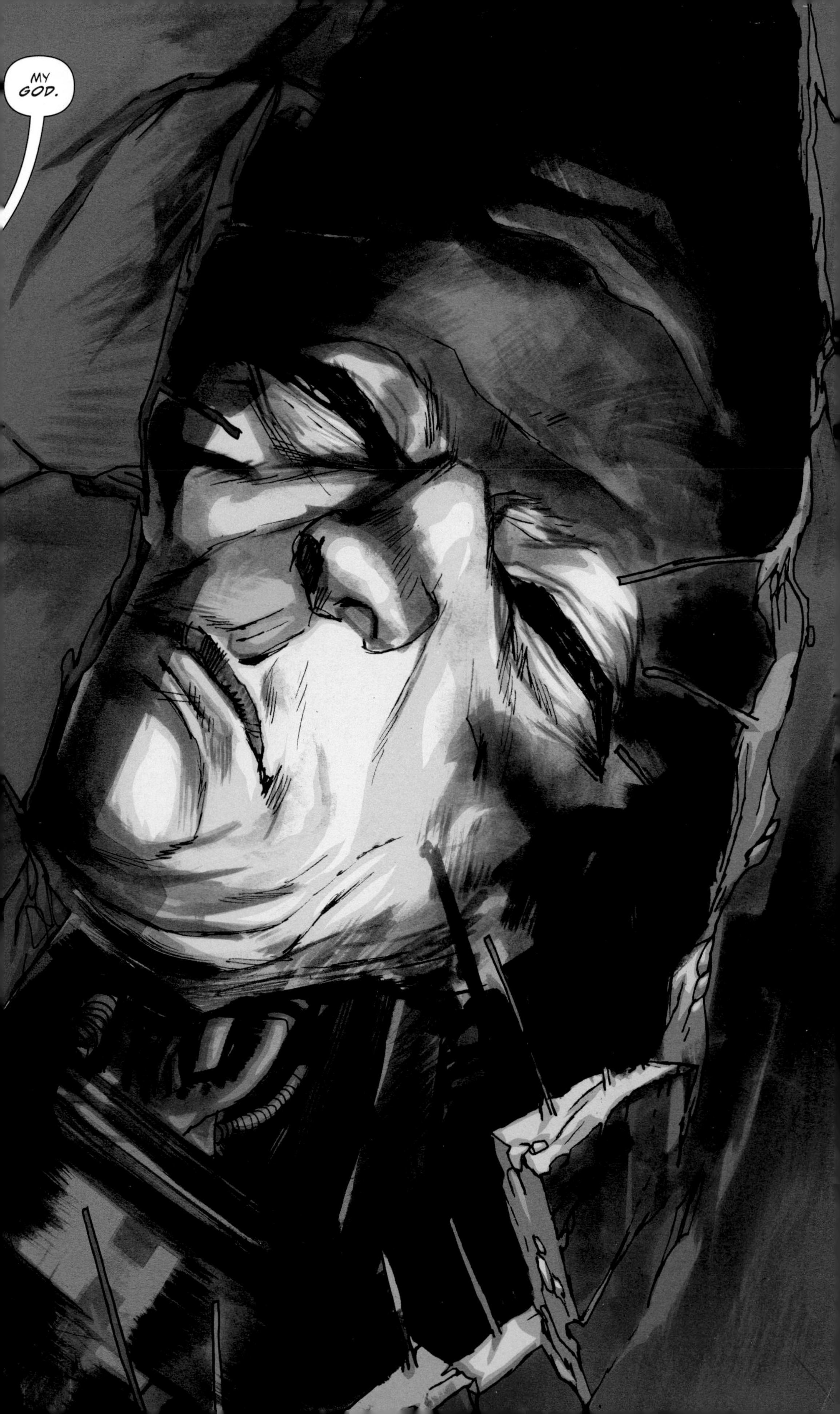
MY GOD.

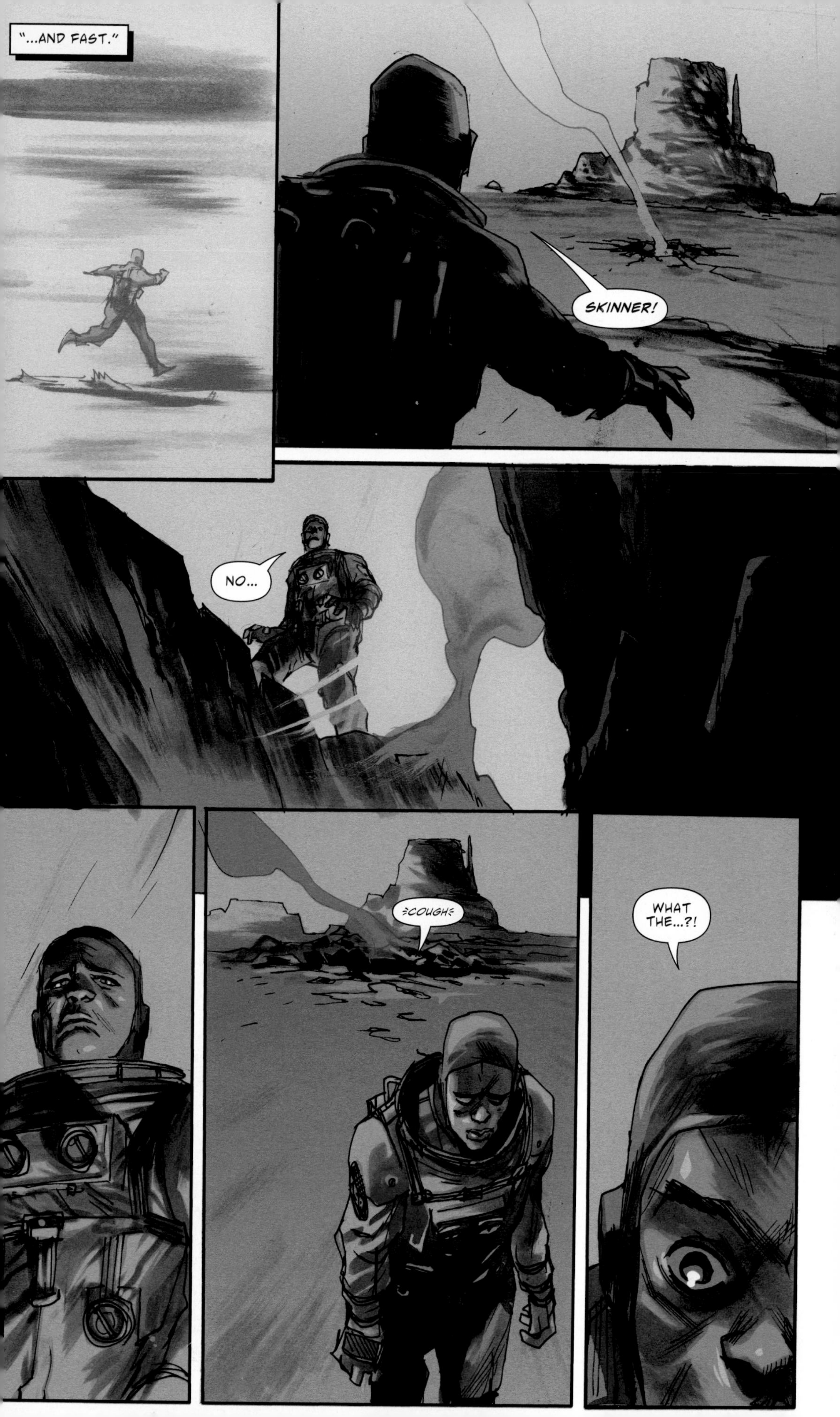
"...AND FAST."
SKINNER!
NO...
≈COUGH≈
WHAT THE...?!

FROM THE *NEW YORK TIMES* #1 BESTSELLING
AUTHOR OF *BATMAN VOL. 1: THE COURT OF OWL*

SCOTT SNYDER
with RAFAEL ALBUQUERQUE
and STEPHEN KING

AMERICAN VAMPIRE VOL. 2

with RAFAEL
ALBUQUERQUE and
MATEUS SANTOLOUCO

AMERICAN VAMPIRE VOL. 3

"At a time when vampire stories engulf pop culture, this one's actually fresh and original."
— ENTERTAINMENT WEEKLY

AMERICAN VAMPIRE
SCOTT SNYDER   RAFAEL ALBUQUERQUE
and
STEPHEN KING

with RAFAEL
ALBUQUERQUE and
SEAN MURPHY

AMERICAN VAMPIRE VOL. 4

with RAFAEL
ALBUQUERQUE and
JORDI BERNET

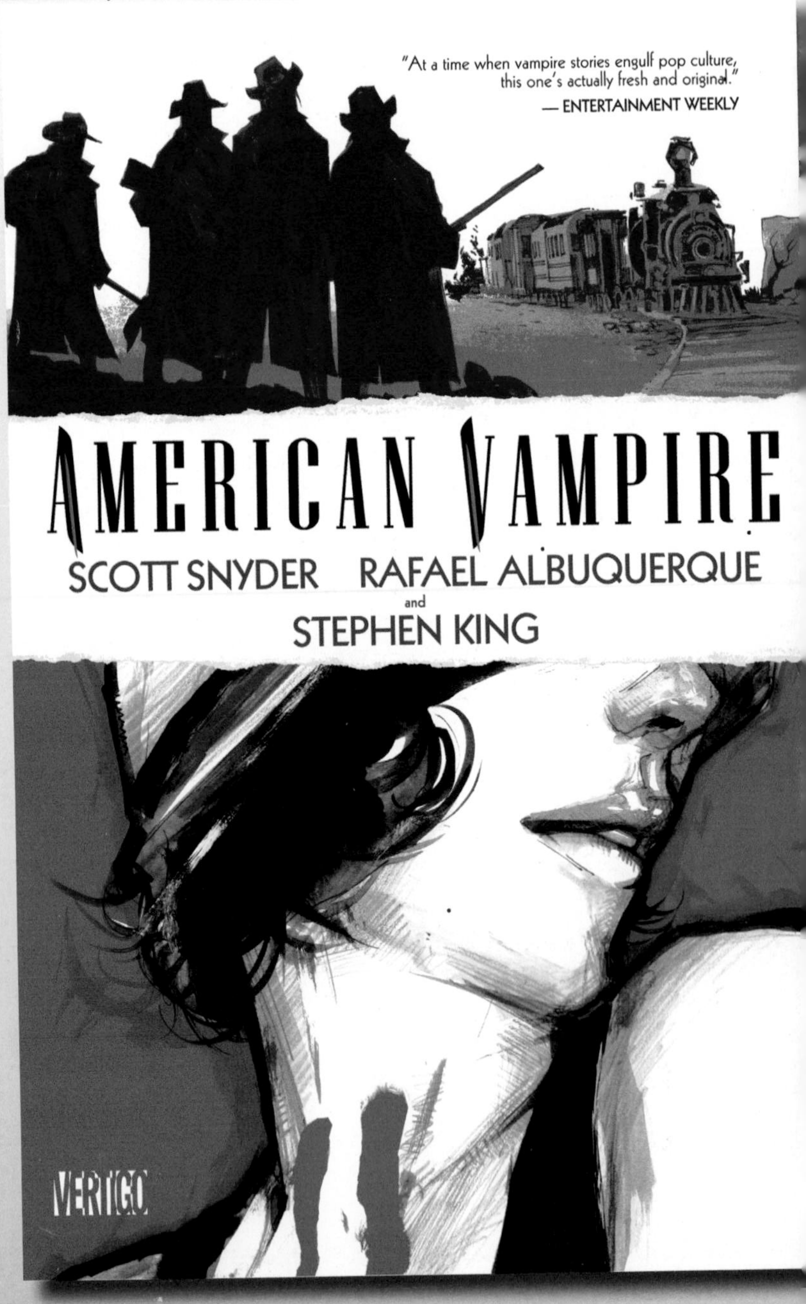